# ROOTS AND FLOWERS

## THE LIFE AND WORK OF

## AFRO-CUBAN LIBRARIAN

## MARTA TERRY GONZÁLEZ

# ROOTS AND FLOWERS

## THE LIFE AND WORK OF
## AFRO-CUBAN LIBRARIAN
## MARTA TERRY GONZÁLEZ

**Abdul Alkalimat and Kate Williams**

LIBRARY JUICE PRESS
SACRAMENTO, CA

Published in 2015 by Library Juice Press

Library Juice Press
PO Box 188784
Sacramento, CA 95822

http://libraryjuicepress.com/

All photos used with permission of Marta Terry González, unless otherwise noted

This book is printed on acid-free, sustainably-sourced paper.

Library of Congress Cataloging-in-Publication Data

Alkalimat, Abdul.
Roots and flowers: the life and work of Afto-Cuban librarian Marta Terry González
/ by Abdul Alkalimat and Kate Williams.
    pages cm.
Includes bibliographical references and index.
    ISBN 978-1-936117-64-2 (alk. paper)
    1. Terry, Marta. 2. Terry, Marta--Political and social views. 3. Library direc-
tors--Cuba--Biography. 4. Women library administrators--Cuba--Biography. 5.
Blacks--Cuba--Biography. 6. Women, Black--Cuba--Biography. 7. Libraries--Cuba--
History--20th century. 8. Cuba--History--Revolution, 1959--Influence. I. Williams,
Kate, 1958- 11. Title.
    Z720.T43A79 2015
    025.1'97092--dc23
    [B]
                            2014047422

# Contents

# Marta Terry: A Poem
## by Abdul Alkalimat

The lady of books

She teases and even taunts
the tales of culture

She collects
classifies
conserves
and collaborates
and always she campaigns

She is a lady of books
a librarian
a cadre in the battle of ideas

She lives now,
but her time is of the future.

—Havana, January 1, 2007

Marta Terry González in 2001. Photo by Kate Williams.

# Introduction

The title of this book describes a contradiction. Roots signify a long, rich, and complex history that is the basis for growth. Flowers signify the continuing affirmation of life: truly new and beautiful things. The two are connected in a rhythm of life, death, and rebirth. The most wonderful time is the spring, when a tree's roots explode energy through the organism and the tree gives birth to a new season of blossoms. This is one way to think of the Cuban revolutionary process: it was a historical spring out of which there was a flowering of new things.

We are writing about a couple of inter-connected themes. One is that the Afro-Cuban experience is not marginal to Cuban history but rather has its origin in one of Cuba's three fundamental roots: Spanish, Indian, and African. This is true in terms of demographics, politics, culture, and soul. Without Africa, there would be no Cuba as we know it. However, this objective fact is not the whole story. The Afro-Cuban had to face the blatant degradation and exploitation of slavery under Spanish colonialism and then segregation and racist devaluation under US neocolonialism. This lasted for 450 years. The Cuban revolution is just over fifty years old. Do the math: the transformation isn't over yet.

We are also focusing on information and libraries. Nothing is more central to the democratic character of a society than how it handles information and what its libraries do. The prerequisite for mass participation in the life of a society is an educated population with access to information. This is done most typically through key institutions, the library in particular. This book is about one person's path through the library, a journey that has lasted sixty-three years and counting. It focuses on the tensions between sustainability and innovation, between

1

standardization to global norms and decolonization to affirm national integrity. In short, tensions between yesterday and tomorrow. The sixty-three years spans the coming to power of Fidel Castro and the July 26 Movement.[1] It also includes the onset of the digital revolution, with the emergence of people using computers to transform information practices. The people and the library converge in our focus on the life of the Afro-Cuban librarian Marta Terry González.

Marta is an eminent librarian of the Cuban revolution, having at various times been the librarian of record for institutions led by Che Guevara, Haydée Santamaría, Armando Hart, and (at the National Library) under the leadership of Fidel Castro. She herself has been a leader in both the Cuban and the international library world.

The authors became involved in learning and then telling this story when Kate met and interviewed Marta in 2001. We interviewed Marta in Cuba, Canada, and the United States. Beginning in 2001, we made eight trips to Cuba, where we spoke with her and others. Marta told her story in an improvisational fashion, giving us a series of dots to connect as best we could. We added what aspects of Cuban librarianship we could learn about in US libraries, particularly in the rich collection of the University of Illinois, but also through the magic of interlibrary loan and the Internet. All three of us began to learn together. Marta very often corrected and expanded the text. She has been a guest in our home. We met her in Toronto where she traveled to a joint American–Canadian library association meeting in 2003. She connected us to others who provided their perspectives: family members, friends, and colleagues, including Dr. Héctor Terry Molinert, Graziella Pogolotti, Julio Rodríguez-Luis, Nancy Morejón Hernández, Emilio Setién Quesada, Eliades Acosta Matos, Gloria Ponjuan Dante, and María Aurora

---

1. The July 26 Movement is named for date of the daring 1953 attack on the Moncada police barracks. The attack was beaten back and the rebels took many casualties, both immediately and under torture in prison. But it was a powerful moral blow, for it rallied a great many Cubans and helped to organize them into the strongest force in the movement against Batista. With an army and an underground organization, the July 26 Movement was able to seize power just six years later.

Soto Balbón, among others. Along the way, Marta's colleagues and others created EcuRed, the Cuban Wikipedia, which we were excited about and grateful to discover. We learned from all of these. At the same time, any errors in the text are ours. We taped and transcribed; we searched and scanned. We lost material to a disastrous theft, but we reconstructed and managed.

What helped make this possible was our broader focus on Cuba. For Abdul, this began in 1957 when Bayamo native Mario Argote joined Abdul singing "Moody's Mood for Love" as they stood in line in their college cafeteria. The two of them then followed the Cuban revolution as closely as was possible from the small college town of Ottawa, Kansas.

Later, representing the Black Liberation movement, Abdul made several trips to Cuba with delegations from the United States. In 1972 he represented People's College as part of a tour for progressive university students and faculty, and made a report on the role of students in the Black Liberation struggle. After several subsequent solo visits, Abdul joined forces with Bill Sales[2] and Rosemari Mealy[3] to organize the Havana conference "Malcolm X Speaks in the 1990s," bringing eighteen African Americans to participate.[4]

Kate first traveled to Cuba in 2001 with a Canadian-led tour organized for North American librarians. The group met Marta in the library she had founded and was directing, the Arca de Papel (Paper Arc) in the Cuban Book Institute. Kate later parted from the tour group in order to speak further with Marta and others in library studies and informatics. The resulting photo report helped provide context for North Americans to understand the then-current battle over Cuban libraries.[5] Marta was a

2. See: William W. Sales, *From Civil Rights to Black Liberation: Malcolm X and the Organization of Afro-American Unity* (Boston: South End Press, 1994)

3. See: Rosemari Mealy, *Fidel & Malcolm X: Memories of a Meeting* (Melbourne: Ocean Press, 1993).

4. Video, audio and text from the conference is available online. Abdul Alkalimat, "Malcolm X Habla En Los 90's / Malcolm X Speaks in the 90's," Malcolm X: A Research Site, http://www.brothermalcolm.net/2002/mx_1990/.

5. Kate Williams, "Literacy and Computer Literacy: The Cuban Experience: Report on a Library Tour of Cuba, February-March 2001/Alfabetización y

key protagonist in that battle, defending Cuba's libraries, librarians and, in fact, sovereignty. This story is told in Chapter 10 and (in Marta's own words) in the documents included in the appendices.

When Marta succeeded in travelling to IFLA Boston—the annual meeting of the International Federation of Library Associations and Institutions—in August 2001, Kate and Abdul invited her to the Midwest. Marta visited the Detroit Public Library, lunched with faculty from the University of Michigan's School of Information where Kate was then a doctoral student, and toured JSTOR, the project to digitize and store entire runs of academic journals. She also spent time at the University of Toledo, where Abdul was director of the Africana Studies program, and in the community with staff and volunteers of the Murchison Center, a local community technology center where we worked with residents and students on digital literacy, gardening, and school reform.[6]

In 2002, we accepted an invitation to share the experience of the Murchison Center at Cuba's International Congress on Information, INFO 2002. A nine-person delegation from the University of Toledo and the Murchison Center traveled to Havana to speak at the conference and see our counterparts in Cuba.[7]

Both of us are faculty at the University of Illinois at Urbana Champaign—Abdul emeritus from the Department of Afro-American Studies and the Graduate School of Library and Information Science (GSLIS), Kate an associate professor at GSLIS. As we complete this biography of a librarian, the school is considering dropping the word "library" from its name. This reflects a global crisis: public cultural institutions

Computadorización: La Experiencia Cubana: Informe Sobre un Viaje de Bibliotecarios a Cuba, Febrero-Marzo 2001," Kate Williams faculty Web page, http://people.lis.illinois.edu/~katewill/cuba/.

6. Abdul Alkalimat and Kate Williams, "Social Capital and Cyberpower in the African American Community: A Case Study of a Community Technology Center in the Dual City," in *Community Informatics: Shaping Computer Mediated Social Relations*, ed. Leigh Keeble and Brian Loader (London: Routledge, 2001), 178-204.

7. Documents from the trip are available online. University of Toledo Africana Studies Program, "Toledo Spiders Go to Cuba," Murchison Center, http://murchisoncenter.org/cuba/.

are seeing surging demand, yet are also fighting for funding and for their continued existence. Libraries are inclusive institutions for entire populations. "Big data" research—including that carried on in the same academic unit as library and information studies—serves corporations and governments. This book is also an argument for examining, sustaining and, where necessary, reinventing the libraries that serve a broad democratic role involving literacy, popular education, and recreation in local communities.

Who should read this book? First and foremost, this is a book about the Cuban Revolution, a narrative about people and one particularly important cultural institution. Anyone interested in Cuba will find this a good read. This is especially true for readers interested in racism and Afro-Cubans. This is also a book for librarians and library students. We need to see libraries in all sorts of contexts, for that is the modern world. The library as a memory institution can be reimagined as a nerve center for society, with its capacity for collecting, processing, storing, and sharing our recorded perceptions. Here is a story of the emergence of a modern library system aimed at decolonization and social justice. Librarians in the Global South,[8] and many in the Global North serving immigrants from the South, will find this a useful study of their longtime colleague Marta Terry. And library students interested in social justice can use this book to understand an important example of a librarian who has made and is still making a sustained and creative contribution.

While it is not possible to completely separate the two topics, this book is in two parts: Marta the Afro-Cuban woman and Marta the librarian. Each part begins with an essay that provides context, which is especially crucial for readers not familiar with Cuba. Chapter 1 is an overview of the development of Cuban identity, focusing on the dialectics of the Afro-Cuban experience. Major signposts here are the ideas

8. The Global South is a term that very broadly identifies the parts of the world which were subjugated and colonized by the European powers after 1500. People and countries in the Global South have since taken a variety of paths towards freedom and equality, but within a context of continued subjugation (cultural, economic, political, and military) by the Global North, especially the US and Western Europe.

of José Martí and Fernando Ortiz. The rest of Part One focuses on
Marta's family, education, and her joining the Cuban revolution. Chapter
2 examines six generations of Marta Terry's family. It begins with her
great-grandmother Marta O'Farrill, born of two African parents and
born into slavery. It traces her lineage through her grandmother, her
parents and aunts and uncles; her son and grandson. (Because her marriage emerged within a particular historical—and library—context, that
story is told in Chapter 6.) Chapter 3 is about Marta's education. Home
schooled until age ten, she was enrolled early in high school where she
earned her *bachillerato*. She then continued on through the University of
Havana and the State Teachers College at New Paltz (in upstate New
York), eventually earning a doctorate at the former. At the university
she joined and shaped a network of friends that has endured all her life.
Chapter 4 explains how she joined the revolutionary movement against
the Batista regime soon after her University of Havana experience.

Part Two begins with Chapter 5, which tells the story of how systems
of information and communication, especially libraries, developed in
Cuba. Early aspects emerged during Spanish rule, and further developed
under American rule by proxy, the Cuban struggle against these two,
and then Cuban independence (and the US blockade) beginning in 1959.
The rest of Part Two focuses on Marta Terry the librarian, while also
touching on aspects of her life during those professional years. For the
majority of her working years she has directed three important libraries:
at JUCEPLAN (1961–1967), Casa de las Américas (1967–1987), and
the José Martí National Library (1988–1997). Chapter 6 discusses her
experience at JUCEPLAN, or Junta Central de Planificación, the Central
Planning Board of the Cuban economy led by Che Guevara, among
others. It also describes her meeting there and marrying the young engineer Luis Antonio Forte Manilla. Chapter 7 tells how she ran the José
Echevarría Library at Casa de Las Américas (House of the Americas).
There she worked with Casa's founding director, Haydée Santamaría,
who led the way in building Casa into a destination and resource for
writers and readers—for cultural and political innovators—from across
Latin America. Chapter 8 covers the ten years Marta served as director

of the José Martí National Library. This time spanned the collapse of the Soviet Union and the ensuing Cuban economic crisis known as the Special Period in Time of Peace, and yet the library system carried on. Chapter 9 is about Marta's experience as a founding professor—although always part-time—of the Department of Library and Information Science at the University of Havana. Marta's five decades of service to IFLA are detailed in Chapter 10. Starting as a young librarian in an IFLA training, Marta rose to being elected vice president and finally honorary fellow of IFLA, one of only twenty-seven so named.[9] Among her achievements during this decade was the first IFLA meeting in Latin America—in Havana. Another of her achievements was repelling an extended US government attack on Cuba and its libraries, orchestrated through isolated American librarians but also including various agents in Havana and elsewhere. Chapter 11 deals with her more recent experiences establishing collections in the Cuban Book Institute (1997–2007) and elsewhere. After retiring for the second time, she joined Armando Hart Dávalos, the early urban combatant against Batista and past Minister of Education and of Culture, to help organize his archive and publish his collected works. So Part Two covers making the revolution (JUCE-PLAN), connecting the revolution abroad (Casa), institutionalizing the revolution (national library), training professionals in the revolution (the university), defending the revolution (IFLA), and finally retiring in the revolution, which has meant continuing to contribute as a librarian, but in new ways.

9. International Federation of Library Associations and Institutions, "Honorary Fellow," International Federation of Library Associations and Institutions Honours Awards Web Page, http://www.ifla.org/honours-awards/honorary-fellow.

# PART ONE

## AFRO-CUBAN WOMAN

# Chapter 1

## NATIONALITY

This book is the story of one person, Marta Terry González. She has many dimensions that bring together the complexity of being Cuban. She is a member of what Cubans call the Centennial Generation, the generation that overthrew the US ally Batista.[10] She is a woman reared in a multigenerational family. Born Afro-Cuban, she became a mother and grandmother, a university-educated intellectual, and a professional librarian. The only way to grasp what it means to be Cuban—or to be human—is to interrogate multiple identities, especially in the life of one individual. It is pointless to privilege one of these identities above another. It all depends on what you are trying to learn about life's experience. In a person's life, all identities are operative all the time, so making such choices is academic at best.

Part One of this book is about Marta Terry, the Afro-Cuban woman. This chapter on her nationality provides historical and cultural context for her growth within her family from a young girl to a mature woman (Chapter 2); her education and resulting social class (Chapter 3), and her crucial decision to remain in Cuba and join in the Cuban Revolution of 1959 (Chapter 4). On the basis of an understanding of Marta

---

10. The Centennial Generation is the generation of those who fought in the 1950s. The year 1953 was the hundredth anniversary of the birth of Cuba's national hero, the independence fighter and writer José Martí, as well as the year of the attack on the Moncada barracks, which launched the final years of the struggle against Batista.

Terry the person, we then examine Marta's professional contributions in Part Two, Librarian.

Cuban nationality was born as a historical process that begins with Spanish invasion and colonial conquest, genocide against the indigenous population, and the enslavement of Africans.[11] The Spanish became Cuban and the Africans became Cuban, meaning they were an amalgamation with each other while at the same time holding onto aspects of their original heritage. For example, white people looked to Spain for their "high" cultural reference while the Afro-Cubans maintained contact with their traditional gods in religious practices such as Santería and others, the survival of the Yorùbá language, and more.[12] Both fought against Spain to end slavery and win the independence of Cuba. They then had to fight against the United States and forms of neocolonialism to create a people's republic under no form of foreign rule. They are different and yet they are one.

This is a challenge for us in this text, just as it is a challenge for the Cubans themselves in everyday life; frequently within a given family their history brings all of these elements together. In this chapter we want to clarify some of the broad conceptual thinking about the issue of Cuban nationality in order to set a theoretical context for our discussion of the life and times of Marta Terry.

The father of the concept of one Cuba is José Martí (1853–1895). Martí was first generation born in Cuba, the oldest of eight children of Mariano de los Santos Martí y Navarro (himself born in Valencia

---

11. For an extended bibliography on Afro-Cuban history, see Abdul Alkalimat, "Sankofa Cuba," *The Black Activist: Journal of the Black Left Unity Network*, no. 2 (2013), available at http://jblun.org/issue/2/

12. Santería is the religion of the Yorùbá region of Southwestern Nigeria and adjacent parts of Benin and Togo, adapted to survive in Cuba alongside the religion of the Spanish Empire, Catholicism. One of Santería's adaptations is the use of Catholic saint names for its orishas, that is, spirits or deities. Kindred religions emerged all over Latin America and the Caribbean, and today Santería is practiced all over the Western Hemisphere and beyond. Useful sources include George Brandon, *Santeria from Africa to the New World: The Dead Sell Memories* (Bloomington, IN: Indiana University Press, 1993); Joseph M. Murphy, Santería: An African Religion in America (Boston: Beacon Press, 1988).

in eastern Spain) and Leonor Antonia de la Concepción Micaela Pérez y Cabrera (born in Spain's Canary Islands). He came of age politically during the Ten Years' War (1868–1878). As a young nationalist he opposed both Spanish colonialism and slavery, and on that basis became the ideological leader of the anti-colonial struggle. He is regarded as the father of free independent Cuba. More than that, he was a leading intellectual for all of the Caribbean and Latin America. His travels took him all over the region, especially to the United States, Mexico, Guatemala, Venezuela, and many of the other islands and countries. His literary and intellectual output is phenomenal for a man who was an activist and who died at the age of forty-three: poetry, newspaper articles, essays, speeches, a serialized novel, articles for children (for a magazine which he also founded and edited), manifestos and declarations, and more.

Martí was a visionary with high ideological ideals. Cubans of all colors, in and beyond Cuba, were active alongside him—many whom he had mobilized. But being white, he could educate and activate other white Cubans while Afro-Cubans could not. In doing so, Martí committed both class and "race" suicide in the interest of a free and united Cuba. He was in direct conflict with the social Darwinist movement, which argued for a hierarchy of humanity and posited the theory that equality was biologically impossible, and in any case the history of change would be evolutionary and not revolutionary. Martí advanced an opposing argument: Races did not exist, hence there could be no "racial" hierarchy:

> The person of color in Cuba is already a fully rational human being that reads his book and knows his waist measure; with no need for the cultured manna to fall from the White sky...rather, let the White Cubans,...give, in the truth of customs, the example of equality that nature teaches, confirms the virtuous and intelligent life of the Cuban of color and which is disguised today in false laws.... In Cuba the Black person does not have to be elevated; proportionately, to tell the truth, as many Whites need elevation as Blacks could need it. In Cuba, out of humanity and foresight, one must be just.[13]

13. José Martí, *Obras Completas* (Havana: Editorial de Ciencias Sociales, 1975, vol. 2), 108–9, as translated and quoted in Dionisio Poey Baro, "'Race' and Anti-Racism in José Martí's 'Mi Raza',", *Contributions in Black Studies* 12, no. 1

While fighting against Spanish colonial rule, he lived in exile in the United States for more than a decade and understood it well. As Martí himself wrote, "I have lived in the monster and I know its entrails; my sling is David's."[14]

Martí was an idealist in the best sense of that word. With respect to "race," he spoke about Cuba as it ought to be, not what it was and would continue to be for some time. The independence movement from the beginning had weak, vacillating positions on the relationship between ending slavery and winning independence from Spain. Living beyond his death through his words and his deeds, Martí became the icon of the one Cuba philosophy.

By the 1800s, the Cuban ruling elite consisted of two tendencies, represented by the Spanish settlers on the one hand and their descendants on the other. Sometimes both were represented in the same family. One was the *peninsulares*, born on the peninsula that most North Americans know as the country of Spain. Continually replenished by new appointees and migrants from Spain, those of this tendency remained colonial government bureaucrats and merchants loyal to the Spanish Empire. Those of the other tendency were the *criollos*, or creoles. Born in Cuba, they developed an island consciousness, looking less and less to Spain. The most powerful of the creoles were the sugar planters; their enormous slave-based operations came to dominate the economy.

The peninsulares and the creoles started out united on maintaining slavery. They differed on the question of Cuban independence. And in order to wage a fight for Cuban independence, the creole plantation elite needed unity with Afro-Cubans, both slave and free. Afro-Cubans were a sizeable portion of the population, and the least loyal to Spain. But in the end, the creoles denied Cuba its independence, for it might also mean the abolition of slavery. Outside of the most elite strata—for instance among the tobacco planters, who were smaller landholders—the

---

(1994): 58.

14. José Martí, "Letter to Manuel Mercado, May 18, 1895," HistoryofCuba. com (History of Cuba Web page: Sierra, Jerry A., n.d.), http://www.historyofcuba.com/history/marti/mercado.htm.

impulse for independence based on Black–white unity was easier to achieve. Unlike tobacco, sugar depended on slave labor and lots of it.

The key figure who emerged as the best spokesperson for this emergent creole national bourgeoisie was Carlos Manuel de Céspedes (1819–1874). Céspedes was a lawyer and sugar planter in Oriente Province. In Oriente, the easternmost province, fewer than 10% of the slave population worked on sugar plantations, and they worked alongside free labor. Oriente was influenced by the sizeable free Black and *mulato* population, that is, people descended from some combination of Africans with Europeans and/or Indians. Oriente was also influenced by repeated low-intensity raids carried out by the maroon communities, that is, runaways living high in the Sierra Maestra Mountains. Céspedes carried out actions that tried to advance the revolution using a slave military force, while making it clear that he was also protecting the interests of the slave-owning elite. His reputation is based on his historic freeing of his own slaves, not all slaves. The same analysis that critiques the US 'founders'—in particular slaveholders George Washington and Thomas Jefferson—applies to Céspedes. In October 1868 he was elected president of the Republic of Cuba in Arms as it fought Spain for power. On the tenth of that month, Céspedes freed his own slaves and declared Cuba's independence; today this date is a national holiday. In November he announced that anyone who helped plantation slaves rise in rebellion would face the death penalty. In December he clarified further that abolition would only be considered after independence: "When we … have forced the representatives of the Spanish government to leave Cuba precipitously, the revolution will take care of this vital question."[15]

And so the emergent national bourgeoisie operated within its own historical limitations. The last two countries in the Americas to end slavery were Cuba in 1886 and Brazil in 1888. So Cuba's slave society was particularly backward and defensive against the global winds of abolition. As every decadent class of slave owners across the Americas

---

15. Philip S. Foner, *A History of Cuba and Its Relations with the United States. Volume 2, 1845-1895: From the Era of Annexationism to the Outbreak of the Second War for Independence* (New York: International Publishers, 1963), 172.

was overthrown, they retreated to Cuba. After 1804 came Haiti's slave-holders. After 1865 US slaveholders joined them and many others fleeing from human freedom.

George Washington, who served as the first US president from 1789 to 1797, was a slaveholder and never made a single move for abolition. Like him, Céspedes is a national hero, a patriot—but flawed. Céspedes made his limited moves half a century later, the same year that the Fourteenth Amendment to the US Constitution legally ended slavery in the United States.

Ten years later in 1878, this contradiction was confronted and resolved in the betrayal of the Zanjón Agreement and the subsequent protest at Baraguá. Growing weary of the battle and willing to compromise the fight for an independent Cuba free of slavery, generals of the independence army signed an agreement to end the Ten Years' War with the Spanish without consulting all of the leadership, particularly Antonio Maceo y Grajales. Maceo, an Afro-Cuban and a general, was committed to fighting on. He saw that the treaty was in fact a betrayal, and his next move made him even more of an iconic national hero than he already was. He was to meet with the Spanish representative at Baraguá. Instead of acting alone, he called all of the other officers who had not yet signed the agreement to Baraguá as well. A total of fifteen hundred officers and soldiers responded with their presence. Maceo was building a new kind of army, one in which democratic discussion dominated political decisions while strict discipline characterized all military actions. This was an Afro-Cuban general of the independence army who by this time was a national hero. And he was now leading the most dangerous opposition to the colonialism and slavery imposed on Cuba by Spain.

The Spanish general Arsenio Martínez-Campos, then also Spain's governor of Cuba, was confident that this would be a moment of great triumph: the surrender of Maceo. But instead he got the shock of his life. Maceo came to discuss the end of slavery and the independence of Cuba and not the surrender that other officers had accepted. Here is the recorded exchange:

Martínez Campos then asked Maceo directly: "That is to say, we are not in agreement?" Not being contradicted he asked further: "Then hostilities will again break out?" "Hostilities will again break out," Maceo replied emphatically. Martínez Campos then asked how much time the Cubans would need before the outbreak of hostilities. "For my part," answered Maceo, "I do not find it inconvenient that they break out right now." ... Thus ended the historic and dramatic meeting.[16]

The actual fighting ended soon afterward and converted Cuba's surrender into a truce. The truce was only possible by means of the leadership of General Maceo. Maceo had been able to beat back the opportunist policy of the sugar-plantation-owning creole elite. They had only wanted to grant freedom to those slaves who fought for independence and their own freedom—they had not wanted to end the system of slavery. Now he was the main defender of independence in general. In fact, after the Protest of Baraguá the strategic unity of the abolition of slavery and the independence from Spanish colonialism was forever linked.

Ada Ferrer sums up the meaning of Baraguá with the following comment:

[Maceo] nullified the argument that Spain, the colonial power, civilized Cuba, its charge. Instead he portrayed the colonial power as the principal obstacle to the progress of civilization. The Spanish—not African—presence in Cuba was classified as the problem. In that meeting at Baraguá, Maceo painted himself and his companions as the bearers of honor and civilization; Spain had lost its claim to both by tolerating and preserving racial slavery. Maceo had skillfully unmoored the categories of colonial discourse that posited Spain as civilizer and Cuba as uncivilized. That this inversion came not from a (white) colonial subject but from a man of color made the inversion that much more of a challenge to traditional notions of honor and place in a colonial slave society.[17]

The Cuba of Martí's idealism was anchored politically in the militant politics of Maceo. But in actual Cuban society, racism continued to

16. Philip S. Foner, *Antonio Maceo: The "Bronze Titan" of Cuba's Struggle for Independence* (New York: Monthly Review Press, 1977), 81.

17. Ada Ferrer, *Insurgent Cuba: Race, Nation, and Revolution, 1868-1898* (Chapel Hill: University of North Carolina Press, 1999), 66.

contradict and challenge the idea of one Cuba. The twentieth century called for a theory rooted in social science research to anchor the mestizo nature of Cuban identity in the systematic study of the empirical reality of Cuba. This notion of identity painted whites as a different cultural category from the Spanish, but still in opposition to the obvious African descendants in Cuba. Fernando Ortiz (1881–1969) emerged as the anthropologist to provide such a theory: transculturation. As one scholar described Ortiz,

> The bulk of his contributions to Cuba's intellectual life and public culture stemmed from his seminal research on all aspects of Cuba's African-influenced, orally transmitted traditions. He validated the use of Afro-Cuban as an analytical construct while insisting that Afro-Cuban cultural forms were integral to a unified Cuban national identity. He also addressed the problem of racism and the workings of race as a social rather than biological category.[18]

Ortiz wrote within the US neocolonial domination of Cuba and faced the legacy of Cuban racist slavery, with its relative degrees of freedom, covered over by the racist segregationist practices imported by the Yankee rulers and their racist categorization based on the "one-drop rule."[19] He began his career as a racist criminologist following the school of the Italian Social-Darwinist Cesare Lombroso (1835–1909), who advanced a biological theory of crime that targeted Black people as slow-witted and criminally inclined. However, Ortiz was active in progressive politics and also interacted with a wide variety of Black people in his research, going deeply inside the Afro-Cuban community. Black people turned him around and he became an advocate of Afro-Cuban humanity.

---

18. Faye V. Harrison, "Fernando Ortiz," *International Encyclopedia of the Social Sciences*, http://www.encyclopedia.com/doc/1G2-3045301836.html.

19. The One Drop Rule was the US practice, codified in law in the early 20th century, that classified a person with just one African ancestor—one drop of African blood—as Black or African American, or in the dominant name of that time, Negro.

Ortiz made a journey from being hostile to Black culture to being an advocate of tolerance and multicultural understanding:

> I am of the opinion that the word transculturation better expresses the different phases of the process of transition from one culture to another.... In the end, as the school of Malinowski's followers maintain, the result of every union of cultures is similar to that of the reproductive process between individuals: the offspring always has something of both parents but is always different from each of them.[20]

The central concept of transculturation is a model of five stages, which according to Ortiz, describes Cuba through stage four, but not yet five: hostility, compromise, adjustment, self-assertion, and integration. He was the scholar-activist who took the ideological orientation of José Martí and brought it into social science. The first and main ideological intervention was the argument that "racial differences" were myth and could only be understood as differences in cultural heritage. Robin Moore states, "Ortiz began to question the validity of racial constructs and to propose that Cubans define themselves in terms of shared cultural heritage rather than shared ancestry."[21] Therefore, change was possible, and his theoretical model attempted to map this change.

The one Cuba thesis of Martí was not so much a description as an ideological belief, a political goal for revolutionary transformation. Likewise, the integration phase of the Ortiz model has never been fully realized in everyday life, though it has repeatedly been affirmed in official documents. Ortiz campaigned for the full embrace of the African content in Cuban culture and the recognition of the many forms of Afro-Cuban organizations. As part of this, he makes an insightful critique of how the Cuban authorities attacked Black self-organization, for instance the *cabildos*. These were Afro-Cuban mutual aid organizations

---

20. Fernando Ortiz, *Cuban Counterpoint, Tobacco and Sugar* (Durham, NC: Duke University Press, 1995), 102-03. This book first appeared in print in Spanish in 1940.

21. Robin Moore, *Nationalizing Blackness: Afrocubanismo and Artistic Revolution in Havana, 1920-1940* (Pittsburgh, PA: University of Pittsburgh Press, 1997), 133.

organized by ethnic group (very roughly by locale of origin in Africa, for people did move around); the groups were allowed to exist because the social services shared among their members lightened the load of state. Ortiz argues that attacking the *cabildos* weakened Cuba's national unity, driving these Black organizational forms underground, thus polarizing rather than embracing these organizations of cultural differences. So he writes in 1921:

> The government persists in attacking the external and antiquated forms and does not take care to note the persistence of the internal essence. Thus disappeared the *cabildo*, together with all of its positive features: mutual aid, the insurance against illness, the bases, in short, of a traditional and rigorous mutuality.... How much better would it be if we today had mutualist *cabildos* and public dances with African drums and not temples of *brujería*, of clandestine or [openly] tolerated nature![22]

Ortiz's main contribution was to provide a rational theoretical framework for grasping the deep contradictions in Cuban society between the two external influences: Spain and Africa.

In effect, Maceo's transformative practice came to power in 1959 with the July 26th Movement led by Fidel Castro, Che Guevara, Raúl Castro, Camilo Cienfuegos, Juan Almeida (who was Afro-Cuban) and many others. This was the third dramatic turning point in Cuban history. The first was launching the war of independence to eject the Spanish colonialists and end slavery. The second was the construction of the Republic under neocolonial domination by the United States. Over the 56 years since 1959, the government and the people of Cuba have been fighting to end the contradictions that developed over several centuries.

The racism of the Afro-Cuban experience has been at the heart of the crisis of Cuban nationality. This is true even though official policy in the abstract has given respect to the thinking of Martí. This has been especially clear at critical historical junctures when the Cuban mainstream

---

22. Fernando Ortiz, "Los Cabildos Afrocubanos," *Revista Bimestre Cubana* 16 (1921): 30, as cited in Stephan Palmié, *Wizards and Scientists: Explorations in Afro-Cuban Modernity and Tradition* (Durham, NC: Duke University Press, 2002), 232.

faced militant action by the working class and the self-organized agency of Afro-Cubans. So Martí's philosophy appears in the Cuban constitutions drafted in 1933 and 1940.

The government that came to power in 1959 advanced a strong anti-discrimination policy for the Cuban revolution. On January 2, 1959, it reinstated the Constitution of 1940. This constitution had never been fully implemented, and Batista had suspended much of it in his 1952 coup d'etat. In February 1959, the Fundamental Law of Cuba replaced the constitution. Both documents included much of the same language, most significantly for this discussion the following article: "Any discrimination by reason of sex, race, color, or class and any other kind of discrimination destructive of human dignity is declared unlawful and punishable."[23] The 1976 Constitution, which continues in effect today with some revisions, affirmed and elaborated on this.

Creating a society to serve Cuba itself ran into direct conflict with US interests. Their massive hostile reaction put a stranglehold on Cuban economic and social life, which they eventually made nearly permanent in the shape of an embargo, or economic blockade. How did this evolve? In March 1959 the Cuban government nationalized the phone company, taking it from the US transnational corporation International Telephone and Telegraph. In May the Agrarian Reform Law was passed, limiting land holdings to 1,000 acres and beginning to democratize agricultural production. In June, US-owned refineries refused to process Soviet crude oil. In response, Cuba nationalized them. In July the United States canceled all orders for Cuban sugar. In August Cuba responded by nationalizing the Cuban assets of all US corporations. In September Cuba nationalized the US banks. The embargo was later tightened, for instance via the 1996 Helms-Burton Act. The economic reality was and has been backed up by military force. All this prevents Cuba from doing business with US entities or others who want to also do business in the United States. It bars Cuba from using international business

---

23. Republic of Cuba, "Fundamental Law of the Revolutionary Government," (Havana: Publicaciones Lewis / Private Commercial Service S. A., 1959), 5.

infrastructure (banking or Internet resources, for example). And it stops US citizens from traveling freely to Cuba.

In 1960, Fidel[24] came to New York and was discriminated against in a downtown hotel. Malcolm X arranged for him to move uptown to Harlem's Hotel Theresa, where he was greeted by throngs of supporters. By 1961 the United States had broken ties with Cuba and was training counterrevolutionaries. In April 1961 the United States carried out its failed Bay of Pigs invasion. In December 1961 Fidel declared himself a Marxist and the revolution as socialist.

Along with passing an antidiscrimination law, the revolutionary government also advocated antidiscrimination from the start. On March 22, 1959, Fidel gave a televised speech. He spoke of realizing Martí's long-held vision of an integrated, totally free society with no discrimination. All of Cuban society was not ready for this kind of "revolutionary" transformation. The Haitian poet and writer René Depestre reported firsthand this reaction:

> The entire white bourgeoisie and most white petit bourgeois, even those who would then have given their lives for the revolution, were panic-stricken as if the Cuban Prime Minister had announced an atomic attack against the island on the following morning.... The whole sinister mythology constructed in the days of slavery resurfaced in men's consciousness along with its imaginary procession of evil instincts, lubricity, physical filth, pillage and rape.... The volcano of Negrophobia was in eruption.[25]

Also in 1959, speaking at the University of Las Villas, Che Guevara urged people to action to implement equality:

> Che told the gathered faculty and students that the days when education was a privilege of the white middle class had ended. "The University," he said, "must *paint* itself black, mulatto, worker, and peasant." If it didn't, he warned, the people would break down its doors "and paint

---

24. As is customary across Cuba and beyond, in this book the name of Fidel Castro is at times shortened to Fidel.

25. Depestre, in Samuel Farber, *Cuba since the Revolution of 1959: A Critical Assessment* (Chicago: Haymarket Books, 2011), 169-70.

the University the colors they like."[26]

In the September 1960 First Declaration of Havana, the National General Assembly of the People of Cuba proclaimed "the right of the Negroes and Indians to 'the full dignity of man,'" and further,

[I]t is the duty of the workers, the peasants, the students, and intellectuals, the Negroes, the Indians, young people, women, and old people to fight for their economic, political and social demands. It is the duty of oppressed and exploited nations to fight for their liberation.[27]

But the government's response to the "volcano of Negrophobia" was to ease up on transformation in two ways. First, they focused on implementing Martí's vision and Maceo's practices in public spaces: employment and education. They left private spaces and changes in racist attitudes to evolve. Second, the government's calls to action did not mean that Black people could organize as an autonomous force. One serious decision made by the Cuban revolutionary leadership was to follow the age-old pattern of closing down all the Black organizations, essentially forcing these networks underground. This policy was part of an antiracist closing down of all exclusively Black and/or white organizations. But applying the same policy equally to the oppressed community as to the oppressor had a crucially lop-sided effect.

Both the white and Black organizations were associated with the Batista regime and as such could have been centers of counter revolution as well. However the Black organizations anchored in the oppressed community had a better chance of being won over to the revolution based on the benefits of policies that limited and pushed back racism in the society.

The fundamental issue of revolutionary policy is to safeguard the agency of oppressed people, or put another way, their means for

---

26. Jon Lee Anderson, *Che Guevara: A Revolutionary Life* (New York: Grove Press, 1997), 449.

27. Fidel Castro, "The Havana Declaration, September 2, 1960," University of Texas Latin America Network Information Center Fidel Castro Speech Database, http://lanic.utexas.edu/project/castro/db/1960/19600902-2.html.

self-determination. The Cuban Revolution impacted Afro-Cuban quality of life via class-focused policy, and great gains were made. One of
the greatest of these projects was the 1961 literacy campaign. But the
legacy of racism was not destroyed, and various developments since
1959 have created new social contradictions that feed the continuation
of racism in Cuba.

The social and economic policies of the revolutionary government
greatly opened up opportunities for people, especially working and poor
people in urban and rural areas. This impacted Afro-Cubans as much, if
not more, than other sectors of the population. But in 1991 the Soviet
Union ceased to exist, overtaken by pro-capitalist forces led by Mikhail
Gorbachev and Boris Yeltsin. Soviet support for Cuba vanished, forcing Cuba into crisis. This "Special Period in Time of Peace" led to a
drastically lower standard of living across the island. Afro-Cubans were
hit especially hard in the Special Period.

Marta Terry was at the National Library when the Special Period
began, and so it will be explored further in chapter 8. But for now, one
sector of the economy best demonstrates the effect of the Special
Period and the Cuban response: tourism. Cuba began to attract hard
currency via joint agreements with global hotel chains for development
of enclave tourism. Employees in this sector were relatively well paid,
often in foreign "hard" currency. Following international norms, Black
people were seldom employed in public-contact positions in the hotels
and resorts and were therefore excluded from the higher-paid positions.
More subtle was the way in which these international norms encouraged
the old racism to rear its ugly head.

Parallel to this, multigenerational poverty emerged and took root,
leading to antisocial behavior and higher rates of imprisonment. This
has been often mentioned as an area that reflects the return to old forms
of racist behavior. But unlike in old Cuba, the government mobilized
people in the affected communities, especially young people. New educational programs tied to practical community projects have facilitated

people taking control of their lives and planning ways to reverse the social situation.[28]

This is the context for understanding the life of Marta Terry González. She matured in sync with a surging revolutionary struggle to end slavery, end racism, and fully unleash the Afro-Cuban people to have full access to all of the institutions of the society, while maintaining their African cultural heritage as part of the historical wealth of the society alongside the indigenous, the Chinese, and the Spanish. Her life story will demonstrate that this has been a valiant struggle marked by great achievements. And the struggle continues into the twenty-first century.

---

28. Miren Uriarte, *Cuba: Social Policy at a Crossroads: Maintaining Priorities, Transforming Practice* (Boston, MA: Oxfam America, 2002).

# Chapter 2

## FAMILY

Chapter 1 examined Cuban nationality, particularly the centrality of the Afro-Cuban in Cuba's culture and development. With that as context, we can begin the story of Marta's own life and work. As with all of us, it starts with her parents, and so family is the subject of this chapter.

Before considering family, it will help to reflect on the historical role of women in Cuba. Women in Cuba have faced the feudal legacy of Spanish colonialism, the feudal and communal legacies of traditional African culture, and neocolonial oppression via the United States. They in turn have shaped Cuban culture as best they could. Their struggle has been for equal rights and against machismo or male supremacy, and patriarchal attitudes and practices. They faced oppression in both public and private life, including the family.

Women played key roles at all stages of the Cuban Revolution and were not going to allow the past to continue without a struggle for gender equality. For one example, the mother of Antonio Maceo, Mariana Grajales Coello, was a revolutionary leader in her own right, besides raising two sons to be generals in the liberation army. She served as nurse and healer on the battlefield and elsewhere. She once said her only regret was that she had only one life to give and she couldn't have more sons to go into battle.

Among the key women fighters leading to 1959 were Haydée Santamaría, Melba Hernández, Celia Sánchez, Vilma Espín, and Teté Puebla.[29]

---

29. Memories and reflections on the contribution of women in the 1950s and

The Federation of Cuban Women formed in 1960 by uniting several large women's organizations. Since that time the Federación de Mujeres Cubanas, or FMC, has been the main women's organization advancing the goal of gender equality.

The first major contribution of the FMC was its role in the 1961 literacy campaign, in which more than ninety thousand women helped to eliminate illiteracy. After a full investigation of the role of women and the obstacles holding back gender equality, the Cuban government passed the Cuban Family Act just before an FMC congress. This comprehensive act covers gender equality in the family, thus setting the terms for women to be free and full participants in the wider society. This kind of legislation does not magically change society, but it creates a context where change is possible. As women have gotten more education, taken up positions in many fields of work that previously excluded them, and become leaders in the party and the government, gender equality has become more of a reality. An example of progress is in the field of health. In 1953 there were 403 female doctors in Cuba and by 1999 there were 34,000. While there is much more to be done, the Cuban Revolution has greatly impacted the role of women in all aspects of Cuban society.

In Cuba and elsewhere, the family is the universal social institution as it provides the most intimate framework for the socialization of the individual. This process gives us our language, culture, and moral values, and initiates us into networks that define our social existence. It is home, the source of those we trust, our strong ties and bonding social capital. As such it is also the primary institution for a nation, as this socialization process always begins a journey into a greater whole, building from family to neighborhood to community and beyond. What is started in the family and its immediate environment is continued through schooling into the wider society.

---

since are detailed in Vilma Espín Guillois, Asela de los Santos Tamayo, and Yolanda Ferrer, *Women in Cuba: The Making of a Revolution within the Revolution* (New York: Pathfinder, 2012).

Families are how all of us become human. We learn what it means to be part of society with all of its social and cultural dynamics. It is our entry point and socialization matrix that gives us our sense of being with others—kinship networks, neighbors, and community. The family is how we learn our place in the power arrangements of control and being controlled, and how we navigate the contending forces so that we can survive. We become skilled in the traditions and rituals that undergird a sustainable lifestyle. The historical dynamics of the last 150 years of Cuban history have twisted and turned family life, especially given the mix of African and Spanish heritage, the fight against slavery, colonialism and neocolonialism, and the ruptures of revolutionary transformation.

The family story of Marta Terry González is a particular narrative of a global experience, how social life has formed national identities, how society has shifted from a rural-agricultural extended family social arrangement to an urban-industrial nuclear family that creates challenges for trans-generational continuity. This is exacerbated by migrations creating a global diaspora. For the current generations another major shift is transforming industrial society into an information society, where much of life is moving experience from the actual to the virtual, from living offline to living online. This is also a challenge for Cubans, straining face-to-face relationships, but also reorienting family members living apart to reconnect online, breathing life into the Cuban Diaspora.

The subjugation of the African in the slave system of Cuba and elsewhere transformed family life in several ways, from denying people their family genealogy and extended ties to entering into sexual and personal interactions with no social legitimacy, thereby forcing people to rely on creating informal improvisational family forms. Sometimes this was the forced concubinage of an enslaved African woman by a slave master, and sometimes it was the relationship dynamics of the Afro-Cuban informal multiple partner arrangements of polygamy (men) and polyandry (women).

The Cuban reality involves a deep connection between the Spanish and the African. The objective reality is that the majority of Cubans share some degree of this dual heritage, but the subjective realty is that

Cuba has been dominated by a Eurocentric paradigm of cultural values and social status. (The Roman Catholic Church played its role here, for instance.) One way this paradigm reveals itself is in the complexity of defining family lineage through naming practices.

However, people are not merely the objects of their history. Even under the most total forms of domination and oppression, we always have agency to codetermine our lives. Under whatever conditions, people can choose and self-create. The African was a victim of slavery and its legacy, but at the same time the slave was an active creator of his or her own self-identity. This dialectic is the key to understanding the family life of Marta Terry. Hers is a trans-generational experience of six generations over 150 years, from slavery to freedom to revolution.

Marta's family experience is to some extent a microcosm of Cuban history, especially the history of an Afro-Cuban woman who embraced and lived in the heart of the Cuban revolutionary experiment. This chapter will discuss six generations of her family, from her great-grandmother to her grandchild. (Marta's family tree can be seen in Appendix 1). Marta has direct experience of five of these generations and helped to shape their lives. She herself was shaped by all six. As Marta has said, she is sometimes a nineteenth-century person herself, because she was educated and raised by a woman of that century.

Family history in Cuba often has been sketchily maintained as oral history. The contradictions of the Afro-Cuban experience have created even more silences. But it does appear that Marta's is a matriarchal family line, from great-grandmother, to grandmother, and then to four aunts and her father. Marta's mother died when she was seven. Her grandmother reigned as the power figure, aided by the four aunts. When asked if Marta acted like his mother, her younger brother Héctor replied, "Oh no, she was a sister. We had quite enough mothers!"

The known origin of the family rests with Marta's great-grandmother, Marta O'Farrill, after whom she was named. Marta O'Farrill lived in Aguacate, a small town forty-three miles (sixty-eight kilometers) southwest of Havana. This first Marta was an enslaved woman who won her freedom from her white owner, Andrés Terry y Dorticós, while maintaining a relationship with him. By agreement, he provided some support while she gave birth to and raised their three children in a so-called informal family. Andrés Terry owned several of the largest sugar plantations in Cuba. His wealth and the terms that were negotiated between him and Marta O'Farrill enabled her and her children first of all to be emancipated. Marta was born a slave; her three children were born free. Second, they had a small measure of material assets that set them apart, as did the symbolic status of the children's color. The children were given the two family names Terry O'Farrill, so the patrimony was asserted, if not acknowledged. The foundation of their status was their freedom.

The historical pattern of the slave trade to Cuba, as well as her photograph,[30] suggest that Marta O'Farrill's parents were both African. So the great-great-grandparents are the family's direct connection to Africa with the profound implications of color and culture. From the Spanish colonial and Eurocentric perspective, the color of the African became a mark of the oppressed. African cultural traditions were misunderstood and demeaned as an unnatural deviation from Western European norms and values. This prejudice and ignorance provided a shield from the guilt and shame that would otherwise certainly have been the reaction of a "civilized" people to the vulgarities and barbarism of their own doing.

The lives of Marta O'Farrill and her daughter Higinia Terry O'Farrill reflect centuries of social control of Africans in slave societies such as in Cuba, the United States, and across Latin America. First, unlike their mother Marta O'Farrill, Higinia and her two siblings each had two surnames, following the norm in Spain and Latin America; the first is from the father and the second the mother. What is more, Marta and Higinia were each *placées*, a French word which translates literally as "placed women," but which signifies more. Each of them were placed—although not quite irrevocably, as we shall see—into a well-identified although precarious middle strata between Cubans of apparent European descent

---

30. See this book's photo section.

and those who were more completely African, whether slave or free. In other words, they were raising extralegal or informal families, and had typically negotiated terms for this arrangement with the men involved.

Juxtaposed with the lives of the mother Marta and her daughter Higinia, the life of the father Andrés (1861–no date) also reveals something about the local and global wealth and power of the Cuban elite.[31] He was the youngest surviving child of Tomás Terry y Adan (1806–1886) and his Louisiana-born French-Cuban wife Teresa Dorticós y Gómez de Leys. Tomás was from an Irish family who were rich from centuries of trade in slaves and more, based first in Europe and then in Latin America. Tomás came to Cuba from Venezuela and made his start buying sick slaves, patching them up, and reselling them. Teresa was the daughter of the governor of Cuba's Cienfuegos Province, himself a millionaire. According to a New York City newspaper story, when the governor heard of the impending marriage of his daughter to the Venezuelan arriviste he was furious, and Tomás simply replied, "I'll be richer than him some day."[32]

In dramatic contrast to the pro-independence slaveholder Céspedes, Tomás Terry sided with Spain during Cuba's independence wars. That enabled him to amass huge acreages of land that Spain confiscated from the freedom fighters. Terry came to own Cardenas, the largest sugar mill in all of Cuba. One account relates that he was "friendly with the Congolese Negroes and gave them quite a bit of help. He even gave money for the blacks to found their *cabildos*."[33] Such *cabildos* were widespread and served as both mutual aid organizations that eased any

---

31. Sources used on the slaveholding Terry family include Kevin Terry, "Terrys in Latin America of Cork Origin," *Irish Migration Studies in Latin America* 7, no. 3 (2010); Kevin Terry, *The Terrys of Cork: Merchant Gentry 1180-1644* (Chicester/Gloucestershire, UK: Phillimore & Company, Ltd/The History Press, 2013); Hugh Thomas, *Cuba: The Pursuit of Freedom* (New York: Da Capo Press, 1998), as well as other sources cited below.

32. Ben MacIntyre, *The Napoleon of Crime* (New York: Farrar, Straus and Giroux, 1997), 130.

33. Esteban Montejo, *The Autobiography of a Runaway Slave*, ed. Miguel Barnet, trans. Jocasta Innes (New York: Meridian Books/The World Publishing Company, 1969), 144.

obligations of the slaveowners to their slaves and were a nonthreatening alternative to the secret male societies known as Abakuá. For Tomás Terry owned sugar lands and mills just as the global North was adopting a sugar-dependent lifestyle and he was keenly interested in maintaining his wealth and power. He became a player on the global commodities markets, which enabled him to protect his wealth and also to gamble. Soon nicknamed the Cuban Croesus, he moved in the 1860s to New York and later to Paris.[34]

Tomás declared in his will, which was contested in New York, that he started married life with "$20,000 and one Negress." Perhaps this was a backward glance at his hostile father-in-law. Tomás left equal shares of his $50,000,000 estate to his eight offspring by his Louisiana-born wife—after deducting the sums he had recorded as given to each of them over their entire lifetimes.[35] In today's dollars, his estate would total $1.28 billion. It was simultaneously an endowment for his white offspring and the disinheritance of the Black ones.

Less information is available to us on Tomás Terry's son, Andrés, who became Marta O'Farrill's informal husband. But by 1893, eight years after Tomás's death, other offspring appear to have left Cuba to live their cocooned lives in the United States or Europe. Andrés Terry was the son listed as owning more sugar plantations than his other siblings who were still holding Cuban sugar properties. Undoubtedly, Andrés' holdings included much more than sugar production, and an 1890s source lists him as living in both Cienfuegos and Paris.[36] And while he

---

34. Croesus was an ancient Greek known to this day for his supreme wealth and arrogance.

35. "A Wealthy Planter's Will: Don Tomas Terry's Disposition of His Property Contested," *New York Times*, November 21 1886. Ely provides a lower figure of $25,000,000 and adds that the richest man in the world was then thought to be William Backhouse Astor with $50,000,000: Roland T. Ely, *Cuando Reinaba su Majestad el Azúcar* (Buenos Aires: Editorial Sudamericana, 1963), cited in Thomas, *Cuba: The Pursuit of Freedom*, 140.

36. J. C. Prince, *Cuba Illustrated*, 6th ed. (New York: Napoléon Thompson & Company, 1893/94), 125-74.

was married with two legal children,[37] he also had three children with
Marta O'Farrill, who lived in Aguacate near one of his sugar plantations:
a son, Anacleto, and two daughters, Candelaria and Higinia.

Higinia Terry O'Farrill was to become the grandmother of Marta
Terry and the matriarch of the family until her death in 1975. But Higinia
began her adulthood by repeating the pattern of her mother: she entered
into a longtime relationship with another sugar baron's son, Francisco
Averhoff. As of 1893, Averhoff men owned three sugar plantations,
one of which was located in Aguacate,[38] forty-five miles (seventy-three
kilometers) from Havana. Placed in Cuban society just like her mother,
Higinia had four children with Averhoff. She later had four more with a
second man, Nicolás Inchaurtieta y García, a lawyer who served as first
alternative municipal judge for Madruga during 1916–1917.[39]

The first three children were given the family names Averhoff Terry;
the remaining five she named Terry Terry, thus excluding both fathers.
Nicolás married another woman, and by the 1940s their son Nicolás
Inchaurtieta Casuso was a doctor working in the preventive medicine
section of Havana's Children's Health Service.[40]

Higinia thus followed her mother's path toward improving the life
of her family by having a similar "outside" family arrangement with a
sugar planter. Now the family had a reasonably large house in Madruga,
nine miles (fourteen kilometers) from Aguacate. They had a small grand
piano and a garden with yellow roses. This was the most one could

---

37. Guillaume de Tournemire, "[Genealogy of] Andrès Terry Y Dorticos"
Geneanet, http://gw.geneanet.org/pierfit?lang=en;p=andres;n=terry+y+do
rticos.

38. Prince, *Cuba Illustrated*, 125-74

39. "Decreto Presidencial Número 281, Publicado En La Gaceta Oficial De 9
De Marzo De 1916," *Collección Legislativa: Leyes, Decretos y Resoluciones* 51 (1916):
339-40; "Decreto Presidencial Número 177, Publicado En La Gaceta Oficial
De 9 De Febrero De 1917," *Collección Legislativa: Leyes, Decretos y Resoluciones* 55
(1917): 190.

40. Angel Argudin García and Nícolas Inchaurtieta Casuso, "Vacunación
Antivariolosa [Smallpox Vaccination]: Trabajo De La Sección De Medic-
ina Preventiva Del Servicio De Higiene Infantil Municipal De La Habana,"
*Revista de Sanidad y Beneficencia Municipal* 3, no. 1 (1943): 43.

expect under such conditions, but upward social mobility was not in the cards for the next generation in Madruga.

Critical to social existence for Afro-Cubans has been the class, color, and cultural dialectics of African and Spanish influences. Your family mix of these social features would likely set the pattern for your quality of life, opportunities for your children, and your ability to avoid the most virulent forms of racism that were always a dangerous threat facing every Afro-Cuban.

The paternal grandmother and great-grandmother of Marta Terry González each combined the fundamental dialectic of the Afro-Cuban: a foundation in Africa on the one hand and an upward mobility into the Eurocentric world of the creole Cuban bourgeoisie on the other. Marta O'Farrill was closer to Africa, but as we will see, Higinia was also very much anchored in the cultural practices of the African in Cuba.

Higinia Terry O'Farrill was a classic case of a *mulata* who managed her Afro-Cuban family and her relationships with white men. But in the town of Madruga, the fates of her four daughters in particular were sealed, and she wanted nothing to do with that. So Higinia decided to move the family to the city of Havana.

The move occurred during a terrible storm, probably the 1926 hurricane that devastated western Cuba. And it was indeed a storm for one woman to uproot her large family of children and teenagers and trade the house—the piano, the yellow roses, the pleasant countryside of a small town—for the uncertainty of the big city. But their life had already placed them permanently on storm watch, and this must have helped persuade Higinia's mother Marta O'Farrill, who came along with them. The stormy move was a leap out of the rural legacy of slavery that was marked on this free family. The big city promised deeper freedom in the form of new work possibilities and autonomy from status dependent on white benefactors supporting their outside families.

What is more, the years of Cuban president Gerardo Machado y Morales were unfolding (1925 to 1933), and with them a new complexity as to how the Afro-Cuban middle class made political moves to survive. While Cuba was so much later than the US in ending slavery, it was well

in advance of the US in terms of Black people voting. And because
Afro-Cubans represented a voting bloc, every president of Cuba managed to have a relationship with them. Machado's approach was this:
he brought certain Afro-Cuban elites into his administration, and they
worked to get reforms that would benefit the AfroCuban population,
especially themselves. As always, there was a price to pay. As Machado
became a dictatorial tyrant, and mass opposition to his rule became a
dominant aspect of political struggle, the Afro-Cubans in his administration were caught in the middle.

And who was Machado? He was manager of the American and
Foreign Power and Light Company, with sworn loyalty to the United
States. US President Calvin Coolidge said this in 1928: "Under Machado
today Cuba is her own sovereign. Her people are independent, free,
prosperous, peaceful, and enjoying the advantages of self-government."[41]
Coolidge said this near the end of the rapid US takeover of the Cuban
sugar industry: US ownership increased from 15% in 1906 to 48% in
1920 and 75% in 1928.[42]

Once in Havana, Higinia's four daughters went to school and her
four sons went to work. This reversal of the usual gender roles set the
family context for how Marta was raised: with the ego strength most
often reserved for men. The first family home was on Cárdenas Street
between Monte and Corrales. The girls first studied in short courses for
teachers which allowed them to become "maestras habilitadas," authorized to teach. They opened a private school for neighborhood children
in the Terry family living room, and so it was that Marta learned to read
and write just by passing through those classes at home.

Thus, as soon as the nine were settled in Havana their urban social
life began to unfold, and marriage and non-marriage became the pattern.

---

41. Calvin Coolidge, "Address before the Pan American Conference at
Havana, Cuba, January 16, 1928," The American Presidency Project, http://
www.presidency.ucsb.edu/ws/?pid=443.

42. Louis A. Pérez, Jr., *Cuba under the Platt Amendment, 1902–1934* (Pittsburgh,
PA: University of Pittsburgh Press, 1986), 188; Moore, *Nationalizing Blackness,*
27.

The four sons—Francisco, José, Fernando, and Marta's father Nícolas—found wives; the wives moved into the Terry house. The four
daughters—Graciela, Luz, Blanca Zilia, and Mercedes—remained single,
except for Graciela, the oldest. Her husband moved into the house. The
six members of the next generation began to appear, six cousins and
siblings: Marta on May 7, 1931, her siblings Pelayo in 1935, Zenaida in
1936, Héctor in 1937, and her cousins Blanca Luz and Félix. Marta's
own mother, Dora González Rivas, moved out of the house, possibly
as early as 1932, when she entered a sanatorium because of her tuberculosis. She died on November 3, 1938.

Higinia's brother Anacleto joined the household from Madruga in
the 1940s. Two more adults moved in to work for the family. Altogether
from the 1920s into the 1960s they were twenty-three people, spanning
three generations.

Marta remembers her first political act as a young child to be defying
a curfew with her grandmother so they could gather cigar butts in the
street for her great-grandmother to smoke in her pipe. What an exciting assignment this must have been, for a little girl to go into the street,
avoid the police, and gather the national commodity, but in an already
used form. Returning from the hunt and pleasing the two matriarchs
was a supreme victory.

The growing Terry household soon moved down the street to the
corner of Cárdenas and Gloria, taking Calle Cárdenas #151 and eventually expanding into #153 as well. Calle Cardenas was a "white" and
privileged street, but nearby were families and households of all strata
and ethnicities. Cárdenas is still just six blocks long, running from the
Havana train station to the Capitolio. The Capitolio, built for Machado
in 1929, is a marble, bronze, and gold facsimile of the US Capitol, and
at that time it housed the Cuban Congress. It was almost immediately
the scene of protest, massacre, and coup d'état.

The household dynamics were likely set before the family even left
the yellow roses in Madruga. By the time Marta was a teen, she would
describe her family as identical to that in Lorca's play *The House of*

*Bernarda Alba.* It was a feminine army squad with minor masculine participation. And it was, in fact, a traditional Spanish family structure.

Marta's grandmother Higinia—Señora Terry to her friends and admirers—was the squad chief. What she said was not to be debated. Her daughters feared her. So did her sons. The children-in-law, all but one of them women, did not like her. She did not like them much, either. The grandmother took control of Marta's upbringing just as her mother's illness left vacant the maternal role.

Marta's Aunt Graciela, who looked white, was the family treasurer. She was the married aunt. Her husband Félix Acosta Nogueras was a captain of one the most important firefighter units in the city of Havana. He was also one of the very scarce sources of money coming into the family. So that put Graciela—whom the family called Lala—in a very favorable position.

Close to the first of each month, Lala collected the money—a little from everyone who had some kind of a job—and did the shopping: rice, sugar, bathing soap, laundry soap; black, white, and red beans; and so on. Meat was quite a problem, but she managed for the whole family to have some kind of daily protein. Children had to have one or two eggs, generally boiled, in the morning.

Eggs were very cheap at that time, provided you had the money. There were two kinds of eggs and two prices. American eggs were cheaper than Cuban Creole eggs, or criollos. The family liked Cuban ones better than American. This was not strictly a question of patriotism. It was a question of flavor and color of the yolk. According to the grandmother and aunts, it was a question of what the chickens ate. Cubans were poorer, but the chickens were raised almost by hand and were fed grass, insects, and so on. The eggs became a family joke. And sometimes a tragedy when there was no money and no eggs.

When Marta was about six, her grandmother or her father or all of them together decided that she was to be baptized so that she could be confirmed and take Holy Communion in church. But who were to be godmother and godfather as required for baptism? None other than

Aunt Lala (Graciela) and her husband Félix—from then on Padrino—were appointed to perform the sacred act.

So in two moments separated by just a few weeks, Marta was a growing girl at La Merced Church, being formally Christianized and tasting the flavor of real salt on her lips. As she remembers it, a movie scene: the salt, the lips, and the invited guests murmuring Ave Marias and Padre Nuestros. The salt was part of her belated baptism, as the Holy Water, if not itself salted, was accompanied by a few grains of salt in the candidate's mouth. The second moment was her first communion, memorialized in a somber photo included in the photo section of this book.

Some years later, when Héctor came onto the scene, Aunt Lala and Padrino decided to adopt him as a son. They had no children of their own, But as soon as they decided to, she became pregnant. And thus arrived Marta's cousin Félix Fernando.

Graciela had studied to be a teacher, and then simultaneously earned two PhDs at the University of Havana: one in Pedagogy and one in Philosophy and Letters. Her sister Luz Maria—Aunt Luli to Marta—followed the same path and later, in the 1940s, even studied at the Law School where she met Fidel Castro.

So Aunt Graciela became Doctora Terry. After Marta earned her PhD, she could never abide being called Doctora Terry. For Marta, one Doctora Terry was enough for the family. Aunt Graciela had a big influence over the whole family and particularly over Marta. She was the one with jewels. She wore beautiful dresses. She was the only aunt who let Marta try on all her finery.

Much later, in 1962, Marta's cousin Félix Fernando left for the US. Only after Marta's grandmother Higinia had died did Félix succeed in taking Aunt Lala with him, and then on the grounds of health. Marta never heard directly from them again.

Marta's early life was full of moments that expressed the duality of Cuban culture under the dominant Eurocentrism, as well as the female power of the Terry family. One of these times was death of her mother Dora González Rivas. Dora passed away shortly before Marta's baptism.

But the schedule for Marta's formal initiation into Catholicism was not adjusted. Three weeks after Dora's death, Marta took her first communion. Dressed in a traditional white dress and veil, Marta epitomized the aspiration of the Afro-Cuban middle class to be accepted as Cuban; that is, as having achieved Eurocentric standards. But around her neck, hidden beneath her dress, she wore the blue and white beads of reverence for Yemayá (Our Lady of Regla), the Yorùbá deity prominent in the pantheon of Santería.

Marta's aunts were educated women with professions as teachers. They matriculated at the University of Havana in the 1940s, and for Afro-Cuban women this was a unique and amazing achievement. They adopted middle-class aspirations and lifestyles that centered on the home. Meanwhile, Marta's father Nícolas was a postal worker who embraced the norms of mass culture. A gregarious man, he was well-known for his skill as a dancer. He was well educated in history and culture through the "people's college" of their household full of interesting books. He was an avid reader who kept up with his sisters. But every Saturday night he would go to the Tropicale, just three kilometers from their home and a magnet for Afro-Cubans and others who could not enter the whites-only dance venues. People would crowd the nightclub's plate glass window to watch him and his partner dance.

He was a community leader as well as a star on the dance floor. The Afro-Cuban community was excluded from the white mainstream, but they self-organized as they have always done in Cuba, exercising their own agency as recounted in Chapter 1. The Afro-Cuban club movement was organized along class lines, with the most elite in Havana being the Club Atenas. There the elite would meet, party, and curry favor with the white Cuban political and economic elites who visited the club. In contrast to that scene, Nícolas was an active member of the Union Fraternelle, an Afro-Cuban workingmen's club. He was at various times the president, vice president, secretary, and director of their council of leaders. He was also an elected leader of the postal workers association. He traveled abroad to sustain linkages with similar associations across Latin America.

Higinia and the aunts reined in Marta's father more than once. Zenaida and Héctor each came to live in the house soon after they were born, even though Nícolas was not married to their mother, Evelina Molinert. He was enjoying the lifestyle of a single man. Eventually he decided to marry a beautiful dancer by the name of Josefina. She signed her name Josefina Rivera S. O. A., which stood for "sin otro apellido" (without other name), acknowledging her own informal family status in a way that became obsolete after 1959. The aunts insisted that she move into the house with the rest of them, to stay close and make sure everyone was provided for. And they insisted that Nícolas get the permission of his daughter Marta to marry and bring a stepmother into her life. Marta, then twelve years old, said yes.

Later Josefina's beautiful mulata mother, Fortuna, would often visit the family. She was there for many January 11 feasts, for that was the Catholic day of San Higinio. It was Higinia's saint's day and her favorite son Fernando Averhoff always managed the feast. Another visitor to the family home was Marta's maternal grandfather Antolín González, who would come on Sundays. That family had something of the same flavor as the Terry family. Grandfather Antolín—Marta's aunts gave him horrible nicknames, for they did not like him—always took an interest in Marta's progress as a student and young woman, and he would help her out with gifts of money. He told her that González was not his real name, that it should have been O'Halloran. O'Halloran was then a well-known mulato family of musicians, one of whom taught in the conservatory that Marta attended. Putting this all together, Marta concluded that if informal families were legally acknowledged, her name would have been Marta Inchaurtieta O'Halloran rather than Marta Terry González.

As she was just becoming aware of her own family legacy, Marta had her first contact with an exhibit of Cuban painting. In it she saw a picture called *Grandmother and Child*. It was a Black woman and a blond child. It was her first personal contact with the public world of fine art. She was stunned to see the familiar in a big art exhibition. It was as if a public secret was being openly acknowledged.

Marta spoke of this when she remembered a fragment of "El Apel-lido" ("My Family Name"), a poem by the Afro-Cuban Nícolas Guillén, thirty years her senior and later the national poet of post-1958 Cuba:

> Don't I have, then,
> a Mandinga grandfather; or Congolese, or Dahomeyan?
> What's his name? Oh, yes, give me his name!
> Andrés? Francisco? Amable?
> How do you say Andrew in Congolese?
> …
>
> Do you know my other last name, the one that comes
> to me from that enormous land, the captured,
> bloody last name, that came across the sea
> in chains, which came in chains across the sea.
> Ah, you can't remember it!
> You have dissolved it in immemorial ink,
> You stole it from a poor, defenseless Black.[43]

As a young teenager Marta would occasionally see her grandmother's first informal husband, the planter's son Francisco Averhoff. Sentimental and audacious at the same time, he would bring his white family—wife and children—along to meet their Afro-Cuban blood relatives. They kept the money "white" while their visit to these Afro-Cubans validated their Cuban identity. The opposite was true for Marta and her family. They were disinherited from the "white wealth," but were brought straight into the complex and contradictory union of their African heritage confronting their historical connection to "whiteness." But there stood two women, one Afro-Cuban and the other of Spanish heritage, both Cuban, looking at each other across a social and cultural divide. And there stood a broader personal complexity as well, since every young family member present was related by blood. Of course,

---

43. Nicolás Guillén, *Man-Making Words: Selected Poems of Nícolas Guillén*, trans. Robert Márquez and David Arthur McMurray (Havana: Editorial de Arte y Literatura, 1973), 75.

there was young Marta, caught in this dialectic of the past, sometimes being called upon by her grandmother to recite a poem for the guests, and always wondering what it might mean for her future in a Cuba to come that was far beyond anyone's imagination. Higinia would run into her second informal husband, Marta's father's father Nicolás Inchaurtieta, in the fields and streets around his office. And later Aunt Luli would take Marta—but never the other children—to his house for a social call.

Two more members of the household were Higinia's sister and brother. Candelaria had children, but they died young, so towards the end of her life she came to live with the extended family. Anacleto, who did not have a family, had remained in the family home town of Madruga where he worked as a carpenter. At the end of his life, he came to Havana to live with Higinia and her eight children and their partners and children. Marta Terry remembers him as a very gentle person. He was also the first person she watched die. Her great-grandmother Marta O'Farrill died before Marta knew her, but Marta felt her legacy in many ways. For one, every Sunday Higinia would take Marta with her to visit Marta O'Farrill's grave in Havana's renowned Cristóbal Colón Cemetery. Marta O'Farrill had been born a slave and won her freedom. She was buried in Colón, but among the poor in that strictly hierarchical cemetery, until Higinia's years of determined effort yielded enough money and political influence for her to be reburied in another section. Other family members were later buried near her, including Luis, Marta's husband.

This was the time before TV; family gatherings and the art of conversation were the entertainment and primary socialization process at home. Marta sat at the knee of her grandmother when the aunts would gather and talk about popular culture and the arts. For them, Charlie Chaplin was good and Clark Gable was bad. The American movie industry was strong, but they also paid close attention to the Spanish, Mexican, and other Latin American traditions which they had access to in those days. They loved the Mexican muralist tradition but also the movies by María Félix and Jorge Negrete. Marta was later to publish her first film criticism about one of Negrete's films in a Mexican magazine. One of the family dramas was her inventive uncle Francisco applying for a US patent on a "valve for lubrication" of air compressors; for three years everyone had moments of hope, despair, and laughter over this, but in the end, patent number 2,425,446 was duly awarded.

The radio was almost a member of the household. Most everyone had their favorite dramas or comedies, during which the family would gather and listen. Marta remembers listening to debates about the 1940 Constitution, large portions of which were drafted by the Cuban Communist Party, as it was then working in the Batista administration. The constitution was passed but never fully implemented until after 1959, when much of its language was adopted for the Fundamental Law of Cuba.

Marta was home-schooled until age ten. One of the reasons for this was her weak health. After her mother died, she was the sickest in the family. The family kept her close in part because of her sore throats and colds. Her thinness made her look all the more vulnerable. Her aunts and grandmother were always afraid Marta would get tuberculosis because her mother had died of it. And it was the entire family who managed for Marta to have her tonsils removed to try to solve her chronic throat problems. They went to great lengths to have her treated in what was then the best specialized private hospital in Havana.

At the same time, health care was one of the aspects of life that anchored Marta's childhood in the Afro-Cuban cultural traditions. Her grandmother was a healer who had lots of pots with herbs that she got from people she knew. She would take the family back to Madruga at least once a year, where they would collect flowers, herbs, and many different kinds of things for her to use to make her healing potions. Marta was frequently treated by Dr. David Cazañas Aldama, but her grandmother would also bring in *babalaos* and spiritualists. The healing story from the spiritualists was that since Marta's mother had died from tuberculosis, her mother's spirit would come to protect Marta whenever she got sick and had colds or was coughing. The story helped Marta feel close to the mother she lost at age seven. Decades later, Marta's bouts of illness were understood—and treated—as stubborn allergies.

Her grandmother would say, "Take the nest of a special kind of ant that grows near the trees. That ant hill, you take it in an infusion of material and that clears up congestion. If the congestion is too strong, you know what you have to use? Grease of the maja [the Cuban boa constrictor]. Take a spoonful of that grease and your congestion goes." Today that grease is recognized by Western medicine. Higinia knew how to lower fever and ease stomach aches and menstrual cramps. She offered potions for colds that Marta found both marvelous and terrible. Poor people had to do this as they had no money for a doctor or his prescriptions. The Terry family was able to afford penicillin and they saved up for the best hospitals of the day— Marta remembers a Doctor Revuelta who removed her tonsils—but the family relied on both schools of thought. As she grew up Marta was one of the generation that coveted pills.

Higinia did not observe many rituals of the traditions, but she was realistic and used everything that worked. One ritual persisted. To protect Marta from people who would be envious of her good looks, Higinia rushed to the door whenever Marta made ready to go out. "Stop! Just a minute!" And she would bless Marta with a leaf from the ficus tree always positioned nearby. The ficus leaf belongs particularly to the three orishas Shangó, Odua, and Egún. Santería uses it to remove impurities and negativities, to banish evil spirits and attract good fortune.[44] Mainstream institutions frowned on and even banned these African-derived beliefs and practices. Followers kept Santería a secret. Afro-Cuban families that sent their children into the mainstream did not pass the traditions on, and over time they became weak. Today, there is a resurgence of green medicine and more openness to different religions

Marta's close friends were curious and admiring of Marta's family. In 2013 she was watching television and they were broadcasting a big official event about education, teachers, and so on. Suddenly there was Graziella Pogolotti talking about the ways, behavior, and wisdom teachers

---

44. Dalía Quiros Moran, *Guide to Afro-Cuban Herbalism* (Bloomington, IN: AuthorHouse, 2009).

must have. As she later confirmed to Marta, she was indeed describing Marta's aunts. Another friend, Marta Vesa (who worked briefly in marketing and publicity before she died young), said a book should be written on the Terry family: Marta's grandmother and the other great character, Marta's father, who was the best Danzón dancer in Havana, not to say in Cuba. Marta Vesa wanted to make a film of Nícolas and his wife Josefina dancing. Marta herself even started to write short stories after another one of her classmates, María Elena Jubrías (later an art history professor at the University of Havana and a prominent ceramist) was mystified by Marta's living arrangements and it prompted Marta to begin to write down her family stories. She felt there was something different in her family, something that ought to be known.

Marta's family had an extended set of nicknames for everyone. The aunts evolved a complete system, now lost, for the nicknames of friends and neighbors. Inside the family, Higinia's nicknames were Mona and also Mamá, although she was always known in the community as Señora Terry. Aunt Graciela was Lala and her husband Félix was Padrino. Aunt Luz Maria was Luly, Lulu, or Lila. Aunt Zilia was Zilita or Zili. Aunt Mercedes was Mercy, Merceditas, or Nene. Uncle Francisco was Panchito. Uncle Fernando was Fernandito or Fernan. Her father Nícolas was either Papi or (to his siblings) Colín. Cousin Félix Acosta was Pipo. Cousin Blanca Luz was Cuchy. Sister Zenaida was Cena. Brother Héctor was Hectico. Brother Pelayo was Pela. As for Marta herself, the family called her la China, or sometimes la Niña. Her brothers and sisters would tease her with the nickname Gira, that is, Giraffe—which is to say, tall and thin. Later her university friends—reflecting the classical aspects of their education—would call her Terricola, the Latin word for "terrestrial." Marta and her extended family were thus embedded in a network of local, citywide, even countrywide relationships.

Marta had dozens of fights with the adults in her family as a teenager. She was the only one among the young ones to rebel this way. Her brothers and sister did as they liked, but never protested so loudly. Why? As Marta put it, the adults wanted her to be the best of the best: best student, best dressed, best at church, best at the Santeros party, best in

English classes and music classes, best in the French classes that her aunt Zilita was in charge of, and in the best of health. Since her mother had died from lung disease, they all seemed convinced she would, too. As one observer wryly commented to Marta, "They did all they could to prove they were right."

Health was just one of the causes of the open struggle between Marta and the older generation. There were other obstacles to overcome: race, poverty, and man–woman relationships, including, of course, sex. Marta was determined that she would not suffer as her aunts did. Meanwhile, they wanted her to be so good that nothing and nobody would be able to hurt her, so good that she would be prepared to face the trials life would bring to her—or rather, to them all, as women, Black, and poor.

After the 1959 revolutionary transformation, the grand extended family leadership began to make its transition. In 1961 the government outlawed all private societies. This included the elite whites-only yacht clubs and country clubs, for they had become organizing centers for counterrevolution. It also included the Afro-Cuban clubs and societies. They had been manipulated by Batista, and then were conspicuously absent from an otherwise broad call for Batista's resignation in March 1958. By 1959, Nicolás Terry's ceaseless organizing and socializing had ended, causing despair and disorientation across the family. Aunt Graciela became seriously ill and her son Félix Fernando persuaded her to leave with him to the United States and get treatment. Marta remembers praying with her not to go to the United States; she died shortly after leaving Cuba. Aunt Luz Maria, Higinia's favorite, died in 1968. Higinia survived until October 5, 1975. Nícolas and Zilia lived the longest, into the 1980s or 1990s.

This was a household caught in the dialectics of generational change. Higinia's mother (Marta's great-grandmother) was of the enslaved generation that experienced and participated in the revolutionary end of slavery and later of direct Spanish colonialism. Higinia herself did as well, but as a little girl, for she was born in 1880, six years before slavery was ended in Cuba. Higinia and her generation experienced the early republic and the great disappointment of American-sponsored neocolonialism during that early republic. The aunts were the generation of Havana-based Afro-Cubans who benefited from the opportunities of the republic, becoming teachers with a university education. This was not enough for Marta's generation. They wanted this and much more.

Within the household, while all of Marta's siblings and cousins achieved successes, the chosen ones were Marta and Héctor. Influenced by Marta and her peers, Héctor joined the revolutionary struggle. He was an early member of the Revolutionary Directorate (founded in 1955), while keeping his grades up to maintain his scholarship funding at the university. Later Héctor went to medical school and rose to the top of his profession in revolutionary Cuba. In many ways, Héctor was to public health what Marta was to libraries. But they were not the only high achievers. Her sister Zenaida also grew up to earn a PhD and to become a librarian, working at the National Museum of Fine Arts.

Héctor married and had two daughters and a son, finishing his medical training after 1959. He rose in the ranks of his profession and eventually became the Cuban Vice Minister of Health for Hygiene and Epidemiology. He provided the key leadership in developing the AIDS policy for the Cuban health care system. Medical care has been one of the policy concerns of Cuba since 1959. As he said,

> In Cuba, nobody lacks economic resources because of being an AIDS carrier. In Cuba, no one dies abandoned on the streets for lack of access to a hospital. In Cuba, we haven't had to open hospices so that patients who have been abandoned have a place to die in peace. In Cuba, no one's house has been set on fire because its inhabitants are people with AIDS. In Cuba, no homosexual has been persecuted because he's assumed to be likely to spread the virus. In Cuba, we don't have the problem of national minorities or drug addicts with high rates of AIDS.[45]

Elsewhere in the same volume comes another statement by Héctor:

---

45. Karen Wald, "Questions and Answers on AIDS in Cuba," unpublished interview with Dr. Héctor Terry, 1989, quoted in Marvin Leiner, *Sexual Politics in Cuba: Machismo, Homosexuality, and AIDS* (Boulder, CO: Westview Press, 1994), 145.

We have the opportunity to stop the disease [AIDS] in our country. It would be irresponsible if we didn't face the situation with courage, knowing we could stop it. We have an epidemiological opportunity that we are not going to lose.[46]

As did her brother after her, Marta married in the context of the early years of her professional career in revolutionary Cuba, a story to be told in part 2 of this book. She and her husband Luís had a son, Claudio, who unfortunately shared her health challenges but has persevered through the years, working when he can as a driver. He married Lillian María González Martínez, a doctor who distinguished herself in service with the army in Angola, part of Cuba's progressive foreign policy leading all countries in the African Diaspora. Claudio and Lily named their only child—Marta's grandson—Héctor Luis Forte González. This honored Claudio's father Luis, Marta's brother Héctor, and Héctor's own son, who was named Héctor Manuel. Claudio had been very close to Héctor Manuel, who died in a tragic car accident while still a teen.

As part of the Elian González[47] generation, Marta's grandson Héctor Luis has only had the experience of the Special Period and after. Marta spends time with her grandson and experiences the great advantages he has compared to when she was young, and yet as a grandparent she hopes things get much better. This is one of the great tragedies of the US blockade, that the youth are quarantined from full access to world culture and opportunities. They want what they don't have and are challenged to get what they want by continuing the revolution or compromising it. It will be their choice.

The family of twenty-three who lived communally under one roof is gone forever as a consequence of the new opportunities after 1959.

---

46. Marvin Leiner, *Sexual Politics in Cuba: Machismo, Homosexuality, and AIDS* (Boulder, CO: Westview Press, 1994), 117.

47. Elian González left Cuba for Miami in November 1999 when his mother took a raft with other would-be refugees. She drowned and he was placed with Miami relatives. His father and others in both countries agitated for his lawful return, which took place seven months later, ending a saga followed closely by media in Cuba and the United States. Although Florida authorities acted otherwise, most Cubans and North Americans supported Elian and his father's rights to be together.

Three people left Cuba in the 1960s; the older generation passed on; the younger ones were able to get their own housing where they raised their families. Marta got her apartment in the Miramar district of Havana with her husband as part of the housing allocated to staff of JUCEPLAN where they both worked. She has lived there now for more than fifty years.

So what in summary can we say about Marta's emergence from her family?

Marta is quintessentially Cuban. Her family combined African and European, Black and white, Catholic and Santería. She had a personal foundation in strong bonds of trust in a trans-generational extended family. The grandmother-based matriarchal structure gave her the gift of a strong ego. Within a household diverse by generation and gender, she learned a great deal about how to assert and withdraw in struggle and diplomacy. As the oldest of her generation, she became a leader.

Marta was reared to be upwardly mobile and achieve professional status, instructed always to be "the best of the best." And yet in doing so, she rebelled against limiting societal norms, mostly with her family's approval. She entered previously forbidden territory. Her family prepared her to negotiate the terrain of status and class and programmed her for high achievement.

# Chapter 3

## EDUCATION

Education is a social process that is necessary for humans to exist as our behavior is not determined by our genetic code; we have to learn how to be human. What we learn through education determines who we are, and in most societies this process begins in the family, but is then turned over to institutions in the society so that everyone in the same society shares language, norms, and values, including historical consciousness. Marta's education began in the family, but as is usual continued in the schools.

Through age nine Marta saw life primarily from the window of the family home, and otherwise shared in the oral culture of family life, both what she was meant to hear and what she was able to get by eavesdropping. When she turned seven, she did go to some classes at the Municipal Conservatory of Havana, as did her siblings. Only later did the aunts decided that it was time for Marta to start school full time and have contact with her peers to prepare for adult life and work. With her extended family foundation, fueled by her ambition and curiosity, Marta left the family cocoon that had nurtured her and ventured out into the world, pursuing her education and experimenting with the diversity of life. It was 1941. She was ten years old and off to school for the first time.

Marta's transition was one step at a time. Most of the other children went by themselves or walked in groups, but Aunt Merceditas would take Marta to school because the family didn't want her to go by herself. She went to a school for girls, #20. The even-numbered schools were for girls and the odd for boys. Nearby was school #21, so Marta's aunts were taking no chances.

As life continued, Marta grew up to be very different from her aunts. They had been cloistered and kept out of the usual social life. Mainly, no men! On the other hand, Marta mastered the iconic and infamous role of the Cuban mulata, though she reversed its usual meaning. Her aunts had been protected against the stereotype of the mulata as sexual object by their mother (Marta's grandmother), thus avoiding the fate of the previous two generations, but Marta lived a different life. She became a liberated mulata, educated and sophisticated, beautiful and working networks of power with finesse. She was not an object for others, she was a subject armed with a strong ego and ambition. She was more in control than being controlled. She was becoming more her grandmother than her aunts.

As such, she worked the contradictions in her family's own hopes for her. She had been schooled by her aunts who had two conflicting desires: for her to be "the best of the best," on the one hand, but to protect her from the dangers in society on the other. They wanted her to be a successful middle-class professional, overcoming the barriers to women, especially those affecting Afro-Cuban women.

At age ten she learned that the Ministry of Education decided that, as of 1944, twelve-year-olds could sit for an examination and be admitted into high school. This set off a burning desire in Marta. At that point she was headed for grade six by age twelve. She felt she could take the exam and pass, so she waged a campaign in the family. The aunts were opposed; they had their sights set on her becoming a teacher. If she passed, it would mean moving from elementary school to upper elementary school for what in the US are the middle grades, and then to normal school at age 14. At the time Cuba had one in each province.

Graduating from high school, by contrast, would earn her the diploma called the Bachillerato. This was the credential for entering the university and all of the offerings there. In the end, her aunts agreed to high school for two years and then normal school at age fourteen to become a teacher. But Marta's real strategy soon emerged: to go to university, and in the end that is what she accomplished. They had taught her to have a mind of her own and she was using it to rebel in the family. And so Marta skipped three grades, sixth, seventh, and eighth! Cuba was changing and Marta was ready.

Marta soon began to interact with all aspects of Cuban society. There were only twenty-one institutes of secondary education in the country, and she attended Institute No. 1. This was the school that José Martí —intellectual, organizer, father of Cuba—had attended as a young boy in the 1800s. One of her first ethnic encounters was with a Jewish community. She remembers them as Sephardic Jews from Germany. This community had been assimilated into Cuban cultural norms and did not wear traditional clothes or hairstyles. Her competitive perspective shaped her memory: "They were good at mathematics and I was very dumb at mathematics."

She had won the battle for high school and entered into a world where she was generally the youngest and the smallest. With her rebellious spirit, she was often not the one with the highest grades. With his top grades, her brother Héctor was going to get a tuition-free high school education, but for Marta it would cost six pesos per course ($6). The family pulled together and budgeted for her education.

High school—more precisely the Instituto de Segunda Enseñanza Numero 1 de la Habana—created the context for Marta's first political demonstration. Instituto #1 was one of four in Havana and only twenty-one in the entire country. All were in cities; there were no high schools for rural children. By 1944 the progressive and popular Minister of Education Luis Pérez Espinós was pushed out, and on January 28, Martí's birthday, the students at #1 organized a protest march. Marta was chosen to hold one edge of the Cuban flag at the head of the march. Her rebellious spirit, miniature size (being so much younger than her classmates) and good looks had catapulted her into a prominent role. They only got a couple of blocks before the police charged the march. Older students grabbed Marta and got her out of there to protect her. This was her first taste of fighting, in this case against the regime of Cuba's tenth president, Ramón Grau San Martín (1944–1948).

In high school Marta was gradually given greater degrees of freedom. She was no longer chaperoned and was allowed to go to parties and have a variety of friends. On occasion could she stay out until midnight, but she was constantly given instructions on what to do and what not to do. The family embraced Marta's friends in their home. These were more girls than boys and that was fine with Higinia and the aunts. Marta's siblings followed her example and so the new generation had influence and began to change the norms and cultural values of their family. The two bottom lines were that you had to be a good student and an honest person.

Cuba has a musical culture that was and is everywhere and all the time. Dancing is merely an extension of walking and moving collectively in a group. A hip rhythm is the logic of life in Cuba. Marta's father Nícolas went outside of the home to dance, and in fact was part of popularizing the evolution of the Danzón, Cuba's distinctive social dance form. Using more syncopation, the Danzón led to the Cha-cha-cha, the Pachanga, and the Mambo. The children of the household could do these dances at home, but their fluid motion and distinctive Afro-Cuban-based art form had to be practiced under the imposed social norms for the middle class, and certainly for the Terry girls: no movement below the waist! As Marta remembers, she was thus blocked from following her father into dancing fame.

But for the youth the import of US popular culture was soon to be a major factor in social life. US neocolonial culture changed the popular culture of Cuba—baseball and rock and roll. The most impactful aspect of this popular culture was the Afro-Cuban connection to African Americans in the United States.[48] Indeed this was both a capitalist import and the music of rebellion. They heard Fats Domino and the Platters, and they heard the white crossover Elvis Presley. Here was a

---

48. For more on this, see Lisa Brock and Digna Castañeda Fuertes, *Between Race and Empire: African-Americans and Cubans before the Cuban Revolution* (Philadelphia, PA: Temple University Press, 1998); Frank Andre Guridy, *Forging Diaspora: Afro-Cubans and African Americans in a World of Empire and Jim Crow* (Chapel Hill: University of North Carolina Press, 2010).

white musician in the United States openly embracing Black music and dance culture, swinging his hips and calling attention to his blue suede shoes. The singer and band leader Benny Moré was king in Cuba, but for Marta's peers Elvis was definitely in the royal court, along with the Platters and Nat King Cole.

The freedom of high school meant that sometimes Marta and her classmates would cut classes. Tuesday afternoon baseball games were free to women and they went to admire the "cute" baseball stars who were well-publicized pop culture icons. They also went to the radio stations to catch a glimpse of the personalities they listened to on a regular basis. While violating the rules of their school, these outings demonstrated that one sure way to get an education is to go and see for yourself, to investigate.

After high school Marta faced the challenge of entering the University of Havana. This was considered the best of the three existing institutions of higher education in Cuba,[49] and it was right in Marta's hometown. The University of Havana was founded in 1728, 220 years before Marta enrolled in 1948. It was a center of resistance against tyrannical governance, against the Cuban puppets of US colonial domination. The Federation of University Students (FEU) was founded in 1923 by Julio Antonio Mella, also a cofounder of the Cuban Communist Party in 1925. Mella was killed in Mexico by assassins sent by Cuban President Machado in 1929. In 1933, two years after Marta was born, it was FEU that initiated a general strike that led to the downfall of the Machado regime. To enter the University of Havana was to enter a liberated zone, thanks to tradition, convention, and student activism. Fidel Castro entered the university in 1945 to study law, and Marta did so in 1948 to study philosophy and literature.

In this environment Marta experienced and participated in the general political motion of the campus in general. She met the already prominent

---

49. Compared to the University of Havana, which was founded in 1728, the others were extremely new: the St. Thomas of Villanova Catholic University, which opened in Havana in 1946, and the University of Santiago, opened in 1947.

students Fidel Castro and José Antonio Echeverría. Echeverría was a revolutionary, elected president of FEU, and founder of the Revolutionary Directorate (RD). The militant students of FEU and the RD were later to pose such a threat to Batista that he ordered the campus closed from 1957 to 1958. In doing so Batista helped organize even more students and others against his regime.

World War II unleashed global winds of struggle for freedom from colonialism. These winds blew through university campuses worldwide, engaging larger numbers of students. In 1945 Ho Chi Minh led the Vietnamese to victory with the creation of the Democratic Republic of Vietnam in the northern part of the country. By 1954 they had defeated French colonialism in the Battle of Dien Bien Phu. In 1945 the fifth Pan-African Congress was held in Manchester, ushering into existence national liberation movements in many parts of Africa. By 1957 Ghana had become the first African country to win independence. In 1945 Mahatma Gandhi and Jawaharlal Nehru demanded that British troops leave India. By 1947 India was independent. European colonialism was being challenged and the fight against US neocolonialism in Cuba would not be far behind. In 1953 Fidel Castro led an attack on the Moncada military barracks in Santiago, Cuba. By 1959 the revolutionaries had come to power.

Marta had an advantage in pursuing a university education: because her aunts had been students at the University of Havana, this gave her the right and responsibility to be there. There was open enrollment; no entrance exam for the university in those days. With your bachillerato (high school diploma) and with money to pay the entrance fee you could attend. If you were poor and allowed the authorities to inspect your family's living situation to prove it, you might be granted free admittance, but her aunts did not want anything to do with that. They were proud to pay and claim the status that went with being able to pay your own way. There were not many who could. Even middle-class families who did not live in Havana were hard pressed to send their children because of the cost of relocating to the city.

After some time the family wanted Marta to take a job as a substitute English-language teacher, for that skill was in demand, given US hegemony, and work while continuing her studies. But because of illness Marta was not able to do that. The aunts thus ended up excusing her from the job market. They wanted her to have a degree, but not at the cost of a gravestone! Marta continued as a full-time student.

Upon entering the university in 1948, Marta had to choose her path. For sure, she did not want to be a schoolteacher like her aunts and their friends. She wanted to be a doctor of medicine. According to Marta, she prayed to God and begged her aunts to allow her to study medicine. They in turn arranged for the family physician, Dr. David Cazañas, to convince her it was a bad idea. Dr. Cazañas was a mulato with some Chinese in his background. The entire Terry family were among his patients. Marta remembers him as a magnificent person and at the same time a sort of victim of pre-1959 Cuba, someone who had to obey Aunt Luz María, the intellectual aunt taking the lead on this matter. He did try to convince Marta, but she saw that he himself was not absolutely convinced in the matter.

Marta remained stubborn and (as she remembers) somewhat childish regarding the decision, so the family brought out their final argument, their deadly weapon: a Black woman could not study medicine because she would end up as a midwife. The aunts had not spent their own lives taking care of her in order for her to become a midwife. As choir director on this matter, Aunt Luz Maria pointed out the supposedly hideous example of an Afro-Cuban woman doctor. In point of fact, this woman became famous across Cuba for her excellent work as an obstetrician.

Marta could not argue any longer. Her grades in science and math were not helping her, and so the family elders won the battle. The Terry that was chosen by destiny—that is, by the aunts—to become a medical doctor was Marta's brother Héctor. Some years later, in February 1959, Marta visited Dr. Cazañas and he said, "Marta, today you could have studied medicine and become a psychoanalyst, I know you would have been a great success at that!" Decades later, Héctor said to Marta,

"The truth is that without the revolution, our destiny would have been nothing but to flee to the United States."

So it was that Marta entered the elite field of Philosophy and Letters, one of the students who all aimed to be the best of the best among Cuban intellectuals. In her school there were 150 students, only three of them Afro-Cubans and all of those women: Marta, Flora Merconchini, and one more. As in wider society, the intellectual content of her university education was not her only challenge. Just as important were the social contradictions that she faced on campus. She was marginalized by some of the white students, offspring of the Cuban bourgeoisie, over whether she was an authentic Cuban Catholic. Marta's grandmother had made sure she learned her catechism and was properly confirmed, but she had gone to a public high school. On the formal basis of religion Marta knew she was indeed a Catholic, albeit one with a Santería flavor.

Marta believed she was an equal to these Catholic girls, but at that time she didn't really understand the deep dynamics of this discriminatory process that created divisions of hierarchy. Nor did many of her classmates, although their experiences and activities sprung directly from Cuban culture. For instance, Marta remembers everyone enjoying duets that she and classmate Carmen Almodóvar would perform (with much noise and fun) from the musical play of *Cecilia Valdés*. This adaptation of Cuba's most famous 1800s novel was in fact a tragic story of a mulata falling in mutual love with her rich father's white son, who then betrays her and is killed by her Afro-Cuban suitor.

In the end, the elite students were able to cover their class and color prejudice against Marta by saying she wasn't a real Catholic because she hadn't gone to a Catholic school (most if not all private schools were Catholic), but to a public school. According to them, the Sunday schools offered at the churches were not the proper or the adequate place to learn the principles and ideology of Catholicism. While associating with Marta in general student activities, they increasingly drew a firm line of demarcation and marginalized her from their inner circles. These differences proved to be decisive as the struggle intensified and separated revolutionaries from reactionaries. Many of these "authentic" Catholics would end up in Florida after 1959, although one of them remained: her singing mate Carmen Almodóvar. Speaking recently as the historiographer she became, she mentioned Marta and others and recalled:

> Professors and students alike defined the circumference of my activities during those turbulent years for the country. Many of those who studied with me and shaped me in the house of higher learning soon emigrated. Others stayed and have made contributions to developing the culture of the country. I remember this period 1948-1952 with nostalgia for lost youth and for dreams that are long gone. But even stronger is the lasting memory of a period that forged my future as a professional.[50]

Marta and her cohort benefitted from a generational dynamic whereby former students became leading university faculty. Students who were activists in FEU and led the resistance to Machado in the 1930s became professors at the University of Havana. They in turn educated the students who were to become activists in the 1950s leading to Cuba's rebirth in 1959. These professors covered the entire spectrum of radical opposition, from liberal reformers to active members of communist organizations, all nationalist patriots fighting for a free Cuba.

A man who had great influence on Marta and her peers was José Elías Entralgo Vallina, a distinguished professor of history. He was a character like the British fictional character Mr. Chips,[51] almost fanatical about discipline, but a champion at guiding his students to a firm intellectual foundation. In the end, after jokes and pranks by the students that included sexual provocation, he won their greatest respect. At the beginning of Marta's fourth year he gave all two hundred students a surprise exam. Out of that exam, he chose a small number of students, about twenty, to be in a special class. At least half of those students became close associates during their university years and later, and were well into future high-achieving careers during the post-1959 revolutionary

---

50. Mildred de la Torre Molina, "Vivo Orgullosa De Ser Maestra: Entrevista a Carmen Almodóvar Muñoz," *Espacio Laical* [Laity Space] 6, no. 24 (2010): 74.

51. Mr. Chips was the protagonist in a 1934 novella about a school teacher, see: James Hilton, *Goodbye, Mr. Chips* (London: Hodder & Stoughton, 1934). The story was adapted for film twice, in 1939 and 1969.

experience. Elías Entralgo himself was already a communist in the 1950s, and he was the first of Marta's professors to suggest that she join the faculty when he was looking for people who could help lead the university after 1959.

But back in that fourth year of Marta's university studies, Entralgo required his chosen ones to attend his special class several times a week at seven a.m. sharp, including Saturdays. To be late meant that you would be excluded that day. In the beginning the students hated this level of strict order, but it became a mark of distinction as their discipline distinguished them from the other students who were on a different, less-demanding schedule. He led close readings of texts and was always serious, even when Marta and others were trying to make fun of him. He also had each of them write an autobiography placing themselves in the context of family and country, suggesting that if each of them understood his or her past, planning a new future would be more possible. They eventually learned that he was helping them achieve the focus and methodological grounding necessary for their future roles in leading key Cuban institutions.

In Philosophy and Letters, everyone took the same classes for the first three years and then chose a special area for the final year. This is when Marta wrote a paper on the Escalera incident of 1844. The year 1843 saw a series of successful slave revolts, one led by the legendary Carlota. The Year of the Lash followed in 1844, particularly the Escalera conspiracy which involved torture and murders, including the whipping of slaves who had been tied to a ladder (escalera). Many years later, Operation Carlota was the name of the first stage of Cuban military support to Angola, which began in 1975 and ended in victory for Angola and further, in helping to end apartheid.[52] As a further culmination of

---

52. Piero Gleijeses, *Visions of Freedom: Havana, Washington, Pretoria, and the Struggle for Southern Africa, 1976-1991* (Chapel HIll, NC: University of North Carolina Press, 2013); Guillén, *Man-Making Words: Selected Poems of Nicolas Guillén*; Gabriel García Marquez, "Operation Carlota," 1976. Marquez's account was published in newspapers around the world.

her studies, Marta wrote a thesis titled "The impact of slavery on white society in the South up to 1850."

One high point for Marta was attending the masterful lectures by Fernando Ortíz in the university's Aula Magna (as they call their large lecture hall) when he first presented his findings, making room on the stage for an unprecedented performance of Afro-Cuban dancing and drumming before the amazed audience. It was one of the most exciting and controversial events concerning new scholarship on the Afro-Cuban experience. While not on the faculty, the great Cuban anthropologist introduced people to his theory of transculturation and invited them to rethink the history and cultural life of Cuba by re-evaluating the role of African-descendant peoples. These lectures were an act of resistance on campus to the popular prejudicial view off campus that devalued and marginalized the role of African culture in Cuba. He introduced a young woman who became a very famous singer and cultural representative of Santería, Merceditas Valdes. She opened and closed the proceedings, singing in the Yorùbá language and dancing all around the lecture hall, which was sacred in its own way to the university community. She danced to Elegguá, god of roads, the one who enables aché (the life force) to flow.

Part of the contradiction of this period is that there were so many people who played a role in one or more instances who later departed, choosing not to be part of the post-1959 revolutionary process. One such man was a professor Marta encountered at the university, one of the most enthusiastic for organizing Fernando Ortíz's lectures: the historian Herminio Portell Vilá. He encouraged Marta and several others to help organize a library for the school of philosophy and literature. He encouraged her to become a librarian and persuaded her to compete for an international scholarship. When she won, he convinced the family to let her travel to the United States. He eventually moved to Miami, continuing as a prolific historian who also did broadcasts for the US government's international radio station, Voice of America. The Cuban revolutionary experience is full of such stories and it is only hindsight that can even try to discern clues as to who would stay the course as patriots in revolutionary Cuba and who would not.

The student networks moved as social units, in classes and in discussions at crucial third places on and near campus. But as the very first school year began and the Catholics rejected Marta and others, the "Group" formed itself. They use that name to this day, although by the second year they also invented another name, playing with Greek and Latin: Pi Kappa Tau, PKT, in other words, the strong explosive letters. The Group was social, sisterhood and brotherhood, and soon they were swept up in the strong left anti-government sensibility of the time. While a large majority of the students in Philosophy and Letters were upper class girls, a minority of girls and boys were there from the middle-class, professional or intellectual families. They emerged as leaders in the class and beyond, as Marta explained:

> We gathered spontaneously, probably driven by the vast majority of students from wealthy aristocrat families that constituted the whole 1948-1952 class, to which we did not belong and with whom we had nothing in common. We were poor, some middle class with professional parents, intellectually driven. We had very little or nothing in common with the vast majority of the class. There were others, some very few from the aristocratic majority, but they did not approach us. They were afraid of us I think. For in the end we were all considered communists.

> But we had examples to follow. Whether first year students or more advanced, we found leaders on campus, the revolutionary people of the student union and the Young Communists, and what was most in fashion at those times: freethinkers. And we met all together and they all gave way to us untypical freshmen.

> Among those freshmen were Roberto Fernández Retamar, Adelaida de Juan, Marta Vesa, Graziella Pogolotti, Mercedes Fernández de Castro, María Regla Zayas, Amalia Rodríguez, Maria Elena Jubrías, and me. Some of us had met, but not been friends, at Instituto #1 high school. And we found others already on campus: Alfredo Guevara, Leonel Soto, Geisha Borroto, Antonio Nuñez Jimenez, Francisco García Valls, Haydée Dias Ortega. And others joined the group later on: Elisa Tamames, Julieta Campos de la Torre, Concepción Arzola. Ricardo Alarcon de Quesada started his studies one or two years after us.

So we called ourselves Pi Kappa Tau, just as a student joke and because we were strong, explosive, and unbearable. But we were at the head of our classes. And when we realized we had a presence and an influence, we understood we had to be the best of the best. Of course, after so many years, you see how we moved and what we did. You will find our distinctive behavior and line of thought.[53]

The Group frequented the FEU coffee shop and the law school cafeteria. Student discussions and debates were free and open, turning classroom theories into debates about the future of Cuba. Their leader, as Marta looks back, was Alfredo Guevara, international secretary of the student union. He was an organizer who kept the network intact and who taught his peers in this revolutionary campus generation, which became the revolutionary generation. Later a filmmaker, he founded and headed the Cuban Film Institute (ICAIC). One of her closest friends at the university was a friend from high school, Graziella Pogolotti (who became an art critic and essayist). Also in the group were Roberto Fernández Retamar (later an essayist, president of Casa de las Américas, and member of the Council of State), his future wife Adelaida de Juan Seyler (later a music and art professor and also an essayist), María Elena Jubrías Álvarez (later a ceramicist and art professor), Mercedes Fernandez de Castro, and Maria Regla Zayas.

The group also included Antonio Núñez Jiménez, who, in Marta's words, was the eternal unelected president of the faculty of philosophy and letters. He wrote the widely used *Geography of Cuba* at age thirty-one and became known as the Third Discoverer of Cuba. He served as captain in Che Guevara's division in the Sierra Maestra. Manolo Corrales, the secretary of culture of the student union, was another member. He arranged for the Alicia Alonso Academy to move to the university sports field after Batista suspended government aid to the company; it was to become the National Ballet of Cuba. There was also Leonel Soto, who became an ideologist and writer. And Haydée Díaz Ortega, today the Director of the Martí Museum at the Plaza de la Revolución,

---

53. Marta Terry, email to authors, October 30, 2014.

and the mother of the current Minister of Foreign Trade and Foreign Investment, Rodrigo Malmierca Díaz. And Amalia Rodríguez Rodríguez, Mercedes Fernández de Castro, and Marta Vesa Figueras. And Elisa Tamames (musicologist), Julieta Campos de la Torre, and Concepción Arzola, who wrote about children's folklore.

The reality was that Marta was the only Afro-Cuban in this crowd, so she limited herself; for instance, not going on certain trips and social outings, in order not to place the group in jeopardy. She saved herself the embarrassment of being discriminated against and protected the group from any test of its affinity or from taking a stand against racist behavior. This is a universal story of people of African heritage who were upwardly mobile, at least in the United States and Cuba. As a result, many white people think any discussion of racism is exaggerated because they themselves have been shielded and are blind to the everyday experience of being Black.

An important relationship Marta developed in library school at the University of Havana was with Olinta Ariosa Morales. Olinta was an Afro-Cuban woman ten years older than Marta, from a middle-class family of specialized sugar mill workers. Olinta entered the one year library studies program at the same time as Marta. She had completed her four year degree (also in philosophy and letters) at the university some time earlier and had been unsuccessfully looking for work for a few years. Olinta was an activist in the movement against Batista and was jailed for her protests. After 1959 she continued with her work building school libraries and in 1962 was appointed head of the Department of School Libraries in the Ministry of Education. In 1976 she was named head of the Library Division of the Ministry of Culture. Armando Hart made each of these appointments, but 1952-1953 was only the second year of library studies in Cuba and only seven students enrolled. It was there that Marta and Olinta began a lifetime friendship and close collaboration; they each grew into accomplished and leading librarians.

Then Marta won a scholarship from the Institute of International Education to attend the State Teachers College at New Paltz. This wasn't one of the bastions of elitism that socialized people into positions and perspectives of power. Although she felt the status differences when others went to elite institutions in the US or Europe, she was in effect a deep probe into the heart of US society. Marta had a common, everyday experience in this society, going to the heart of the matter and not to the periphery of privilege.

In 1953, as Marta made ready to travel to the United States, the entire family mustered its resources. They finally sold the piano Marta could never learn to play—eighty pesos, then the equivalent of eighty dollars. But the money they pooled was not enough. So Aunt Graciela repeated the old saying, "Licking doesn't make the dog fat." In other words, they had to find some real money! And the word she used—*lambiando*—sounded like an African word. Aunt Graciela dipped into her secret stash so Marta could travel to the United States. She had done this for tuition payments—Marta's grades did not get her the scholarships that Héctor won—and for pencils. This family funding was to set the standard for all her trips abroad: make a success with a little less money than was needed, usually by cutting back on fun, and even on food.

While at New Paltz she was engaged socially, from the diversity of international students on campus to the intimacy of joining a sorority. Marta also carried out a three-week internship at the Columbus Memorial Library of the Pan-American Union, the predecessor of the Organization of American States. She worked there with Marietta Daniels, who worked indefatigably for US contributions to Latin American libraries., Marietta kept Marta in mind, later offering her several jobs in the United States and elsewhere in Latin America. Marta's work at this early library for all of Latin America and the Caribbean was part of her preparation for her twenty years, 1967–1987, at Casa de las Américas.

While spending the year in the United States, Marta had experiences that educated her about the class reality of capitalism and the racism that plagues the Black experience. Her contacts with the Quakers arranged a scholarship for her to go to a summer camp on Orcas Island off the coast of the state of Washington. She took a bus trip from New York to Seattle that lasted four days, always sleeping on the bus. She got the whirlwind tour of the urban and rural landscape through the bus windows, while also reading *The Big Money* by John Dos Passos. Dos Passos attacks the corruption inherent in the capitalist greed of always striving for big money. What an antidote to the seductive consumer society of the United States! Plus, Marta was both strapped for cash and a librarian in the making—not on any kind of track to making big money.

Her experience with racism was still more direct. A soft experience of this was also an example of a universal experience. Black people can have lots of subjective feelings about being Black, but there is at least one objective fact that must be dealt with, and that is hair. People of African heritage have hair that is uniquely structured for styling that can be as simple as cutting it in designs or taking lots of it and doing forms of hair sculpture. Racist values attack Black people's hair as "bad hair," so this racist perspective concedes that while white people can have a bad hair day, Black people are assigned a bad hair life! Marta had to travel twelve miles from New Paltz to Poughkeepsie in order to find an African American hair salon. Of course, this was at the same time an affirmation of Black culture, as salons for Black women are hubs of bonding, discourse, and cultural production. In one sense, visiting this salon was a proxy for home. On the other hand, when commenting on the New York weather, Marta wrote home that she sometimes felt "like a frozen fish in the refrigerator."

More raw was her experience with public accommodations. During December 1953 she was travelling on the New Jersey Turnpike from New York City to Washington to visit Mr. and Mrs. Milton W. Fisher, an African American couple connected to the postal workers organization, who were friends of her father. The Fishers and their friends often visited Cuba and Marta was a rare return visitor. On the trip, Marta was refused entry into a café, and the nation's leading African American daily told the story in a profile of Marta, quoting her directly:

> "Some say [the United States] is beautiful and wonderful. Some say it is bad. I want to know this country so I come to see for myself, to feel it, to know the people, then I can say I know America." [...]

Marta says that although there is some discrimination in Cuba, the

American variety puzzles her.

She went with a French girl, also an exchange student, to a restaurant in Maryland. At first she was refused service, but when the proprietor found out that she was a foreigner, she was quickly served.

Cubans, she said, are so mixed up that no one can tell who is a Negro and who is not, but she said it is estimated that 25% of the people are Negro. They are not referred to as Negroes, but as "people of color."[54]

These international students were studying in the United States and being trained to prefer the United States, while at the same time facing the reality of racist discrimination. Their crisis of consciousness was to decide whether racism was an aberration that could be ended or was endemic to the society and only to be ended with a systemic transformation. This crisis remains.

Marta's uncle Fernandito died suddenly and in summer 1954 she was called back to Cuba two weeks earlier than she had planned. Her travels took her through Alabama where she confronted the crude racist designations of separate bathroom facilities for different "racial" groups. This final act of racist apartheid in the United States, the depth of Jim Crow segregation in the Deep South, sealed her view of the United States as a country that did not represent the future she wanted for Cuba. The similarity between New Jersey and Alabama was decisive.

Upon her return the family was worse off than she expected. Her uncle had passed away just one month after she left Cuba for her year in the US. As her father took her home from the Havana airport, he told her point blank: "Cry all you want now so you won't cry at home. We held back the news because we knew you would end your time in the US as soon as you heard. Everyone is still distraught. Things are more tough here than ever. We sorely need you back, and we need you to be strong."

---

54. "Marta Terry of Cuba Here 'to See US for Myself,'" *The Chicago [Daily] Defender*, (National Editon), July 17, 1954. See Appendix 2.

# Chapter 4

## JOINING THE REVOLUTION

A revolution is not an event so much as an historical process full of multiple events both simultaneous and sequential. Within the revolutionary process there are more events than can be counted; and while some that get recorded make up the great historical record, the most important in the long run are the often unnoticed day-to-day processes that change the people in their everyday lives. It is the people upon whom any successful revolution must depend. Policy and structural change, yes, but the people's everyday lives are what count most of all.

As already noted, Marta had many experiences of rebelling against forces of authority, from family to school to the state, whether it was fetching cigar butts after curfew, or protest marching with fellow students, or resisting family authority figures and fighting siblings, or being mischievous in a university classroom. Undergirding this was her upbringing as a proud Afro-Cuban, aspiring toward upward mobility, yet always having to work in opposition to the prevailing norms which would relegate her to the margins. To be both successful and Afro-Cuban, you had to rebel against those norms even if not on a fully developed ideological level.

Marta was also a young woman in love with high cultural attainment, from the fine arts of museums and symphonic concerts to the popular culture of movies and dance music. She was in search of being truly human, embracing all of the expression of what it meant to be so. For many this might be considered normal, but for a person of an oppressed and marginalized community this requires rebellion, even if one is not always conscious of it. Often being the only Afro-Cuban on a scene, in a racist society with the lingering legacy of slavery, this had to be an act of resistance or submission. She lived in a sea of subtle yet horrendous human acts of discrimination, from facial expressions to body language to slips of the tongue. In this context, Marta marched forward with her head up, backed by the strength of her family's multigenerational experiences, its social capital, and academic achievement.

Marta's direct connection with the revolutionary motion began on campus with the support of her brother Héctor. He was an activist, nurtured in his pre-university years by Marta and her friends, who sought freedom in what to them was a repressive society and cultural mix. They performed this desire for freedom of expression during many social occasions at home with Marta and her aunts. Indeed, her friend Graziella was a Marxist whose parents maintained a revolutionary spirit from their origins in Italy and Russia. Marxism was just one ideological focus within the broader cultural and intellectual currents searching for freedom that led them to rebel against all forms of arbitrary authority. This dynamic was the social force that guided friendship networks like Marta's.

By 1948-1949 Héctor, not even a teenager, would read the student newspaper Marta brought home from the university, the *Alma Mater*, and learn about the politics of the student movement. Marta knew the leaders of FEU and would often have them as guests in their home where politics would inevitably be the main topic of conversation. Héctor graduated from high school in 1953, the year after the Batista coup d'etat. This was also the year that Fidel led the attack on the Moncada barracks and launched a new stage of militant armed struggle. Héctor became directly involved with the student movement when right-wing forces tried to destroy the monument of the founder of FEU, Julio Antonio Mella, who had also been one of the founders of the first Cuban Communist Party. One student was killed, and Héctor was so moved that from that point on he became a militant in the movement. Students in Santiago de Cuba were also shot. Héctor and others ran into the street to demonstrate but were met by machine gun fire from Batista police, forcing them to run and escape.

Since it was an underground movement, most of the revolutionary student organizing and political work was hidden, though there were also various forms of progressive thought, including Marxism, that were discussed openly by faculty in the relative safety of the campus. A friend once told Marta and her female classmates to come to a FEU political forum to see and hear what was going on, but to watch for his signal to leave immediately. It was likely the meeting would shift from political debate to physical combat. What an exciting time! The idealists of the campus were forging visions and networks that would later be the guiding force for the transformation of the country. Fidel was on the scene, as well as others who later became stalwart militants of the struggle.

After returning from the United States Marta continued her social life in this group, which had its origins during her university years. At the core were Graziella Pogolotti, Julio Rodríguez Luis (later an author and professor of Spanish in the US), Severo Sarduy, Marta Vesa, Nicolás Farray, Carlos Ruíz de la Tejera (today a humorist), and Marta. On weekends they would often gather at Graziella's apartment, since everyone admired her father, the painter Marcelo Pogolotti. They would listen to music and then go out to some cultural event. This group was trying to be something that 1950s Cuba was not: open and free, embracing culture and a desire to live a life stretching the limits of what it could mean to be truly human, transcending the limitations of gender, color, country, and class. They would walk up and down Old Havana's Paseo del Prado talking about everything, as they said, from the human to the divine: literature, politics, films, the New Wave. There was a favorite movie house, one that later became known as the Cinemateca, and various theaters.

Marta was a librarian trained at the University of Havana with one year of study in the United States and some professional experience, but she found it difficult to get stable work in her profession at home in Cuba. This was discouraging and forced her to begin thinking about emigrating. Even more than not getting a job was the depressing experience of the repressive Batista regime. Her family increasingly had divergent political views and could not contain her.

In 1955 Marta was able to work part time at three jobs: as a translator in the Batista Ministry of Finance, as a librarian at her former high school Instituto #1, and as a substitute teacher of English at a special center for working people—all of those English students trying either to get ahead in Cuba or leave for the United States. None of these jobs gave her job security. In 1956 she was hired by the Office of the City Historian, where she was trained by the eminent historian Emilio Roig de Leuchsenring. There she continued the vanguard work of Roig, librarian Fermin Peraza, and others who founded the Library of the History of Cuba and America under the auspices of the City Historian's Office. It was an early public library, hosting visiting school classes, doing outreach including on the radio, and generally being part of the democratic impulse of 1940s Cuba. During 1956–1958 she also worked in the library of a non-governmental organization called the Cuban United Nations Association; the library of the Cuban Sugar Technicians Association; the private library of noted movie critic and professor José Manuel Valdes Rodriguez; and even the Ministry of Finance. Her good friend Olinta Ariosa worked with her in the lending library of her old high school, Instituto #1. There her supervisor (and former professor) Ofélia Pérez Daple muttered one day, "I pay my maid more than you earn here, I am ashamed of this!" She shortly left for the United States. Another time, at that same library, Marta heard explosions: it was March 13, 1957 and an urban battle was in process centered on attacking the Presidential Palace. The Revolutionary Directorate, which included her brother Héctor, had planned and carried it out. That day saw several policemen shot and several dozen young people killed.

The struggle against Batista was heating up. On December 2, 1956 the July 26[55] rebels had landed on the coast from Mexico on their boat *Granma*. Militant armed resistance was launched and urban violence

---

55. See footnote 1 above.

began to escalate. On March 13, 1957 the student-led Revolutionary Directorate led an armed attack on the Presidential Palace in an attempt to kill Batista and seize power. Echeverría's part was to interrupt a hugely popular radio program and deliver a three minute speech, which was the length of time that the insurrectionists calculated they could hold off the police. He succeeded, but was killed immediately afterwards by the Batista police not far from the famous granite stairs into campus. This demonstrated how dangerous the situation was becoming, since the campus was usually considered a safe zone. In a useless attempt to defeat the students, Batista closed the university completely from August 1957 to June 1958.

Héctor was a founding member of the Revolutionary Directorate, but because it was an underground organization he was not publically identified as a member. When they had printed materials to be distributed, he brought Marta into the process to spread them to her contacts and friendship network.

Héctor was arrested and imprisoned from November 30, 1957 to February 23, 1958, during which time he went on a hunger strike. The family visited, especially his grandmother who went each day to the prison. Spirits were very high among the prisoners, and Héctor obtained two shawls woven by the so called "non-political" prisoners. For Christmas he presented a black one to his fiancée Carmen and a white one to Marta, which she has kept for more than fifty years.

The Supreme Court ordered that the incarceration of so many people—revolutionaries accused of various crimes without trials and habeas corpus—had to end and that they should be released. On the same day in 1958 that Héctor was released, the July 26th Movement kidnapped Juan Manuel Fangio, a champion Argentine race car driver. The move kept him from starring in a Batista showcase, a Formula One race in Havana. It exposed the regime and demonstrated the power of the revolutionary forces. At that point, Batista suspended the constitution and declared martial law.

Many militants were in prison and the police went on a violent spree, killing many people. The July 26th Movement began planning a general strike for April 9, 1958, and Héctor threw himself fully into that effort. After this, in May, Héctor left Cuba for Miami. He had gone to the US embassy in Havana and gotten a tourist visa after stating his intent to travel via the United States to Spain to study. Why did the United States give him a visa? They were interested in turning Cubans into agents of the counter-revolution to advance US policy interests. Héctor negotiated his way through three months in the United States, eventually moving to Mexico where other expatriates were regrouping and planning to go back to Cuba as an armed revolutionary brigade.

The years 1957 and 1958 were horrible for young people. There were no safe places to go without being under surveillance by Batista forces. The intellectuals retreated. Only declared communists and radicals dared to manifest their political sympathy toward Fidel and the revolutionaries. More than a few decided to join Fidel in the Sierra Maestra mountains. Others escaped arrest, or worse, and went to advance their study and work abroad. For instance, Alfredo Guevara went briefly to Italy to learn filmmaking.

There was no way for young people in Cuba to publish their work, so some of the writers in Marta's peer group—including Severo Sarduy, Julio Rodríguez Luis, and Antón Arrufat—seized on the idea of publishing a young intellectuals' journal, putting their literary and artistic works in print. As they forged ahead, Marta jumped out in one conversation—like a tiger, she remembers—to say that the true youth of Cuba were in the mountains or in exile, suffering and fighting for a new state of things. Her brother had already been jailed for participating in urban insurrection. Marta argued that the best any other young person could do was to keep silent as a sign of respect for those fighting and dying. In her view, the would-be publishers were too cowardly to either join or denounce the rebels. Antón shot back, "Fidel in the mountains doesn't care about us!" Marta answered: "Fidel knows what he's doing."

The publishing project was abandoned, and shortly after January 1959, Severo visited Marta's family's home, hugged her tight, and thanked her for stopping their silly venture. Over the decades, the young intellectuals rose to prominence in and beyond Cuba: Julio as a professor of Spanish in the US, Severo as a novelist in Europe whose writing was always deeply Cuban, and Anton as a renowned novelist and playwright in Cuba. Each of them they remembered Marta as the person who was able to stop that big mistake. (Of the three, Severo has passed away; Marta regrets that this occurred at a time shortly before he was to visit Cuba.)

Marta was a Cuban patriot, but like many before her in the tradition of Martí and Maceo, her patriotic rejection of a corrupt and repressive regime led her to consider leaving Cuba. She had been offered a job in Washington, DC, by Marietta Daniels, a hugely energetic American librarian who had seized on the idea of building up a powerful Latin American collection for the Organization of American States (OAS, OEA in Spanish)—the group of nations that was to implement anti-Cuba policies after 1958. Marietta was recruiting the best of the best for that project, so in December 1958, Marta gathered up her savings, said her good-byes, and was on her way into a new life. But the demands of patriotism in that year were the same as they had always been: to regroup in some way and renew a life of struggle. The first task would be to seize power and change the government, and then to take up the task of rebuilding Cuba. This generation had the awesome task to realize centuries of hopes and dreams for a better life, for a free and independent Cuba. Marta was not isolated; she had a younger brother who would reach out to her at that critical moment and redirect her energies back into the revolutionary process. He contacted Marta from Mexico, while she was still on her way to the United States; she was now a courier carrying documents to comrades working with Héctor. Leaving Cuba led her back even deeper into the Cuban revolutionary process.

Héctor connected her with the revolutionary movement in the United States. She agreed to accept the assignment of being a courier between the United States and Mexico. Marta was sent to Mexico carrying documents and money from comrades in the United States. As part of the process she ultimately met up with Héctor. Héctor and his comrades there had been raising money and gathering weapons for an expedition to join the rebel forces in Cuba. The Mexican government was not being very cooperative, but when Batista abdicated and left the country on New Year's Eve, Mexico's lukewarm talk of military intervention became moot. The task for Marta and Héctor was to get back home as soon as possible and join in the process of reconstruction.

On January 7, 1959 Marta and Héctor were able to get on the first flight from Mexico City bringing Cuban revolutionaries back home from exile. They landed at the airport to see the militants from the mountains with long hair and olive drab uniforms—Marta mistook them at first for a band of women soldiers. The revolutionaries were in control and practiced no deference to the norms of civility that had been the legacy of Spanish and US colonialism. These were Cubans of a new type, a type that opened up imaginative possibilities for everyone who had been held down and silenced.

Everyone in the family welcomed them fully, although not everyone agreed with their politics. Standing tall in this context was their diminutive grandmother. When Marta and Héctor first entered their home after returning, Higinia, then seventy-nine years old, raised her fist and shouted "Viva Cuba!" Sister and brother were home in a new postcolonial moment of rebirth. This grandmother was born to an emancipated slave, and her response to their return called forth the aspirations of the Mambises, the fierce independence fighters who rode with Maceo and carried the spirit of Baraguá. Marta always remembered her telling about how she ran away from home with her playmates just to welcome General Maceo when he camped nearby, and how he gently scolded them for risking their lives to meet him.

One of the complexities of the struggle is the way in which Afro-Cubans were often tied to the existing government administration. The Afro-Cuban middle-class leadership always reached out to the government to get concessions for their community, including financial support for Black organizations and jobs. This tied Black leadership to such corrupt regimes as those of Machado and Batista. Marta's father got caught in this trap and was out of touch with the necessity for the 1959 revolution. On the other hand, it was his spirit and the general political culture of their extended family that provided the moral and political force behind Marta and Héctor. When the new government eliminated the Afro-Cuban clubs and societies, it succeeded in cutting back the influence of pro-Batista forces, but lost the longstanding self-organization that could have helped link Afro-Cubans closer to the revolutionary path. Nícolas Terry and some of his groupmates sought shelter for their network among some Freemasons.

Things were chaotic, with the revolutionaries moving into key sectors to take power and begin sweeping changes while also relying on the people in place to keep things working. This meant that the theory of revolutionary change was not at all consistent with the actual pace of change. Furthermore, the business class and patriotic government bureaucrats were not necessarily in favor of the deep revolutionary changes toward an egalitarian, anti-racist society that was being articulated as Cuba's future by Fidel and the other leaders. Many Cubans deserted their homeland and fled to other countries, especially the United States. This exodus hit health care hard, since many doctors left and most faculty of the medical school expatriated as well.

Food shortages started. Before rationing had been implemented, Marta once came home for lunch. Aunt Lala had cooked some beans. Marta said without thinking, "I don't care for this," and pushed it away. Her aunt's eyes welled with tears of frustration as she said, "If you knew how difficult it was to get those beans, you would eat them without a word!" Marta promptly ate them. She and her family were to repeat those words over many decades of food shortages and rationing.

Marta found a job with UNESCO because of her friendship with Carlos Victor Penna. He was from Argentina and had married a Cuban woman. Penna was beginning his career at the Havana-based UNESCO regional center for the Western Hemisphere. Armando Hart Dávalos (Ministry of Culture from 1959 to 1965) signed the 1959 letter that appointed Marta to this job, her first permanent and full-time library post. She worked as assistant librarian to her former professor Raquel Robes for two years at the UNESCO Center of Pedagogical Documentation. Marta also began volunteering to set up libraries in schools and communities with her close colleague Olinta Ariosa Morales. There were no school libraries before 1959, so they began to volunteer at Elementary

School #2 in the Marianao district of Havana. They had several boxes of books and provided some library services for the children. This was possible because one of Marta's aunts had worked in the school and helped open doors for these two volunteers, who were full of patriotism and the desire to serve their people with the professional librarian skills of their university education. Carlos Victor Penna, their former professor, was also UNESCO's staffperson for the development of libraries in Latin America and the Caribbean, and he advised and supervised the two volunteer librarians.

Shortly after returning to Cuba in 1959 Marta got the shock of her life. At that time the National Library was an elitist institution, as the staff reflected the old, pre-1959 Cuba. No Afro-Cubans were being hired there in professional or paraprofessional positions. But Marta's friends were encouraging her to apply for a position. The director, María Teresa Freyre de Andrade, was the first librarian to head the institution and had also been Marta's professor of library reference at the university. Marta had a deep fear of what would happen and a sick feeling in her stomach. But respect for her friends and the honorable responsibility she felt as a revolutionary patriot won out. She went for an interview. Nothing positive came of the interview, which left her feeling hurt and angry. No explanation was given for not offering her a position. Her peers were hired, but not Marta. She cried about it and was mad because this was her professor from the university library rejecting her. But Marta was not in any way deterred from her path.

Later, in 1965, Marta got a call from María Teresa Freyre de Andrade, who was director of the National Library, asking her to join the staff as her executive assistant. By this time the ideological and political confusion of the staff was getting out of hand and was impacting library service and collection management. Marta was clearly the choice to save the situation because she combined being red and expert as the Chinese revolutionaries phrased it after 1949; that is to say, she had both political and professional skills. Maria Teresa wanted to save her reputation as the leader of the national library in a situation she could not handle. Marta was working then in JUCEPLAN's new building across the street, and remembered looking out the window at the National Library as the two of them spoke. She told Maria Teresa she could not move. Marta was director of her own library and knew better than to put herself in a confused and chaotic situation that could backfire on her, something she had nothing to do with creating. Marta's time at the National Library would come later.

These early days were very tense indeed, as people began to take sides over the policies being implemented by the new revolutionary government. Marta was a patriot fully embracing the changes that were opening things up for the people, including Afro-Cubans. Libraries were part of this new democracy. For example, the Ministry of Finance took over a former Dominican convent and turned a big space on the first floor into a library, but they had no books. At the same time the government was taking over the houses of the Batista forces and the upper classes who were in flight out of Cuba. The Ministry of Finance took the lead in reorganizing the books into collections that were then used to launch new libraries.

Marta was entering the revolutionary process primarily as a volunteer, innovating via grassroots efforts. She and her colleagues—especially Olinta, because the two of them were Afro-Cuban women with the best training available but without full access—had to move on their own. This was just the beginning, as the revolution was soon to open up and affirm the need for a new library system led by these new librarians.

# PHOTOS

Marta on her First Communion Day.

# Family

Marta standing behind her three siblings,
L to R: Pelayo, Zenaida, and Héctor.

Marta O'Farrill, great-grandmother of Marta Terry González.

Grandmother Higinia O'Farrill, four others, and Marta on left.

Dora González Rivas, daughter of Antolín González and Mercedes Rivas and mother of Marta Terry González.

Father Nícolas Terry Terry.

On December 18, 1965 at the marriage of Marta and Luis Antonio Forte, her family stood with the couple for this photo. From left to right, 1 Marta's uncle Francisco Averhoff Terry. 2 Stepmother Josefina Rivera. 3 Aunt by marriage Chichita Padilla, wife of Francisco Averhoff. 4 Sister Zenaida Terry Molinert. 5 Cousin Blanca Luz Averhoff, daughter of Celina Herrera and Fernando Averhoff Terry. 6 Sister-in-law Carmen Berro García, wife of Héctor Terry Molinert. 7 (front) Niece Blanca Graciela Terry Berro, daughter of Carmen and Héctor. 8 Brother Pelayo Terry González. 9 Husband Luis Antonio Forte Manilla. 10 Father Nicolás Terry Terry. 11 Marta Terry González. 12 (front) Niece Carmen Cristina Terry Berro, daughter of Carmen and Héctor. 13 Aunt Graciela Terry Terry. 14 (back) Brother Héctor Terry Molinert. 15 (back) Cousin Félix Acosta Terry. 16 Aunt Blanca Zilia Terry Terry. 17 Cousin by marriage Magaly, wife of Félix Acosta Terry. 18 Grandmother Higinia Terry O'Farrill. 19 Aunt Luz María Terry Terry. 20 Aunt Mercedes Terry Terry.

Marta with husband Luis and son Claudio.

Marta's son and his family: Lily, Claudio, and Héctor Luis.

# Education

Professor Elias Antralgo and his Philosophy and Letters undergraduate students. Marta is fourth from left.

Marta at front with other University of Havana classmates who together formed their own club, Pi Kappa Tau, otherwise known as the Explosive and Strong Letters.

Marta with other 1953 pledges to the sorority Arethusa at the State Teachers College at New Paltz, New York.

Marta and friends in the United States during 1953-1954.

# Joining the Revolution

Marta and Graziella Pogolotti.
Photo courtesy of Julio Rodríguez-Luis.

Marta leading a discussion in the local FMC (Federación de Mujeres Cubanas, or Cuban Women's Federation) in front of her apartment building.

Marta on volunteer labor with Casa de las Américas coworkers Manuel Galich and Marta Cortizas.

Shaking hands with Fidel Castro.

# Librarian

JUCEPLAN.

Casa staffmembers at the home of director Haydée Santamaría and Armando Hart Dávalos. Left to right: unidentified woman, Haydée Santamaría, Marta Terry (standing), unidentified woman, Armando Hart Davalos, Roberto Fernández Retamar.

Newspaper photo of Marta as
library director at Casa de las Américas.

At the National Library.

Marta and others with Fidel Castro.

Left to right: Unidentified woman, Alfredo Guevara, and Marta.

# International

Robert Wedgeworth naming Marta an Honorary Fellow of IFLA in 2006.
Photo courtesy of Robert Wedgeworth..

With US librarians Betty Turock and Al Kagan, and the library educator E. J. Josey,
at a Social Responsibilities Roundtable reception, part of an
American Library Association conference. Photo courtesy of Al Kagan.

With Joan C. Durrance and C. Olivia Frost, faculty membees at the University of Michigan School of Information, during Marta's visit to Ann Arbor. Photo by Kate Williams.

Visiting the Toledo Spiders in Ohio.
Several of these people traveled from Ohio to Cuba in 2002.

# PART TWO

## LIBRARIAN

# Chapter 5

## LIBRARIES AND INFORMATION TECHNOLOGY IN THE CUBAN CONTEXT

No society has been possible without an information system. As vulnerable social animals, humans need ways to relate to each other and need to understand their environment. Our brains process the information we get from our sense perceptions. Language, vocabulary, and semantics make sense of what we experience and enable us to communicate with each other. There have been great revolutions in how the world's information is created, stored, organized, and shared based on aural, visual, and written practices such as music and art, written language, printing, and more. The vast majority of the world's collections of recorded information are in libraries. These libraries are part of society's information infrastructure—along with publishers and printers, readers and writers, books, magazines and newspapers, movies and art, and more. Libraries depend on that infrastructure and they also shape it. What's more, since the late twentieth century, in different ways but in every part of the world, computers and the digital tools and techniques that follow from them have become central to that information infrastructure. They, too, depend on and shape the rest of that infrastructure.

The world's first libraries were for the elites, because literacy was for the few and powerful. The rise of industrial society helped create the need for a literate public and a scientific approach to knowledge. In the West, important breakthroughs took place in the nineteenth century in understanding nature (Charles Darwin, 1809–1882), society (Karl Marx, 1818–1883), and technology (Charles Babbage, 1791–1871). As a scientific approach to knowledge became the foundation of modern society, the library everywhere became an important location for economic and social development.

Libraries were not a high priority in colonies for anyone except the settler elite. Thus in most colonies the main libraries were private collections for the colonizing elite. Even the official colonial records were usually not kept in the colony but in the so-called mother country. Marta explains how this happened: "The Archivo General de la Isla de Cuba was founded by an order of the Queen of Spain in 1840. In 1888 the Captain General of the Island, by order of the Madrid government, sent to Spain 2,300 documents of great historical value. An official decree of December 20, 1904 established the island institution as the National Archives."[56]

As the Spanish settlers were replanting themselves across the generations in Cuba, a nascent national bourgeoisie began to develop private libraries to serve their class, supporting economic development and cultural life. The library of the University of Havana was established in 1721, although the official position of a library director wasn't created until 1918. While it did not serve a wide public, "The first public library in Cuba was established in 1793 by the Sociedad Economica de Amigos del Pais, Cuba's oldest cultural society, whose history is closely related to the vicissitudes and development of Cuba's economic, cultural, political, and social history."[57]

José Martí wrote a biographical essay about his high school principal, Antonio Bachiller y Morales (1812–1889), who is better known today as the father of Cuban bibliography.[58] Bachiller y Morales was the first

56. Marta Terry González, "Cuba," in *World Encyclopedia of Library and Information Services*, ed. Robert Wedgeworth (Chicago: American Library Association, 1993), 236.

57. Josefina Mayol and Jerrold Orne, "Cuban Libraries," *Library Quarterly* 22, no. 2 (1952): 95.

58. Ana Cairo Ballester, *José Martí Y La Novela De La Cultura Cubana* (Santiago de Compostela, Spain: Universidade de Santiago de Compostela, 2003), 137. José Martí first published the essay "Antonio Bachiller y Morales" in 1889 in *El Avisador Hispanoamericano*. Martí's high school was Instituto #1, and close

to carry out scholarship on Cuban letters, most notably his major bibliographical work, *A Catalogue of Books and Pamphlets Published in Cuba from the Introduction of Printing to 1840*.[59] Just as the war for national liberation was emerging, so was a national literature documented by this path-breaking bibliographer.

The first Association of Cuban Librarians was formed in 1949 and was active until June 1959. During this period they published a quarterly journal *Boletín*, which had three editors in turn: Rosina Urquiza García, Raquel Romeu Fernandez, and Ana Guerra Deben. Many of the leading librarians of this organization left Cuba after the revolution, just as the nation's libraries were turning from serving middle-class elites to serving the public. The professional organization was re-established by Olinta Ariosa, Marta Terry, and a new generation of patriotic Cuban librarians in the early 1980s.

In 1950 the first Cuban library school at the University of Havana was established by the same librarians who had started the association in 1949. The entering classes were small and studied in both classrooms and in apprenticeship relations with the faculty. The faculty tended to be working professional librarians who taught part-time.

Libraries are the main institutions in society for the preservation of information and as such are fundamentally involved in national culture and social and economic development. But in general they are often the expressions of the ruling classes. What is important about understanding Cuba today is that the Cuban revolution has its own special history of information production and preservation. What is more, some of the librarians of the 1950s were active combatants in the anti-Batista, anti-imperialist fight.

The revolutionary movements in the 1950s began a stream of innovative informational practices. It begins with an active clandestine and

---

to a century later it was Marta's as well.

59. Antonio Bachiller y Morales, *Catálogo De Libros Y Folletos Publicados En Cuba Desde La Introducción De La Imprenta Hasta 1840* (Ciudad de la Habana: P. Massana, 1861)

guerrilla press.[60] A particular achievement was the publication of the speech given by Fidel Castro while he was a prisoner and on trial for the 1953 attack on the Moncada military garrison. The speech, "History Will Absolve Me," was smuggled out of the prison. Haydée Santamaria and Melba Hernández, who were the first two Moncada combatants released from prison and the only women, led the effort to publish and distribute it. The story goes that Fidel asked for one hundred thousand copies to be printed. The comrades apologized that they were only able to do ten thousand while also evading the police. Fidel replied, "Fantastic, if I had asked for ten thousand maybe we would only have five hundred!"

By 1956, the main underground press was *Aldabonazo*, which means a sharp knock on the door, or a simultaneous release of weapons.[61] That year, with the landing of *Granma*, the boat carrying Fidel and eighty-one other revolutionaries from Mexico to Cuba, fighting began in the Sierra Maestra, Cuba's eastern mountains. As the revolutionary fight started, the paper became *Revolución*. These publications were first mimeographed. Later the July 26 Movement was able to purchase and use a series of multilith presses. Eventually the movement had publications coming from all over the island as well as the rebels in the mountains.

These printing ventures continued a trend of all revolutionary movements, especially under repressive regimes. There is a level of secure secrets needed to maintain production and distribution of any underground publication. Of course, there is also the contradiction of producing a written document while the most important target audience does not have a high level of literacy. This requires careful writing with the liberal use of graphics and photographs. Equipment and supplies had to be moved on a regular basis and sometimes people had to be trusted on the basis of family ties, not political agreement. The success of these

---

60. Unión de Periodistas de Cuba Executive Committee, *A Sketch of the Clandestine and Guerilla Press Covering the Period 1952-1958* (Havana: Instituto Cubano del Libro, 1971).

61. One memoir of the time took the same name: Armando Hart Dávalos, *Aldabonazo: Inside the Cuban Revolutionary Underground, 1952-58: A Participant's Account*, trans. Mary-Alice Waters (New York: Pathfinder, 2004).

publications was based on a two-step process of communication, from the revolutionaries to their readers, and then by oral communication to the networks of the readers. This is a universal process for any information flow, from primary consumers to secondary consumers via networks.

The next major innovation was the creation of a radio station called Radio Rebelde (Rebel Radio) to more aggressively spread information from the July 26 Movement. The historical background for this is that Cuba had been one of the first countries in Latin America to have radio. International Telephone and Telegraph, a US multinational corporation, started this in 1922. Also, in 1950 Cuba was the third country in Latin America to get TV. The Cuban public was ready for electronic communication.

Rebel Radio was first set up under the rebel army's media team led by Che Guevara, and then transferred to where Fidel was based in the mountains. They began to broadcast twice a day, always beginning with the anthem of the July 26 Movement. By the time of liberation there were thirty-two separate radio stations comprising the Cadena de la Libertad (Freedom Network). The revolutionary leadership used the radio for speeches and reports on the battles since the Batista press often went silent or lied about the progress of the struggle, even telling the lie that they had killed Fidel.

One of the innovative moves for international solidarity with revolutionary movements was Cuba's use of its radio capacity to impact the revolutionary movement inside the United States. From 1962 to 1965 they broadcast a three-hour program hosted by Robert and Mabel Williams, African American freedom fighters living in exile in Cuba. They advocated open rebellion and armed resistance to US racism and national oppression on their program called Radio Free Dixie.[62]

The adoption of this new form of communication after the revolution came to power was not automatic. After January 1, 1959, there was an information crisis because of the lack of electricity in the rural areas.

---

62. Timothy B. Tyson, *Radio Free Dixie: Robert F. Williams and the Roots of Black Power* (Chapel Hill, NC: University of North Carolina Press, 1999).

The main historical proclamation had been made by Lenin: "Communism is Soviet power plus the electrification of the whole country."[63]
Cuba, like all countries, had to bring electrical power to the entire nation.
There have been three stages in this process. Prior to 1959 there were
four electrical utilities in Cuba. After 1959 they were consolidated under
the Ministry of Basic Industries. The state called for rapid development
of this sector of the economy. First, from 1959 to 1989, the Soviet
Union was the major trading partner to purchase Cuban sugar and
provide crude oil to expand the Cuban energy capacity. The Cubans
expanded electricity to more than 95% of the country, far exceeding
their expected ranking among Latin American countries. Energy in
all its forms has been one of the biggest economic challenges for the
Cuban revolution and for Cuba.

Then they had to face the collapse of Soviet communism and the
ensuing economic downturn of the Special Period beginning in 1990,
which cut energy resources. This placed a great burden on industry and
the public transportation system, but it was met with great creativity:
the introduction of bicycles with the help of Vietnam, motorized bikes,
and most of all, the Cuban "camel" invented for the moment. This is
an 18-wheel truck that has a redesigned trailer to provide passengers
with a two-level space—humped like a camel.

After 2004, Cuba's energy needs were met by a new relationship with
the oil-rich country of Venezuela. President Hugo Chavez made strong
ties with Fidel Castro and became a leader in the region opposing the
global neoliberal policies of the United States, the World Bank, and the
International Monetary Fund. Venezuela and Cuba signed an agreement
to exchange oil for medical help. This level of international solidarity
led to the establishment of the Bolivarian Alliance for the Peoples of
Our America (ALBA). Based on this new regional alliance Cuba seems

---

63. Vladimir Ilyich Lenin, "Our Foreign and Domestic Position and Party
Tasks: Speech Delivered to the Moscow Gubernia Conference of the R.C.P.(B.)
on November 21, 1920," in *Collected Works*, 4th English ed. (Moscow: Progress Publishers, 1965), 31:419.

to have energy stability for the current period, although there are worries about possible Venezuelan oil shortages.

The other informational challenge in 1959 was illiteracy. 1961 was the year that the government organized a countrywide campaign to eliminate illiteracy. It moved Cuba into being the most literate country in Latin America. Fidel Castro challenged the people not to believe, but to read and to think for themselves. Of course this created a great demand for reading material. By 1964 they had established thirty-four public libraries. By 1987 this number had increased to 328.

How did this happen? When the revolutionary forces took power illiteracy was everywhere; it was over 40% in rural areas. The first realization was the need to educate members of the army, many of whom were illiterate. They took a national survey and found 1,000,000 illiterate people out of a country of 6,901,000, about 15%. They set a goal to eliminate illiteracy in one year. To do this they recruited 268,420 teachers, including 100,000 who were between 10 and 19 years of age, as well as 30,000 factory workers.

Each literacy volunteer was equipped with a pair of boots, two pairs of socks, an olive-green beret, two pairs of pants, two shirts, a blanket to sleep on, and two manuals. [64] *¡Venceremos!* was a teacher's manual and *¡Alfabeticemos!* was for the student. A modern gas lantern was also issued to each volunteer to facilitate night classes. They also were given a patch to wear to memorialize a young Afro-Cuban volunteer who had been killed by counterrevolutionaries trying to stop the campaign. His name was Conrado Benítez, murdered at the age of eighteen. Cuba's schools remained closed for eight months in 1961 because so many young people were involved in the literacy campaign. Once every member of a family was certified literate, they could hang a red flag above the doorway to their house. Once all the houses in a town were certified, the town itself could raise a larger red flag, to signify that it was free of illiteracy. The

---

64. Comisión Nacional de Alfabetización de la Ministerio de Educación, *¡Venceremos!* (Cuba: Gobierno Revolucionario, 1961); Comisión Nacional de Alfabetización de la Ministerio de Educación, *¡Alfabeticemos!* (Ciudad de la Habana: Imprenta Nacional de Cuba, 1961)..

final exam for each person learning to read was to write a letter to Fidel. All of these letters are housed in a Museum of the Literacy Campaign.

The Cuban government placed a strong emphasis on publishing to feed their newly literate public. A major world innovation was the publishing of Cuban posters, especially by the Organization of Solidarity with the People of Asia, Africa, and Latin America, better known by its Spanish acronym OSPAAAL. A highly creative team of graphic artists was mobilized to produce very colorful posters about the revolutionary experience in Cuba and throughout the world, notably the fights for national liberation in Vietnam and South Africa, and the Black Liberation struggle in the United States. These posters were printed on newsprint, folded, and were included in the OSPAAAL journal *Tricontinental* which was distributed throughout the world in four languages (Spanish, English, French, and Arabic).[65]

Finally, there is the major innovation of Cuban films. Santiago Álvarez Román (1919–1998) was an early filmmaker who was close to the revolutionary forces. His early experience was during a progressive film showing when the Batista police broke into the theater and arrested everyone, audience and film crew, and grabbed the equipment and films. Alfredo Guevara, one of Marta's close colleague from her campus days, later became one of the founders and the first director of ICAIC, Cuba's national film institute. Movies have been one of the main vehicles of the revolution to popularize the history of the country, the revolution, and a progressive view of the international situation.

Marta was also involved early in computer innovations related to librarianship. In the early 1960s she and others puzzled over how Cuban economic planning might use a mainframe—if they could get one. Brainstorming, experiments, and transformations in library practice continued through the decades. In 1994, as head of the host committee for the first IFLA annual meeting in Latin America, she teamed with others in IFLA to shift that hosting task from letter and fax correspondence to email.

---

65. Lincoln Cushing, *¡Revolución! Cuban Poster Art* (San Francisco, CA: Chronicle Books, 2003).

The collaboration—working around the ever-present US blockade—managed to be both cutting edge and extremely welcome by librarians in the developing world, where email was slowly being adopted.

We have been discussing the way the Cuban Revolution used information technologies that were available and mostly had their origin in prerevolutionary times. But the last stage of this process is a post-1959 technological revolution that itself is impacting the social revolution. The digital revolution of computers, the Internet and the World Wide Web is impacting every society, including Cuba.

The origin of the digital revolution—the Internet—is first and foremost political, and on that basis is both an economic and a technical development. The US blockade has slowed development in most sectors of Cuban society, if not stopping it completely. In the Special Period when Soviet trade ceased, its overall impact on the economy was devastating. The US blockade has also been an obstacle to international collaboration on scientific and technical matters. But the computerization of Cuba has progressed, and along with it access to and use of the Internet. As early as 1992 the medical and scientific community in Cuba was using email for internal communication. During 1993 the number of Unix computers internetworked across the island went from three to twenty.

Official Cuban access to the Internet was established in 1996 with the domain .cu and administered by the Center for Automated Exchange of Information (CENIAI). Cuba then established a Ministry of Technology, which became the main institution administering Internet connectivity and the distribution of computers throughout the island. There were originally four networks with dial-up connections to the Internet: CENIAI, TINORED, CIGBnet, and InfoMed.[66]

---

66. Each of these networks predate the internet and so were not originally connected. CENIAI, the National Center for Automated Data Exchange, began in the 1980s. TINORED networked the country's youth computing clubs that were started in 1987 by the Young Communist Clubs. Since 1991, CiGBNet has provided networking and information resources for the Center for Genetic Engineering and Biotechnology in Havana and similar institutions. Since 1992, Infomed has provided the same for health workers and

The first connectivity for the entire island in 1998 was a 64 Kps satellite connection administered by SPRINT based on special terms to bypass the US embargo. This only developed after a wide-ranging debate over how the Internet would be beneficial but also a vehicle for greater US imperial penetration. Over the past twenty years this possibility has been demonstrated time and again all over the world, given the revelations by Edward Snowden over the US National Security Agency spying on the entire world via the Internet and all digital communication.[67] Two examples were revealed just in 2014. First, a Twitter-like service called ZunZuneo was uncovered as a secret US government effort to attract Cubans into relying on a short-message network that would promote antigovernment politics and influence Cuban public opinion.[68] Soon after, another secret project was exposed; it hired young Latin Americans for low wages to visit Cuba as tourists and cultivate dissent.[69] Neither of these US government efforts were successful.

After the 1998 Sprint network, the next major advance in Cuba's international Internet connectivity was a joint venture between Cuba and Venezuela to lay fiber optic cable linking Cuba to Venezuela and Jamaica, and through them to the entire world. This has the potential to provide 640 Gbps bandwidth. It began to handle internet traffic in 2013.[70] As of 2010 about 30% of Cubans were online.

In 1987 the Young Communists created a demonstration Youth Computer Club (YCC) to teach young people computer literacy, applications, and programming, and also repair and maintenance and even

---

institutions across the island.

67. Glenn Greenwald, *No Place to Hide: Edward Snowden, the NSA, and the U.S. Surveillance State* (New York, NY: Metropolitan Books/Henry Holt, 2014).

68. Desmond Butler, Jack Gillum, and Alberto Arce, "US Secretly Created 'Cuban Twitter' to Stir Unrest," *Associated Press* (wire service), April 4, 2014.

69. Desmond Butler, et al., "US Sent Latin Youth Undercover in Anti-Cuba Ploy," *Associated Press* (wire service), August 4, 2014.

70. Doug Madory, "Cuban Fiber: Completo?," *Renesys*, (blog), January, 23 2013; Empresa de Telecomunicaciones de Cuba S.A. (ETECSA), "Cable Submarino Alba 1 Está Operativo Y Se Comienzan Pruebas Para Tráfico De Internet," *CubaDebate: Contra el Terrorismo Mediático*, January 24, 2013.

circuit design. Today there is a network of 611 locations, or one for every 18,000 Cubans. This is slightly more than the number of public libraries in Cuba (400), and on a par with the number of public libraries in the United States, one for every 18,000 residents. What is different is that the infrastructure of YCC is distinct from that of the public libraries. In the United States, after a wave of experimentation and innovation in the 1990s and early 2000s, there is no ubiquitous community computing facility on a par with the public library. In Cuba, community computing and public libraries developed separately.

Cuba's strategy with the computer clubs has been to put computer learning and use where the people live, and to raise a generation (or more) who could continue to learn computers and be the foundation for computerization of the island's economy and culture. The emphasis was on a national intranet rather than the global Internet, because of cost and because Cuba chose mass digital literacy and production over an information onslaught from the United States. In fact, the early 1990s saw a wave of e-bombing from Florida—overwhelming Cuba's fragile networks with massive spam. Twenty years later we learn that the US government secretly funded Zunzuneo as a cell phone texting network aimed at creating chatter to overthrow the Cuban government—all while continuing its tight economic blockade of Cuba. Cuba's intranet-oriented approach—building up domestic computer literacy—involved software development and linkages to open source efforts around the world.

As of 2004 there were four hundred Youth Computer Clubs, which served all ages, and a survey found that they did indeed impact the workforce: 95% of young people who used a center went on to further computer study, and one-quarter of the workforce had used a computer club. The clubs operated one of Cuba's first four networks (Tinored), which were dial-up networks to and from Havana and one very slow international connection. One US observer wrote, "It is ironic that some Cuban children have email connectivity, while children in many inner-city schools in the U. S. do without computers altogether."[71]

---

71. Larry Press and Joel Snyder, "A Look at Cuban Networks," *Matrix News*.

In 2002 a new Universidad de las Ciencias Informáticas was established.[72] This is an important development, as the main impact on
economic development comes from a country having its own capacity
for software development. Rather than adopting the digital tools from
another country, where one has to adapt to their model, it is important
to develop tools that are organically linked to the needs of one's own
country.

Although every school had in-house computer access and training
by 2004, the YCCs carried on. Of course, it has to be stated that this is
a weak system and frequently has problems that slow things down or
bring them to an abrupt halt. Repairs are difficult and routine upgrades
are few and far between.

Paralleling the computer clubs, another piece of Cuba's digital infrastructure is EcuRed, Cuba's own Wikipedia, which began in 2009. In
2011 it was widely publicized on the TV channel University for All. As
of May 2014, EcuRed is the 28th-most visited site on the island,[73] with
120,000 entries, 16,000 registered contributors, a downloadable edition,
and a mobile phone app.[74] It is supported by several government agencies, and a 2012 EcuRed event in Havana brought together one hundred
editors to celebrate and brainstorm how to continue to grow the site.

As a result of the literacy campaign begun in 1961, Cuba had the
potential to become a country of avid readers. The government established a Book Institute to make sure that book publishing and distribution
would be developed on a nationally coordinated scale. The institute runs
weekly book programs, especially at its Havana headquarters, as well
as a very important annual international book fair. In 2011 at the 20th
Book Fair, Cubans bought 1.7 million books. The institute runs eight
publishing companies and produces three hundred titles a year that are
distributed to over three hundred bookstores throughout the country.

---

72. The name translates as either Information Science or Science of Informatics. See the university's website at http://www.uci.cu.

73. Alexa, "How Popular Is EcuRed.cu? Alexa Traffic Ranks," http://www.
alexa.com/siteinfo/ecured.cu.

74. Ecured, "EcuRed: A Cuban Encyclopedia," http://www.ecured.cu.

In summary, there is a long history to the production, storage, and distribution of information in Cuba. The central institution in this process is the library, and yet the library changes, as do all of these forms of information production. The digital information revolution is fundamentally changing the library in the twenty-first century. Leading up to this and being part of the first stages has been the librarian Marta Terry.

# Chapter 6

## JUCEPLAN, THE CENTRAL PLANNING BOARD

Perhaps the most basic aspect of society that was first on the agenda of the Cuban Revolution was the economy. Fortune—as well as her own strengths—placed Marta, in her role as librarian, at the heart of this process, as this chapter will recount.

It is only after a revolutionary force takes power that the greatest challenges to transform the society must be faced. This was certainly the case for Cuba in 1959. A small guerrilla army, joined by its comrades in the urban underground movement, seized power and had to immediately transform themselves into an administration in charge of a government bureaucracy that had been run just the day before by their adversary, Fulgencio Batista. They first had to consolidate military control, establish the security of the borders, and create an internal defense against counterrevolutionary subversive action. They had to mobilize public opinion in support of the revolution beyond the euphoria of the anti-Batista celebrations in the streets. They had to consolidate political power.

At first there was one mass campaign after another that activated the masses of people and kept their revolutionary consciousness fueled with patriotic enthusiasm and selfless sacrifice:

1958: The fight to take power: the small army worked in tandem with an urban underground movement and several local newspapers and a radio station

1959: The fight against opposition movements: once Batista was ousted, many different tendencies moved to take over sections of the society in opposition to the July 26th Movement

1960: The fight against the internal counterrevolution: armed groups began to create a counterrevolution and began a process of selective assassinations

1961: Bay of Pigs and the Literacy Campaign: the fight to defend the country against US-sponsored invasions and the campaign to liberate the masses of people from the illiteracy that had been the official policy of Batista and Machado before him

1962: The Missile Crisis: the mobilization of the entire population facing the threat of a US invasion based on their outrage that the USSR had created missile bases in Cuba with nuclear warheads capable of hitting every US city

1963: Eloy Gutiérrez Menoyo had been a leader of the Second Front in Escambray during the revolutionary war, but turned against the revolution and tried to support an invasion organized by Alpha 66, a terrorist organization based in and supported by the United States

The whole world was watching and waiting to see what was going to happen. The economy was not owned by Cubans themselves. This is how then-US Senator John Kennedy put it: "At the beginning of 1959, United States companies owned about 40 percent of the Cuban sugar lands—almost all the cattle ranches—90 percent of the mines and mineral concessions—80 percent of the utilities—practically all the oil industries—and supplied two-thirds of Cuba's imports."[75]

The first initiative was to focus on land reform, to implement the policy of "land to the tiller." The Land Reform Law was published on May 17, 1959. The revolutionary leadership prohibited large capitalist farms (banning all farms over one thousand acres), and set up the National Land Reform Institute (INRA) to manage the process. While they faced the legacy of the mono-crop agriculture of sugar, their initial attempts to drastically reduce this dependency led to a crisis of a drop in foreign exchange that hurt other aspects of the economy. The

---

75. John F. Kennedy, "Speech of Senator John F. Kennedy, Cincinnati, Ohio, Democratic Dinner, October 6, 1960," The American Presidency Project, http://www.presidency.ucsb.edu/ws/index.php?pid=25660.

challenge was to maintain Cuba's trade while at the same time setting in motion a plan to feed the Cuban population, focusing both on the global market and the home market.

The next major step was to institute a planning process to reorient the entire economy. They created the Central Board for Planning and Economic Development, JUCEPLAN (Junta Central de Planificación). This agency was organized at the ministerial level. The board included the Prime Minister; the Ministers of Finance, Commerce, and Public Works; the President of the National Bank; a delegate from INRA; and the Minister of Economy. The planning agency was to set economic priorities, coordinate cooperation between the ministries, plan government budgets, and organize a standardized approach to economic statistics, on the basis of which government planning and coordination could take place. JUCEPLAN issued its first plan in 1962, then began to follow the Soviet model of issuing multiyear plans. The Organic Law of the Budget was passed in December, 1962.

In general, the economy had been dominated by a chaotically unorganized set of capitalist institutions, all dependent on the United States. The real planning of the Cuban economy had been done in New York and Washington. The contradiction facing the new Cuban leadership was whether to place priority on technical expertise or on political agreement with the direction of the policies of the revolution. In the realm of the economy a famous story is relevant here, and whether true or not it has become part of the folklore of the revolution. Fidel was alleged to have been leading a meeting late into the night with the leadership and people were half awake and half sleeping. He asked, "Are there any economists in here?" Che woke and raised his hand, but after getting an explanation he said, "Wait a minute, I thought you said communist, not economist." And that, they say, is how Che became the key figure leading the transformation of the economy. The point of the story is to make a joke about a serious matter: that ideology and political loyalty to the revolution was given priority over technical background and skill. Over time, Che played many roles in leading the economy:

head of INRA, the Minister of Industry, the Minister of Finance, and
President of the National Bank.

In a 1965 speech in Algeria, Che reflects back on this experience:

> We have had to learn from practice, by our errors ... that planning and
> socialism go together and that one cannot plan everything when the eco-
> nomic conditions present do not allow it.... The revolutionary leaders
> consisted only of a group of fighters, with high ideals but insufficient
> knowledge.... The superstructure of the capitalist neo-colonial state was
> intact; we had to work to destroy it and to rebuild our society on new
> bases.... We had to change the structures, we began to do so without a plan.
> The revolutionary group, with Fidel Castro at the head, first issued
> the Agrarian Reform Law. This indispensable law ... revealed a terrible
> instrument: the class struggle—and it pushed the Cuban Revolution to
> its limits.[76]

In pre-1959 Cuba, as a neocolony, there was little emphasis on training economists and building a national capacity for the management
of Cuba's economic affairs. At the University of Havana there was a
program in accounting but not economics per se. This was to provide
a support staff for the government and corporate bureaucracies, keeping track of things but not building models for national development.
What educational focus on economics that did exist was at the private
St. Thomas of Villanova Catholic University. They taught capitalist
economics and were closed down in 1961 with the nationalization of
education; at that time former faculty left Cuba and founded a school
in Miami.

It is important to reflect on how Cuba adopted socialism as its official policy for reorganizing society. The central figures of the Cuban
revolution had been Fidel Castro and his close circle of comrades, who
began their earliest affiliation at the time of the attack on the Moncada
Garrison in 1953. This was not a homogeneous group as they were
from different tendencies of the radical movement. This goes back
to the University of Havana where there were communists, anarchists,

76. Che Guevara, "Che Guevara on the Mistakes of the Revolution; from a
Speech Made in Algiers on February 26 1965" in historyofcuba.com (website),
ed. Jerry A. Sierra, http://www.historyofcuba.com/history/che2.htm.

Trotskyists, independent Marxists, and an amalgam of freethinkers and patriots. Various organizations joined with the July 26th Movement led by Fidel, notably the Revolutionary Directorate and the Communist Party. In 1959 Fidel held out the possibility of a national democratic revolution being carried out without such an explicit ideological orientation. However, the Cold War orientation of the United States would have nothing to do with a Cuba having friendly and robust trade relations with the USSR. The Monroe Doctrine was alive and well in Washington, D.C. The United States was squeezing Cuba, forcing it to seek stability in a stronger alliance with the USSR and highlighting the need to rethink reorganizing the economy and society in general. Thus in 1962 the United Party of the Socialist Cuban Revoluation (Partido Unido de la Revolución Socialista Cubana, or PURSC) came into being. In 1965 this organization gave way to a newly re-established Cuban Communist Party (Partido Comunista de Cuba, or PCC). Among the key actors in this process none was more important than Che Guevara.

Marta had been part of a network of revolutionary patriots based on her family and activities as a student. One day in 1961, while at her UNESCO position, she got a call from a military official. She was summoned to his office, and while she didn't think she knew him she went as requested. This was Lt. García Valls. When she got to his office, she went in and he didn't say a word. She was surprised as she didn't recognize this formal military person at all, but it was Pancho! He had been a close friend at the university, and while she had heard that he had gone to fight in the mountains with Fidel, she had no word about him since. He had been very active in the communist tendency on campus and was much respected. They embraced and Marta was happy indeed.

And Pancho, Lieutenant García Valls, brought great news. Marta was to be given her first big opportunity to directly serve revolutionary Cuba in an official capacity. Pancho was asking her to become library director at JUCEPLAN. Not only was this an exciting assignment, her close colleagues at her UNESCO job were already suggesting that she move someplace that was more integrated into the revolution—they

saw, and she ultimately agreed, that she was too much of a sympathizer
with the Cuban revolution to be content at that agency.

In her new position, Marta worked at the epicenter of economic
planning for the new Cuba. There were many issues, the first being the
need to educate the staff, many of whom were more revolutionariess
than trained economists, and not everyone was college educated. There
was the need to provide information on many approaches, including
capitalist and socialist, to economic planning. Marta was a professional
librarian and she not only had ideological battles to fight, she also had
to impose order and the professional standards of a library. The bottom
line is always that the library should have the books and journals that
the patrons need, and when a book is taken out it is expected that it be
returned in good shape and in a timely manner!

At its start, JUCEPLAN took over a building that had housed an
institute for the study of social and economic matters serving the Cuban
bourgeoisie. They had office space and a small library and were centrally
located. They occupied the first eight floors of this building, with the
library on the sixth floor and the executive offices on the fifth. Che
was a key figure in this process as president of the National Bank, and
a leading figure in the top leadership groups of the revolution, in the
party, and the government. Each morning the staff gathered at the
elevators along with various luminaries of the revolution. People took
note of when Che would come in and planned to be there at the same
time. He often came in with a big dog for security, saw the line at the
elevator, waved, and then took the stairs. Once, at an unexpected time
he showed up, and only Marta was there. They got into the elevator and
Marta says she was so anxious that she punched the buttons for all of
the floors. Then she looked at Che, and they both laughed.

The JUCEPLAN library was an example of how a revolutionary
transformation has to rebuild virtually everything. Here was a dilapidated,
out-of-date facility on which the economic planning of the country
would depend. She had to find new shelving and reorganize the collection. She had to find, hire, and train her staff of three people. This
was a tough process, as every agency was going through the same thing

and she had to find supplies and argue for her library as a priority. This, of course, is one of her greatest assets: knowing how to make a case, muster the support of her network, and get things done. Marta rebuilt and transformed this library.

There was a small reading room, but people tended to take material to their offices for study and research. This set up a struggle between the library staff and the more high-status professional staff of JUCEPLAN. Multiple tactics had to be used to keep the materials circulating and not become de facto personal property by remaining on one person's shelf indefinitely. They had to make regular staff visits to collect the materials, and use the tactic of calling them out and by so doing use embarrassment to build discipline and a respect for library practices. It is important to remember that the freedom to rebel in taking power had to be replaced with the discipline to rebuild a new system. These were relatively young people and full of the romance of freedom.

There were new conceptual and theoretical issues that faced librarianship in Cuba. JUCEPLAN was mainly staffed by technical personnel: engineers, statisticians, and specialists in various aspects of the economy. They craved current information and pushed the library in the direction of being a documentation center. Marta had a background in literature and philosophy and was convinced that economic planning had to be carried out within a broad perspective of culture and history. She carried this out by organizing in her small reading room discussions with key cultural figures she could mobilize, again because of her network going back to her university days. She was campaigning for an inclusive approach to planning, and it worked because the engineers and economic specialists were revolutionary thinkers who could easily see that it was only with a comprehensive view of a society that one could carry out economic planning.

A defining moment in her taking control of the library was a strenuous debate over a roomful of dusty items. A number of JUCEPLAN staffers claimed it was time to throw out old material that did not reflect the new thinking. Marta argued otherwise. She was fighting to preserve history and not fall victim to the blindness of dogmatism (point of view) or pragmatism (scarce space). The debate escalated. Che was brought in to use his status to settle the matter. With his asthma, the dust in the archives on the sixth floor threatened his health. But he saw the valiant fight being waged by this slight Afro-Cuban woman. She pointed out that this was the official government serial reporting the nation's official deliberations and decisions. The origins of the *Gaceta Oficial* went back to 1790. Che leaned over to her and whispered, "Chica, do we need this material for the revolution?" Marta said, "Commandante, we must understand our history so we don't repeat it." Che quickly turned, waved his hand and said, "Keep the material." Marta had already become a librarian of the revolution; now she was approved by the romantic revolutionary icon Che.

Another conceptual issue concerned the Dewey Decimal System, the numbering scheme for locating books in a library near other books on the same subject to facilitate use. Marta organized the JUCEPLAN library according to Dewey, but faced a clear problem. The Dewey system was created in the US. While it is regularly updated, its outlook is that of the United States. So it identifies and locates everything related to Marx and Marxism as 335.43 on the library shelves. This forces the classification of a wide range of material within very limited numbers: philosophy, history, political economy, and many other subjects dealt with in the Marxist tradition. This put the Marxist material a great distance from books on the corresponding subject by non-Marxists.

What is more, this book shelving problem—which was making it hard for JUCEPLAN staff to find their material—was also a computerization problem. Marta became the representative from JUCEPLAN to the advisory council of a new organization—the Institute for Documentation and Scientific and Technical Information (IDICT). She heard about this project from Olinta, who was in there trying to get something useful out of the new ideas being debated. Marta saw a change coming and went back to Pancho: "What are they doing?" He answered, "Who knows, but I want you to be in on it!" So she joined the IDICT scientific council representing JUCEPLAN, going to study sessions, and digesting presentations by Soviet advisors. This was Marta's entrance into the world of computers and their 80 column punch cards:

> Those were very complicated, both the machines and the thought of working with them. One of my best friends at JUCEPLAN was Ventura Montes, the engineer who helped to lead the installation of television in Cuba. And then there was the engineer Enrique Salcedo in the statistical section. Toward the end of my time at JUCEPLAN, we were starting to see if we could do some automation, with some kind of vocabulary for economic affairs. Starting from the Dewey decimal classification system, little by little. What a terrible mess with Dewey number 355.411 [logistics] and the theories of Marxism and communism. We tried to work within that Dewey logic. 338 was economics. And even within that we were adapting and inventing from the sixteenth edition of Dewey [1958]. We needed the seventeenth and eighteenth editions [1965 and 1971] and so on and they wouldn't sell them to us because of the blockade.[77]

Marta and her colleagues were facing the problem of organizing knowledge when the content and shape of knowledge was changing dramatically, without being able to see how others were doing it, as reflected in the Dewey classification system.

One manifestation of this is the ambiguity and complexity of negotiating classifications systems in librarianship. The Dewey system was weak on Marxism and the socialist countries, so all Cuban librarians had to learn from the Soviet experience and at the same time become inventive and adopt new innovations, because the Soviet system had its weaknesses as well. This was a new and challenging time, in both professional and personal ways. The Cuban Revolution was young, the revolutionaries were young, and they faced new problems on all fronts.

This classification problem was just one instance of the puzzles that a developing country, a country developing a new approach, has to solve. The library's mission was to create a future which had been impossible under the old regime (Batista) and the old knowledge regime (mostly exported from the US and Spain). Marta was confronting the limitations of professional library standards created by colonial powers. At

---

77. Marta Terry, interview with the authors, March 26, 2014.

the same time, Soviet influence began after the US blockade, connected to their sugar price supports and other forms of aid. That gave Marta access to Soviet library theory, practice, and colleagues. The Soviet Union used yet another numbering system for information: the Soviet Library-Bibliographic Classification, or BBK. Cuban librarians considered changing their cataloging system from Dewey to BBK, but they found that BBK was unsuited to Cuba as well, although it did classify Marxist theory better than Dewey. Worst of all, it was entirely new to a nation of librarians who knew Dewey more or less by heart. Neither Dewey nor BBK incorporated the understanding of the peoples of Latin America.

The JUCEPLAN library was organized by Dewey with alterations that Marta devised, sometimes in concert with other librarians. Today it is still impossible to get current editions of the Dewey manual, for Dewey is from the US, proprietary and not provided freely online. The island's public libraries still use Dewey with adjustments today. The national medical library uses the United States' Library of Congress system, also with adjustments. Other specialized libraries use the Universal Decimal System, developed in Europe.

Many Cubans were applying the just-emerging digital tools to Cuba's practical problems. But not everyone was convinced that this new approach would be the new norm. The Soviet technical advisors helped; all of them were committed to what they called the "scientific technological revolution." The basic tool was the computer. Almost as if by some magical spell, information was punched into 80-column cards and statistical analysis would produce precise calculations on large data sets. While initially driven by engineers and economists, this new technological system became popular and spread to many parts of the government and many other parts of society. Part of its beginning was in JUCEPLAN.

IDICT has been a very important organization. Marta explains:

In the early years of the creation of IDICT, there was little or no expertise in Cuba on scientific information resources and delivery systems, regulations, and objectives; and even less on issues in the information world's ongoing debate about methodology and the handling of documents, given the overwhelmingly rapid discoveries and developments that had been taking place since the early 1950s.... Perhaps IDICT's most impressive achievement of that era was the way in which it became, practically speaking, a clearinghouse for professional information, and a source of information for our country on all the latest information technology.[78]

This was important as it was the beginning of Marta's exposure to computers and the coming information revolution that would transform everything.

Part of this process was JUCEPLAN being advised by experts from the USSR and their socialist allies from Eastern Europe and China. In fact, one of the key tasks was translating material from the languages of the socialist countries, especially Russian. A Russian language translator was added to the staff of JUCEPLAN. He was a person with a Spanish background who had spent time in the USSR. Another JUCEPLAN translator was Zoia Barash, a Russian woman married to a Cuban. She and Marta became friends and Zoia later became a well-known film scholar.

While JUCEPLAN was a place for specialists, it was also part of the general organization of society and subject to how the society was being organized and mobilized as part of the Cuban Revolution. Marta was involved in both the Committees for the Defense of the Revolution (CDR) and the militia. Each CDR was based on the geographical location of the population by residence and (at that time) by workplace. At JUCEPLAN one CDR spanned two floors in the building. The CDR for the library and the executive floors held regular discussions about the policies of the revolution and how JUCEPLAN staff could contribute to and apply these policies. Marta was the CDR president for all of JUCEPLAN, and as a result also participated in the higher level Estatales CDR that included CDRs from all the big ministries located nearby.

---

78. Marta Terry González, "Special Libraries and Other Information Institutions in Cuba," *World Libraries* 13, no. 1/2 (2003), para. 25, 28. Reproduced in Appendix 9.

The militia was constantly in motion as the first few years were full of counterrevolutionary attacks and acts of subversion. These motions often brought out a contradiction between the loyalists of the revolution and people who were not sold on the need for this level of armed vigilance. Marta found an olive green outfit that belonged to a cousin who was one who had not bought into the need for mass readiness. She wore it one day to JUCEPLAN and caused quite a stir. It was a bold statement of her patriotic commitment to "¡Patria o muerte!—¡Venceremos!" (Motherland or death—We will win!)

All of this moved from speculation to reality with the missile crisis of October 1962. This became a major focus for CDR discussions. The United States had positioned missiles in Turkey near the border of the USSR, and was threatening to invade Cuba. The failed US-sponsored Bay of Pigs invasion took place in April, 1961. The missile crisis was eighteen months later. The USSR leader Nikita Khrushchev made a pact with Cuba to establish missile bases to enable Cuba to ward off the threat of a US invasion or to be able to launch an effective counterattack. US President John Kennedy and his military establishment, upon finding out about this development, prepared for war, and this would have been a nuclear war since that was what the Cubans had. The crisis lasted for two weeks and ended with no winners. In particular, the USSR made a deal with the United States without the full participation of the Cuban leadership. Out of this crisis Cuba was even more committed to maintaining full military capacity to protect itself from the United States. While this has been effective, it has also placed a tremendous burden on the national budget of Cuba. The CDR and the militia were validated as necessary in the minds of most Cubans.

Cuba struggled to realize its policy of being a socialist country, and its relationship with the Soviet Union was critical. They were part of the Soviet sphere of influence via trade and defense agreements, a structural alliance that helped Cuba survive the brutal US embargo. At the same time, Cuba was adamant that it not compromise its national independence and right to develop its own policies.

Of course, not all of Marta's experiences at JUCEPLAN were political or professional. The staff at JUCEPLAN was young and full of energy. They ate together at their local cafeteria, they partied together, and generally were a social group. They were full of the moment. Marta as a beautiful young woman had an active social life. Men vied for her attention, some with noble intent and others full of the macho cultural style that was a holdover from the past. It was here that she met the love of her life, Luis Antonio Forte Manilla. Luis was a young engineer, somewhat shy but a leader among his peers: the director de organización (director of organizational management) of JUCEPLAN. He was head of the militia at JUCEPLAN and commanded the respect of everyone. He was generally shy and somewhat quiet, while Marta was outspoken and full of confidence. They epitomized the belief that opposites attract, but this had more to do with their public style than their relationship as it was an experiment in gender equality.

Marta and Luis married on December 18, 1965. Although Marta remembers that at the time she did not care one iota about family approval, her aunts approved. Both families immediately began to help the couple. They went to live with Luis's parents, Fausto Forte and Mercedes Manilla. He was a successful tailor, even managing a staff; she was a housewife. Without much money, the newlyweds did not have their own bedroom furniture. This time her aunt Luz Maria spoke to Marta for the Terry family: "Each time you have needed money, who gave it to you? You will do now as you have always done. Lala will pay. You can pay it back another time. Find that furniture!"

On November 3, 1966, Marta gave birth to their son Claudio. Sometime later Marta and Luis had a quarrel. Marta snatched up the baby and went back to her family, who had been living at Gervasio #122 in the El Vedado district of Havana since soon after the revolution came to power. Everyone welcomed her, fed her, listened to her, and played with the baby. A while later, she made ready to arrange her old room for her and the baby. But her aunts said, "No, this visit is over, it's time for you to go back to your house and your husband." Marta was stunned. Only one of her aunts had a husband or children, but they all felt that

Marta had to face her life and work through problems if she was to realize her future as a wife, mother, and an adult woman. After she left, they changed the lock on the front door. She laughs when she recalls that they never gave her a new key.

In fact, the aunts were part of the problem, as they had so sheltered Marta that she lacked the skills most young girls got at home in preparation for marriage and motherhood. Marta was reared to be a professional, a leader among her peers. The young couple lived with Luis's parents. The grandparents took care of Claudio, and the four adults worked family matters out as best they could, Marta relying on her experience negotiating a household of 23. They settled into an apartment in Miramar, one of those allocated to JUCEPLAN to house its staff. Today, Marta continues to live in that same apartment.

When Marta went to JUCEPLAN in 1961, it was what she calls the beginning times. Everything was starting. And, surprising to her, she made a success of it. The man who was the day-to-day director of JUCE-PLAN, minister really, was Regino Boti León, the son of a renowned poet from Guantanamo Province. One day Boti called her and let her know that at a particular time she should report for work at Casa de la Américas, because Haydée Santamaría had asked for her. This was 1967.

# Chapter 7

## CASA DE LAS AMÉRICAS

Cuba did not close itself off to make a revolution in isolation from the world. Cuba identified its mission as being part of world revolution, especially in relation to Latin America, the Caribbean, and Africa. Being a small country without access to economic power, the Cubans had to emphasize moral, cultural, and political support for movements and countries engaged in projects of social transformation. Only four months after seizing power in January of 1959, the new Cuban government created a new cultural institution headed by Haydée Santamaría: Casa de las Américas (House of the Americas). Its role was to embrace the cultural workers and artists of the hemisphere and support them as they created art that challenged oppressive regimes.

Haydée, affectionately known as Yeyé, was one of two women who participated in the first major armed attack of the revolution at the military garrison of Moncada. She went on to fight in the mountains and distinguished herself as a revolutionary fighter in many different roles. Despite having something less than a university education, she became a steadfast militant in the highest ranks of the revolution, both before and after 1959, including leading a major intellectual institution of writers and artists.

What is interesting is that the nickname Yeyé is not common in Cuba, although it is usually associated with the name Haydée. What is more, Yeyé is a Yorùbá word that means "mother of us all," and that is fitting for a woman so central to the origin of the Cuban revolutionary process and a founder of one of the most important Cuban institutions, Casa de las Américas.

On a personal level, after the Moncada attack, Haydée was captured along with many of her comrades. First her brother, Abel Santamaria, and then her fiancé, Reinaldo Boris Luis Santa Coloma, were tortured and killed. The torturers presented her with her brother's gouged-out eye. She declared that if after losing one eyeball he did not talk, then for sure she wouldn't utter a word. Fidel told this story and acknowledged her deep sacrifice in his speech at his trial, a speech that she helped publish as "History will Absolve Me." She would face many such moments of hearing of the injury or death of a close comrade, including Che Guevara in October 1967.[79]

Casa set out to form a network of artists and writers to impact people across the hemisphere, starting with Cuba. It had to facilitate production, distribution, critical evaluation, and preservation of cultural artifacts of all kinds. From its first year of operations, Casa began to award literary prizes that reached out to all of the Americas, across a variety of genres and subject areas. Progressive literary figures were not being recognized in their own countries and were frequently being persecuted and hardly ever published. Casa, led by Haydée, changed this not only by recruiting juries and helping them make literary awards but also by establishing a publishing house to make sure that readers could find the works of these writers in Cuba and beyond. They added publishing journals to their capacity and became a formal institution of record for Latin American literary and artistic production.

Casa was a literary center for all of Latin America. Popular movements were surging. People were fighting dictatorships and sometimes

79. Before 1959, Haydée married another combatant, Armando Hart Dávalos, who served as Minister of Education and later as Minister of Culture. He was a member of the Communist Party Political Bureau for twenty-six years; she served on the Central Committee for fifteen years until her death. They had two children. In the end, differences emerged and they divorced. On July 28, 1980, six months after the death of fellow veteran revolutionary Celia Sánchez, Haydée committed suicide. It was a shock to the many people who knew and admired her, although perhaps not to those who also knew the pain of losing so many comrades and loved ones.

fleeing for their lives. Cuba was making itself known. It was logical and necessary to link literature with political analysis and history. In this context, the library at Casa was important for many reasons. It served as research support for the general work of Casa and its participation in international discourse and policy formation, it was a home library for exiled writers and artists from Latin America and the Caribbean, and it was a research location for Cuban students, journalists, and government officials. In addition, it became the repository for the material sent in for the prizes awarded by Casa.

Casa de las Américas was in Havana and thus served the leading intellectual and artistic community of Cuba, including university students. In fact, it was located very near a large dormitory for students in the arts and humanities. They used Casa as a research resource for their studies. Casa also had public programming, which featured cultural figures from abroad and from Cuba as well. The students challenged the cultural workers for the limited seats in the library and in most cases for the books, as in general the library held only a single copy of each title.

Eight years after its founding, Casa had built up its own library, named after the student leader and revolutionary José Antonio Echevarría. Marta was asked to come and manage the library and its staff.

Marta remembers dealing with the news that JUCEPLAN was to release her to start working at Casa. She knew Casa well as a library volunteer and a participant in its programs. She was now thirty-five, already a valued librarian in a crucial institution, and pregnant. But as Marta looks back, she was spoiled—or indulging herself—"crying and wanting to die," unable to decide what course to take. On the steps of the University of Havana she ran into her former art professor, María del Rosario Novoa Luis, who told her sharply, "I don't know why you even want to be that thing of a librarian. You should come back here and teach art history!" But Graziella Pogolotti was waiting for Marta that same day and insisted, "Listen, you have to go Casa de las Américas. You are needed there. Haydée needs you there. There are many critical issues there and you must go there." And in the end, Marta was at Casa for twenty years. She accomplished many things there and learned a lot. It was a perfect match for her education and talents.

Even before being hired or volunteering at Casa, Marta had begun to connect with Casa. In 1959, still hoping to work in history and wanting to learn in any case, she joined one of the classes taught at Casa: History of the Americas. That was her scene! She made friends with the teacher. He was the Argentinian writer and critic Ezequiel Martínez Estrada, who for a time directed a Center for Latin American Studies within Casa. Although Marta didn't make it to every class, Haydée and others began to keep their eyes on her. Finally one day Haydée wanted her to come and work at Casa. But before that day, as we saw, there were other moments when Marta helped Casa. Early in her relationship with Luis, they volunteered together to help rearrange the stacks in the Casa library; his engineering skills were needed for that task. She was becoming the Casa librarian one step at a time, based on joining the intellectual programming of Casa and the practical tasks of rebuilding the Casa library.

Haydée presided over the Latin American Solidarity Conference (OLAS) from July 31 to August 10, 1967. The staff of Casa and its friends across the city were thrown into the mix of this international challenge. From her position at JUCEPLAN, Marta took on the work of helping prepare background papers and bibliographies for the conference.

When Marta was hired as librarian of the José Antonio Echevarría Latin American Library of La Casa de las Américas, she had to contend with two struggles: one conceptual and the other practical. On the conceptual level, Haydée said that Casa staff must be in the second row, to help the intellectuals, the creative people who are in the first row. Marta took this very much to heart, but then a curious debate began—is the library a diamond or a pearl? A diamond shines for all to see, but a pearl develops over time, layer by layer, and then is discovered when the shell is pried open. Haydée argued for diamond, and Marta for pearl. Both seem true, for from her perspective as the director of Casa, Haydée saw the need for a diamond; but as the librarian in the trenches of the stacks, Marta saw the reality of the pearl. As she later told it,

> I had been a library director at JUCEPLAN, a task that was professional, political, and cultural. I was familiar with Casa. I came feeling ready to master any kind of situation. But it was not like that and I had to manage among a sea of troubles I knew nothing about.[80]

Perhaps unconsciously demonstrating her suitability for the international cultural work of Casa, Marta was quoting Shakespeare's Hamlet here.

> Inner life at Casa was a constant movement. I did not have the strong engineers backing my positions. Quite the contrary! I had been given the space; now I had to learn how to do and how to behave.

> Haydée's ideas about the internal organization, I can see now, were quite clever. At the front were the intellectuals or I'd rather say the creators. Those who had both the gift of art and feeling and the intelligence of understanding the new ideological and political set and with all that the ability to work together. The second row were let us say the administrators, but what kind of administrators! They had to be intelligent, with great capacity for adapting to the talented and gifted. At the same time adapting meant creating—along with the creators! And so many of those administrators were themselves very eminent and talented: as poet, essayist, painter, composer, film director...[81]

They all developed a Casa approach to things, without a lot of speeches, manuals and the like. For as Marta said, "The ultimate goal of Haydée was to clarify and sustain the role of the intellectual within our new society."

The practical struggle was over the role and leadership of the library. When Marta joined Casa as director of the library, she had a colleague who had preceded her in the library named Olga Andreu. Olga was part of the artist subculture at Casa: her husband was a playwright with a

---

80. Marta Terry, interview with the authors, March 24, 2014.
81. Ibid.

growing reputation and she was an artist in her own right. They had been out of the country until after 1959, during the struggles leading to victory, but then became vital forces within Casa. Olga worked in the library but was not a professionally trained librarian, which was why Marta came in as the department head. Casa staffperson Silvia Gil was made director of acquisitions for Casa covering books and art, something she excelled at and which made important contributions to Casa, although this work went on outside of the library. She was adept at writing letters and building a network of contacts that proved beneficial for Casa. Marta, on the other hand, combined her professional skill and political acumen to transform the library into one of the most important library centers in Cuba. She was trained in Philosophy and Letters to the highest standards at the University of Havana and she rooted herself in a dedication to advance the interests of working people, with a special affinity for Afro-Cubans.

One of the tactics Marta would use in order to play the great status games that would emerge in dealing with famous people, who sometimes took themselves too seriously, was to speak in terms of the numerical Dewey Decimal Classification system for library organization. Instead of bowing with great deference, she might say, "You are an 861," that is, Spanish poetry. She was not an admiring audience. She was a professional librarian to be respected just like everyone else. In a library, all books have their place, the famous ones and the seldom-read ones, for even those are important to their particular readers. There is a profound simplicity and democratic leveling performed by the classification scheme that maps all books.

Another aspect of life at Casa was style. Cuba—Havana in particular—was famous for style and flair in language, music, dance, and dress. And in Casa there was a concentration of the arts, and even more of a focus on creativity. Even with small incomes, one can make style choices and there was some competition in this matter at Casa. Marta learned the concept of being overdressed from a fellow Casa executive board member, painter Mariano Rodríguez. This mattered for Marta's work because in a workplace where the personal becomes political, psycho-social conflicts can get in the way of work. Marta remembered Rodríguez's comment when she returned from Denmark wearing a blue top with an orange skirt: "Something new is happening at Casa!" The color caught the painter's eye and he approved.

During this period Marta became a professor at the university and began publishing books on the profession of library science. She had the politics of a cadre member in the service of the Cuban Revolution, humble and egalitarian. On the other hand she had the ego and professional standing to be a person of authority and honor. Because there were others who exemplified the opportunism of grandstanding and ambitious climbing up whatever ladder they could be on (institution, government, party, public notoriety), Marta made a point of confronting this opportunist tendency by refusing to play the diva role, though quite a diva she has always been.

As at JUCEPLAN, Marta again faced the challenges of building a library whose mission was part of a global anticolonial movement using professional library standards created by colonial powers. The classification problem at Casa was that Dewey classifies Cuban literature as Spanish literature along with other countries formerly colonies of Spain. At Casa, Marta devised and implemented more adjustments to Dewey, and once again that was one of her foundational achievements. Such adjustments have been developed by specialists even in the US, because the Dewey system does not reflect their knowledge. The classification system has also been roundly criticized for its conservative viewpoint.

Haydée was clear on the role of the library at Casa that Marta had been given leadership over: "I believe it has to be a library specializing in the problems of our continent, able to serve academics (and others) both within and without. The library currently has more than 77,000 volumes, almost all devoted to Latin America."[82]

Building the library collection at Casa was not primarily based on using Cuban foreign exchange, which has always been in short supply.

---

82. Betsy MacLean, *Haydée Santamaría* (Melbourne; New York: Ocean Press, 2003), 62.

Instead, as well as drawing Cubans into its activities, Casa was a hub in a network of artists, writers, and intellectuals across Latin America whose anti-imperialist stance placed them at odds with their own governments and with the United States to the north. When invited to Casa—or when finding their own way as a result of repression and exile—they brought their own and other books. This was part of Casa's acquisitions policy. It resulted in a unique collection built from cultural resistance and good community organizing.

Casa's prizes for literature, poetry, and so on amounted to an effort to create a new canon that would be used on campuses and elsewhere. It was a rejection of canons that had been imposed from outside Latin America by empires past and present.

Marta soon made a contribution to the way in which decisions were made regarding the Casa prizes. The key to the process was how people were recruited for each jury to make the evaluations and award the prizes. The first system was more subjective, meaning the executive board would compile a list and select a committee. Marta was part of the process to anchor the jury selection in more objective criteria. She began to compile résumés and bibliographies of potential jurors and prizewinners so that their backgrounds would lead to more democracy, more opportunity to add diversity, and more inclusivity. This is not to demean the early choices, but to point out that democracy will not spring from the past unless a process is established that overcomes past practice and includes people based on merit and is inclusive of those who have been marginalized in the past. The library's carefully built files on individual writers eventually grew into Casa's Center for Literary Research.

Marta had a very personal relationship with Haydée, as did many, as her style of management was to be intimately close to her associates and weave them together as a close-knit team. Haydée was a master at building and maintaining cohesion despite differences. On many occasions Haydée would give Marta a ride home from working at Casa, as they lived in the same general area. She finally allocated one of Casa's cars to Marta so that she would have the convenience of mobility around the city on her own. But she didn't micromanage. In one instance, when there were some personal conflicts developing, she challenged Marta to directly engage the relevant people in an open meeting. Tension and anxiety filled the room, but it was precisely what needed to be done, as she was confident that Marta could not only explain herself to others, but would do so in such a manner that the conflict would be deflated and people would be won back over to a comfortable working relationship.

However, one critical issue remained unresolved between Haydée and Marta: racism and the Afro-Cubans. The main line of the revolution was that this issue had been resolved by affirmative action policies in education and employment. The basic position was that when the issue had been resolved in public spaces, this would lead to a resolution in private spaces (family, recreation, etc.). The fundamental issue was class, and other issues would eventually be resolved. Marta lived at the experiential vortex of this issue because, while she was a militant party member and upheld the line, she was also aware of the ambiguity of that position as Cuba was far from completely eliminating racism.

Sometimes it manifested itself in ignorance of Afro-Cuban cultural practices. Once Haydée asked Marta why Black people often wore white, as if ashamed of the color black. Marta knew that this was nothing to be ashamed of, as people wore white to publically proclaim their reverence and respect for the orisha Obatalá. On the other hand, Haydée elevated Marta to the executive board of Casa, demonstrating that she had no reservations about color when embracing a comrade of high standards.

There was also the other tendency for some Afro-Cubans to always fall back on racism as the ultimate explanation for every shortcoming and bad result in their lives and work. Some wanted to use the library for that sort of whining and Marta would have none of that. She upheld the line: "In the revolution everything, otherwise nothing." The most important and only acceptable approach was to go through channels, to present your case and engage in the democratic process. Also, she promoted principled public discussions where ideas and feelings could go through an open process. Society had to be transformed via democracy and not by promotion of sectarian secrets and gossip.

Another aspect of this is the definition of revolution. The struggles within a revolutionary process can fall victim to a romantic memory to resist the misinformation of the imperialist enemy and to provide motivational memory for the succeeding generations. To face the future with revolutionary resolve, the past must be seen through a materialist lens that is inclusive of all contradictions, while at the same time not ignoring the main tendency of the revolutionary process. Revolutionary people are revolutionary, but they are also people who carry with them the norms and values of their social origins. Haydée was a soldier of revolutionary love, as best described by her close comrade Che:

> At the risk of seeming ridiculous, let me say that the true revolutionary is guided by great feelings of love. It is impossible to think of a genuine revolutionary lacking this quality. Perhaps it is one of the great dramas of the leader that he or she must combine a passionate spirit with a cold intelligence and make painful decisions without flinching. Our vanguard revolutionaries must idealize this love of the people, of the most sacred causes, and make it one and indivisible. They cannot descend, with small doses of daily affection, to the level where ordinary people put their love into practice.[83]

Marta was invited to an important UNESCO course for teachers of librarianship that was being held in 1968 in Denmark and Haydée asked her to go. She was hesitant because of her fear that it was too early to leave her son, and this became a great challenge—to serve self and family or to serve the Cuban Revolution. But in serving the revolution she was just starting at Casa and now was being asked to leave and serve in another way. Life was not going to be easy, but lived in a sea of ambiguity about how best to serve, even if one was being selfless. Haydée insisted that this trip was the best way to serve, as she would learn things that Cuba needed her to learn. She went, but only with family approval—and such help as getting clothes for Northern Europe.

---

83. Che Guevara, "Socialism and Man in Cuba," in *The Che Guevara Reader*, ed. David Deutschmann (North Melbourne, Australia: Ocean Press, 1965), 225-26.

Casa used its journal, *CASA*, to build exchange relationships with other journals. This journal was founded by Roberto Fernández Retamar, a former student colleague of Marta's at the University of Havana. He has been the director of Casa for the last twenty-six years. As new journals came in, most of them via donation or exchanges with Latin Americans, Marta introduced the use of routing slips that indicated the sequential list of names of persons to get the journal in turn, each with a date so that people would get used to reading and passing along the journal in a timely manner. The slip also helped to locate a journal if there was a slowdown in distribution.

The library as pearl or diamond: the conceptual debate helped structure Marta's thinking and practice. She described one aspect of being a librarian like this: "I cannot prepare the readers—they prepare themselves—but I can prepare the books for the readers. This is what I do." Marta tended to stress the library as a secondary function in Casa, but her actual experience involved making the library central to the intellectual life of Casa, especially via regular discussions she organized in the library reading room. Building the library's depth of capacity—the layers of the pearl—Marta began to train people out of the working class for library work. She put an ad in the newspaper calling for working people who wanted to qualify for a technical job as a librarian to come to Casa and take classes. While she remembers this as something that "just happened," it is in effect a form of class struggle, elevating the working class into the occupations that run society, for libraries are an important part of that. They had served the rulers of capital and now they must be transformed to serve the working class.

One of the stories that can help us to understand the importance of Marta's work is her relationship with a working-class Afro-Cuban woman named Dámasa Reyes Rolando. When Marta was about to make her first international trip to Denmark as a librarian representing Cuba, she found that as a new mother she had gained weight and her winter clothes from 1953 to 1954 did not fit. That's when she found Dámasa, who was a seamstress. Not only did Dámasa take the workplace classes, Marta also hired her to pull together a small wardrobe. She turned out to be a wonderful seamstress and seemed to know exactly what Marta needed to be comfortable and to maintain her stylish standard of excellence.

The Cuban Revolution was moving rapidly to open new opportunities for its working class; people were being challenged to raise their aspirations beyond what anyone could have earlier imagined. This was especially true in relation to literacy and education at all levels. Dámasa had dreams of being a college graduate, a goal that would enable her to maximize her potential and make a greater contribution to society. She had taken up sewing in order to support her family, so her sisters and brothers could afford to study. Now, with the new opening up of opportunity, it was going to be her turn. She turned to Marta for help.

This proved to be a difficult question, because Casa was a regional organization with its main focus on relationship between Cuba and artists, writers, and intellectuals from other countries. So, could it accommodate a worker-oriented educational initiative for Cubans locally? This proved too difficult to manage, so Marta was faced with a contradiction of her revolutionary commitment—world revolution and transformation of a particular Cuban situation.

Marta made a "revolution in the revolution." This phrase was first used by Fidel when he celebrated women as they formed the Federation of Cuban Women. Here, Marta was confronted with a working-class Afro-Cuban woman who wanted to break out of her limited social existence, a primary objective of the revolution. Yet at the same time, she was the librarian in a very important institution carrying out an important aspect of Cuban foreign policy. She chose to do what many did; she embraced her revolutionary duty to work as a librarian by day and became Dámasa's tutor at night.

Dámasa had been taking a class in librarianship at IDICT—where she met Marta's younger sister Zenaida, who was already a librarian. Dámasa also took classes at the Capitolio and the Sugar Cane Institute, all set up for workers. She then began to work as an English translator at the Academy of Sciences and began to study library science. Following this she began to work with Marta at Casa, which led her to enter the university and get a library degree in 1978. She had been working and studying via the courses set up by the party and the trade union in order to advance worker education. Dámasa is a good example of how workers have benefited, and Marta among others are exemplary party members who gave of their time to make sure that these programs were a success.

Marta understood the relationship between reading and revolution. Fidel had said it: "Don't believe, read!" And Marta carried that philosophy forward to rationalize the existence of a comprehensive library of all the books, quoting S. R. Ranganathan: "There are no books that cannot be read. Each book has its user, its readers. Not all books can be read by everyone. That is the power of the library." Casa was the leading institution at the cutting edge of intellectual and cultural developments in all of the areas of the arts, and in addition the library collection provided the material foundation for all that Casa represented. This included the visual artists, the musicians, the writers, the performing artists, and the cultural intellectuals in general.

Even while at Casa, Marta was linked to the broader professional network of librarians. She was teaching them at Casa and at the University of Havana (see Chapter 8). She had close friends and working relationships with people like Olinta and some of her former professors. Olinta and Marta, with a few others, planned and carried out the rebirth of the Cuban professional librarians association, the Asociación de Bibliotecarios Cubanos (ASCUBI), while Marta was at Casa in 1981 (see Chapter 10).

Haydée's suicide in 1980 (see footnote #79 above) sent Cuba into shock, especially the Casa staff. She was Yeyé, the mother of the institution, who held firm command and the loyalty of the staff. She had endured torture and loss as part of the Moncada attack that inspired the revolution. Her great status in the revolution was shared by everyone at Casa. With her gone, she began to be reinterpreted by each subgroup in terms of their special relationship, and as with any complex organization, when one or another tendency takes the lead and changes the whole, then something new comes into being. So there was the period of Casa under Haydée, and then Casa became something different after that.

Cuba changed as well, and other cultural institutions began to develop alongside Casa. This change began when Haydée and Armando Hart got a divorce; Marta was close to Hart, but her visceral connection was with Haydée. The personal once again became political.

# Chapter 8

## JOSÉ MARTÍ NATIONAL LIBRARY

There were many factors that led to Marta's moving from Casa de las Américas to the National Library. She had been turned down at the beginning of her career as a professional librarian by María Teresa Freyre de Andrade, her former teacher and then director of the National Library. Years later, María Teresa tried to hire her as an executive assistant, an offer that Marta declined. By then Marta had her own library at JUCE-PLAN and she felt it was "better to be the head of a mouse than to be the tail of a lion." But 1987 was a different matter. One aspect is that Casa was no longer what it was in those heady days of idealism and forging new ground under the leadership of Haydée Santamaría. Her death was a deeply personal loss and shock for all of the staff as they had become a powerful and intense collective.

Marta lost her comrade Haydée in 1980, and then lost her husband Luis to a heart attack on May 12, 1987. At his funeral, her colleagues Olinta Ariosa and Lucía Sardiñas mentioned to her that the Minister of Culture Armando Hart wanted her to leave Casa de las Américas to become head of the National Library. In the coming crisis every institution was going to be challenged to keep to the course of the revolution, and this required leadership. The demand was to make sure that every institution did not fail, but survived.

What was the institution that she was stepping forward to lead? How had it arisen?

The National Library was established in 1901 by the US military governor ruling Cuba, Leonard Wood. Just months before the founding of the Republic of Cuba, Wood issued Military Order #234 establishing the National Library. The historian Domingo Figarola Caneda was appointed as its first director. In its first years there was little careful attention paid to the National Library and the books were almost always at risk. They were packed up and moved, only to be packed up and moved again and again. At one time the collection was stored in a prison. Every move entailed losses. Finally, in 1941 under the first Batista administration, a one-half cent tax on every bag of sugar was levied to raise funds to construct the building that today houses the National Library.[84]

From its founding in 1901 at the start of the US neocolonial period until the 1959 revolution, the National Library was not involved in serving the Cuban public directly or in collaboration with any other libraries. It primarily served the function of storing official documents of the national government and what private collections had been donated, many of them unique. Over time, as the revolutionary government took library matters into its hands, the National Library began to work with other libraries and took on the role of coordinating regional provincial libraries, municipal libraries, and all public libraries. It fully developed this role under the leadership of Marta Terry.

After 1959 Cuba's libraries were challenged to anchor the development of a new national library system. A critical turning point was the 1961 literacy campaign, which brought Cuba's literacy rate from roughly 75% to more than 95%. When Fidel said the Cuban people must read, and not just believe what they were told, he created more demand for library services to provide relevant documents, books, and journals. In other words, "Think for yourself," because only by the people taking control of the society could the Cuban Revolution be fully realized. In an institution this meant that not just from the top, but from the bottom up, people must read, think, and develop the policies and practices

---

84. Commission on Cuban Affairs, *Problems of the New Cuba* (Foreign Policy Association, 1935); Mayol and Orne, "Cuban Libraries; Lilia Castro de Morales, *Biografía De La Biblioteco Nacional* (Ciudad de la Habana: Editora Biblioteca Nacional, 1957); Emilio Setién Quesada, "Libraries and Library Science in Cuba," *IFLA Journal* 20, no. 2 (1994).

that were needed. This created the social basis for demanding that the National Library be transformed from an elite institution into one that served national and popular needs.

Changing the class nature of an institution is not something that can happen by fiat or by top-down policy. In every case the people decide (staff and library patrons), so change involves persuasion over time, and lots of trial and error. The leadership guiding this change needed to be respected by all involved. But any library, and especially the National Library, changes in sync with the general social, political, and economic climate. Marta became the director of the National Library at a time of great change, a change that impacted policy and the everyday experiences of the entire country. She had to take control of an elitist institution and turn it on its head, to embrace the workers, both professional and clerical, unleashing and legitimizing them as the real content of the Cuban revolutionary process.

The changes in world relations were so dramatic when Marta became the director of the National Library that it is necessary to provide more detail regarding what the Cubans call the Special Period. After 1959, when the United States turned on Cuba, the Cuban leadership was forced to turn to the USSR and was embedded within their global political and economic sphere of influence. This reached a high point in 1972, when Cuba became a member of the Council for Mutual Economic Assistance (CMEA), the global organization for preferential trade and foreign aid support with the USSR. For some years the USSR was Cuba's main trading partner, assuring an oil supply to the island and buying Cuban sugar at a stable price that was often above the price offered on the world market.

But by the 1980s the Soviet bloc was struggling with economic failures. Mikhail Gorbachev became General Secretary of the Communist Party in the USSR in 1985 and head of state in 1989. This signaled a change in their political orientation. Gorbachev launched the policies of restructuring (*perestroika*) and opening up (*glasnost*) that led to the total capitulation of the Yeltsin regime (1991–1999). More than giving socialism a human face, they reversed socialism and ended the revolutionary experience founded by Lenin based on the theories of Marx and Engels. Capitalism was unleashed and even the USSR was dismantled, as different republics became countries in their own right. Each country had to fend for itself in the face of global capitalism and in some cases unleashed fascist elements that had been suppressed since World War II.

Gorbachev's policies were not welcomed by Cuban leaders. Cuba was determined to be guided by its own policies, practices, and beliefs. It was facing the hegemonic United States still hell-bent on implementing the century-old Monroe Doctrine, by which it gave itself de facto ownership and control of the Western Hemisphere, including Cuba. Gorbachev visited Cuba in April, 1989, and indicating that there were even greater changes coming for his country, tried to get Cuba to join in. Just two years later, Marta was in Moscow for the 1991 IFLA conference and saw with her own eyes that the Soviet Union was collapsing.

As a result of the dismembering of the USSR and Russia's turn toward capitalism, Cuba lost its major trading partner. The country lost approximately 80% of its imports, 80% of its exports, and its gross domestic product dropped by 34%. This was indeed a special period. The United States took this as an opportunity to squeeze Cuba even further by the Helms-Burton Act of 1996. They advanced more penalties for any country doing business with Cuba. During this time the Cuban transportation system was strangled for lack of oil and food shortages forced everyone to feel the crisis close to home. All of these conditions hit the National Library hard and placed Marta in the difficult position of leading it in these trying times.

Adapting the library to survive and provide better service was something Marta knew. She had been working on different assignments from the Ministry of Culture even while working at Casa. She was asked to coordinate removing the José Martí papers from the National Library in order to place them in a new institute dedicated to the study and preservation of the ideas of Martí. On the Martí project she worked with one of her classmates from the University of Havana, Roberto Fernández Retamar. Some of the staff were not enthusiastic, thinking of the collection and not the demands of the wider society, wanting to keep everything at the National Library. At another moment she was assigned to organize the archives and library of the famous Lyceum Lawn Tennis Club, moving them into the National Library. The facility that had housed them then became Cuba's first house of culture (*casa de cultura*), with special emphasis on service to children and the general population. A battle Marta lost was the plan to keep the most important works of art in the neighborhood houses of culture, near the people. The two major collection relocations, into and out of the National Library, demonstrate the critical role Marta played in the Ministry of Culture in helping to reorganize the library and archival holdings of major Cuban institutions for more effective use as times and tasks changed.

A third example of Marta's role in institution building and adapting to change concerns Juan Marinello Vidaurreta. He was both a leading intellectual as a dean at the University of Havana and a founding member of the first Communist Party of Cuba. In 1948 he was the party's candidate for president of Cuba. After his death in 1977, his house passed to the Ministry of Culture and Marta was assigned the task of building his archive into the archives of the Ministry of Culture. The memory of a country is socially constructed and preserved. There is the politics of organizing what resources and human capital are needed to get the job done, and there are the professional issues of holding to the highest standards possible so that the project is creditable, sustainable, and legitimate. In Marta Terry, the Cuban Ministry of Culture had someone who could do both.

Until 1959, and on occasion thereafter, the National Library was run by intellectuals who were steeped in the content of the books but did not have professional library training. This was also true of how the party organization in the library had been set up: headed by intellectuals who were not at the core of the library staff. This created two related problems—neither political nor professional leadership was anchored organically in the workings of the staff. This had to be fixed.

A political party has an authority structure with higher-level leadership able to issue policy directives and expect people to follow them.

However, this never works in the long run unless people agree with the policies and respect the leadership as one of them, not above them. When Marta was appointed to head the National Library a major reason was the need to have better political leadership that could consolidate the staff, deepen their grasp of the prevailing policies, and motivate them to work under increasingly difficult situations. After implementing new procedures, which grew the party and led to electing party leadership from the staff, a new stage of political consolidation helped forge a new level of practice in the National Library. The party grew in numbers and in the respect of all the workers and patrons.

Her first day set the stage for her leadership. She decided to show up on a Saturday without any notice as her first day at the National Library. There were many people waiting patiently to use the services of the National Library, but what shocked Marta was that the police were there as well. This was the kind of experience that had been common under Batista. Historically, police meant repression and control. Obviously, some of the staff had requested the police to keep them comfortable in the face of having to serve the public. Marta was having none of this. She dismissed the police and took the pressure off. The people were just living their lives, which included going to the library. They had to be respected. The success of socialism is demonstrated when the masses self-organize and are served by institutions without the police enforcing the rule of law. As of that Saturday, the National Library was changing.

When she reported this to Minister of Culture Armando Hart, he was stunned to learn that Batista-type practices were continuing decades after the revolution took power. A new generation had grown up after 1959, and they did not have the experiential grounding in the struggle and so were influenced by the revolution as well as the past. This was her first day and her decisive action affirmed the importance of Hart's appointment of Marta. She was needed there at exactly that time. At this time the Vice Minister of Culture was Omar González, who was later the president of the Cuban Book Institute and then the film institute ICAIC. He agreed with Marta on the importance of the National Library and while she was in direct contact with him at least weekly, he arranged for Marta to have at least monthly contact with her old comrade Hart, his boss. This included adding the national library, represented by Marta, to the board of the Ministry of Culture. Of course, this is exactly what Hart wanted: a key person helping the revolution stay the course in the interest of the people of Cuba.

Another interesting aspect of her leadership had to do with the class struggle over sound in the library. The National Library had a history of being an elite institution. More people were allowed to become patrons, but different classes were accustomed to different noise levels. The library had been about strict limitations, including the global control mechanism of the librarian's own noise: the Ssh! or the warning whistle. Marta convinced the staff to apply this rule in a way that would win more patrons. Librarians have to meet their patrons and their communities where they are, developing new standards and methods, and striving for mutual understanding. In fact, patrons at the National Library governed themselves. When the noise level got to be too much for anyone, they found new ways to handle it.

Deeper into the reality of the National Library was the role of the Cuban Communist Party, as it had to be in any revolutionary institution or workplace. The stubborn continuation of the elitist culture in the library meant a poor or limited esprit de corps. The militant staff members had retreated and did not insist on a more egalitarian atmosphere. In fact, the party was limited to a few people who were not even on the library staff. Marta believed that the party could not be effective as a hierarchy of control but had to be an organic part of the workplace based on respect and democratic choice by the staff. She immediately began to rebuild the process by building a new party organization starting with herself, the leading member of the communist youth, and a militant staff member. They became transparent and accountable to the staff, building mutual respect.

Marta hired one of her best students and got an interesting reaction to how she was proceeding as director. The student said she was acting more as a politician than as a librarian. What an important insight—one that applies to any managerial position that privileges process with people over the cold mechanisms of a bureaucratic structure. People are organized within a given division of labor, but must learn and agree to work with each other and have a process of resolving conflicts when they occur. When the people don't work well together the institution doesn't function as it should. This is universal, whether one is talking about a hospital, a factory, or an army unit. In this case it applied to the National Library of Cuba. But the student was wrong to delink the political task from the professional task. Marta's political role was made possible because she was a professional librarian with an outstanding public record from her university days including her tenure at JUCE-PLAN (1961–1967) and Casa de las Américas (1967–1987). She was red and expert: trained and experienced in both the politics and policies of the Cuban revolution and the profession of librarianship.

Marta redefined the role of the director in the National Library. She changed the structure from vertical to horizontal, emphasizing democratic discussion and consensus building. Her first move was to set an open door policy. Any staff member who wanted to could come and talk with her, because her office door was literally kept open. If someone saw her in conference with someone it would not be a secret, and they could simply wait. She would also go to the cafeteria and wait in line like everyone else, dismissing the high-status routine of having a special lunch in private. She remembered Che waiting for the elevator at JUCEPLAN like any one else. Unaccustomed to such practices, her staff began to insist that she take advantage of having her coffee and lunch delivered to her, since renouncing the privileges of the director also took them from the staff who directly served the director. This demonstrated that staff had internalized the old bourgeois elitist prac-tices and this would take time to deconstruct.

A major part of transformation at the National Library was bringing a new level of professionalism to the technical aspects of building and running a major library, which was especially needed at the national library center for the entire country. Marta was the third professionally trained librarian since 1959 to head the National Library, after Maria Teresa Freyre de Andrade (1959–1967) and Olinta Ariosa Morales (interim, 1976–1977). Maria Teresa had been on the faculty of the new library science academic program at the University of Havana, so as a student in the first class Marta studied under her. Olinta was Marta's close friend, and as Afro-Cuban women they worked together and shared the common experience of having to prove themselves in government jobs and teaching at the university. They both won respect to the extent that they were selected to serve their country in very high positions.

The workers in the National Library were professional librarians, and as such were not willing to be commanded by intellectuals who were not librarians, and expected to be served by them. It was necessary to embrace the division of labor among intellectual workers and not assume that professionals from any given field, e.g., historians, would be elevated above any other. A library needed to be led by a professional librarian. (Sometimes a large or highly visible library accomplishes this via a vice-director.) But for political and professional reasons Marta was chosen to lead the National Library to consolidate and guide it through a very difficult period.

Her strategy was to embrace the staff and affirm their "ownership" of the policies and practices that they had developed over time. Marta would sit in on departmental meetings, not to intervene directly, but to respect and listen to the voice of the staff. Of course, her presence had a powerful impact because it made mischief-making more difficult and some of those most opposed to the new policies simply left because the transparency took the wind out of their sails.

One of the most productive members of the staff was Tomás Fernández Robaína. He was becoming a prolific bibliographer and historian, especially on issues of Afro-Cuba, but was socially disconnected. He was in conflict with Marta over several policies and carried forth an idealistic set of critiques. One approach would have been to isolate and expel him from the library as an irritant. But this was not Marta's style. He was valuable as staff and if he could be transformed into someone who was helping to solve problems and not create them, he could be a model for everyone on the staff. Marta helped to bring him forward as a leader in the trade union at the National Library and introduced

him to the big picture of all the problems and the difficulty of finding
an instant miracle cure. He began to take leadership in the transformation of the National Library. Marta had become as adept as Haydée
at solving problems among the people and not confusing them with
problems with the enemy.

Marta was clear that she was not there to deconstruct but to recon-
struct the library. She wanted to affirm the staff. Plus, she was able to
make some innovations. She created a department to prepare the annual
national bibliography. This was a process that had not been working very
well, so in creating a department she was able to stabilize and raise the
level of this important function of the National Library. She delegated
the leadership of this project to the scholar Araceli García Carranza,
who did a great job. She also created a department of research. This was
mainly to facilitate historical research using the materials in the National
Library collection. Librarianship itself was added as a research area. All
of this was important because it maintained a connection to the history
profession and academic scholarship without allowing it to dominate
the librarians who were serious professionals in their own right.

Another critical decision she made had to do with classification and
issues of space. As is typical in most of the world, where books are
expensive or hard to come by, only library staff could access the shelves,
"the stacks" as they are called, not the public. When Marta arrived at
the National Library the stacks were organized according to the Dewey
Decimal System. Because new books had to fit into this system as they
arrived, this required more space. Because newer material was more
spread out, this meant more distance for staff to cover to retrieve the
most-requested material. She decided to shelve new material by order of
accession (acquisition), as was common in the Soviet Union and much
of Europe. She had to convince staff that Dewey was a shelving method
for open stacks, where libraries could afford for patrons to browse a
topic. The shelving for new material would now be by accession number
to speed up staff retrieving books, for the newer material was more
sought after. The Dewey classification system would be maintained for
the card catalog where patrons browsed and selected items.

One of the continuing issues for the National Library and every other aspect of Cuban society was how to negotiate the isolation caused by the US government's blockade aimed at stopping all trade with Cuba. There were several particular relationships that did continue, however. The US Library of Congress agreed to send copies of all books by US authors on Cuba, which were then added to the collection of the National Library and some regional ones as well. This served both institutions, for the Library of Congress itself needed Cuban books.

Cuba had to connect with many countries to get the material it needed. This problem began early and persisted; while at JUCEPLAN Marta had written for a subscription to the US business magazine *Fortune*. They answered that they couldn't send it because of the blockade. One might think that the US government would want to get such journals into the Cuban library system. On the other hand maybe such information would be too incriminating in the hands of Cuban revolutionaries.

One of the craziest transitions in the political context for Cuban librarianship was the movement from the US system of doing things to the Soviet model. Once the blockade was set in motion Cubans oriented to the Soviet Union, and people were sent there for professional training in all sorts of fields. They were served by an aggressive approach to publishing technical books in Spanish as well as to providing consultants who advanced the Soviet model for doing things. Of course, when the Gorbachev intervention ended Soviet ties with Cuba, the US paradigm presented itself as a primary frame of reference, but so did a more multilateral approach.

One of the most telling stories of what Marta and her staff faced during the Special Period is about the one lightbulb. When all budgets were slashed to the bare minimum—and supplies were limited even if one had the money—people had to face the crisis with a sense of humor and vigilance. At one point the stacks were dark because of a shortage of lightbulbs. They used the working ones to light the reading rooms until there was the need to fetch a book from the stacks. On one occasion a young staff member grabbed the one lightbulb that was allocated for the purpose of going to the stacks. Several of the other staff members ran after him to prevent an accident. Why? His nickname was "Fumbles." As this story was told over and over people had a good laugh, and at the same time reminded themselves of the need to be disciplined and vigilant.

## Chapter 9

### TEACHING AT THE UNIVERSITY OF HAVANA

Although she has taught and trained librarians for more than forty years, both at the university and in her workplaces, Marta didn't set out to be a teacher. She chose instead the practical profession of organizing and managing libraries, helping patrons find what they sought and providing service to others with material and opportunity for discussion. It became her part in the Cuban Revolution. But she found herself training librarians and designing educational programs in her workplaces and at the University of Havana campus. This chapter traces her path from a volunteer university instructor to a long-standing paid adjunct professor who helped reestablish and reinvent the pre-1959 library education program that she had completed as a student. She developed her own pedagogical methods, curricula, and textbooks. She chose and relied on particular contemporary influences, along with the practical needs of Cuban libraries. She cast a keen eye on applicants, students, and graduates, then and now.

Before she ever taught at the University of Havana, during the tumultuous years of 1956-1958, Marta would make the rounds visiting her university professors. Batista ordered the university closed in the spring of 1957. Street actions and executions of student rebels were the local expression of national misery and impatience with the status quo. José Elias Entralgo Vallina and María del Rosario Novoa Luis were just two of the professors who suggested (before and after 1959, respectively) that she come to teach at the university.

Marta didn't really want to be a teacher. Although her aunts did not teach at the university level, teaching was their world. She, however, wanted to be a librarian.

Marta's former professors in the Faculty of Philosophy and Letters were very fond of her. Professors see the dynamic of groups. They knew she could lead a class and get ideas across. But most of them felt that library work was not a high-status field. Librarianship was within that division of the university, but it was not a field to which the high achievers were directed. As elsewhere in the world, the field was devalued relative to other intellectual tasks, although Cuba was the home of at least one relentless, internationally renowned library organizer and visionary, Fermin Peraza. As an energetic bibliographer, and as the director of the Havana Municipal Library, Peraza understood the centrality of librarianship and was part of every pre-1959 library education program on the island.

Building and working in libraries was a socially responsible thing to do, however and it was an important aspect of the cultural and social justice movements of the 1930s, 1940s, and 1950s. Although always facing challenges, libraries became far more possible and numerous after 1959. The country's memory had to be decolonized. Key to this work was a corps of librarians who could develop and maintain the memory collections and institutions known as the library. As it transpired, Marta chose the work that most represented her love of culture and her commitment to change: being a librarian in revolutionary Cuba. But as this chapter explains, she quite soon found herself to be educating librarians as well.

The University of Havana had started offering a one-year course of study of librarianship in 1951, simultaneous with a similar course launched outside the university. These were designed for people working at the National Library or the few other libraries that existed, as well as any interested graduates of Philosophy and Letters. Marta herself had completed the second such university course as soon as she was eligible as a university graduate, in 1952–1953.

Just six years later, in 1959, so many professors had fled the country that the professorial ranks were very thin. Trained librarians were more needed than ever, with more schools and libraries to build and support the 1961 Literacy Campaign. People were stepping forward to do the work; they were excited, but also needed skills and knowledge.

Although ten years her senior, Olinta Ariosa was one of Marta's library-course classmates, colleagues, and close friends. They had volunteered together to build and operate various libraries, starting with a library for Philosophy and Letters. Olinta was imprisoned for her activities against Batista, but resumed library work when UNESCO library leader Carlos Victor Penna guided her, Marta, and others in establishing one of Cuba's first school libraries, in Marianao Elementary School #2. In 1959, Olinta was asked to join the government to lead the development of school libraries. Soon after, she was also asked to help train librarians at the university on a part-time basis. The particular course had been called Bibliology before the revolution; now it was History of Books and Libraries, to be taught by Olinta Ariosa.

As had been their practice when building the Marianao school library, Olinta wanted Marta to work with her. And Marta wanted the same. As Marta recalled, they were always together. Olinta was the head and she was the advisor. They were a team. So Marta joined in, teaching and assisting on a volunteer basis.

Classes met in the evening, so they came to class from their day jobs twice a week, getting home at eight or nine in the evening. In the first years after the revolution came to power, many people worked in several places at once. It was a time of freedom, of starting new things, of herculean efforts.

Olinta walked with a limp in an era before disability rights.[85] She also had a very soft voice. Especially after 1961, when the Literacy Campaign

---

85. Every country has made advances in this area since Olinta began her work, and Cuba is no exception. In 1980, the Asociación Cubana de Limitados Físico Motores (Cuban Association of People with Physical Disabilities, http://www.aclifim.sld.cu) was established. In 1995, despite the Special Period, a national action plan for services to the disabled was put in place. In 2002, Havana was the site of an international disability rights conference.

got so many more people reading and seeking education, school libraries multiplied and Olinta began to find teaching a challenge. The students were demanding the kind of attention she was not comfortable with giving and had no time for. Little by little, Marta began to take on more of the teaching responsibilities. The course finally passed entirely to Marta, but she was still an informal volunteer.

By 1965, Marta's former professor Vicentina Antuña was the dean of Philosophy and Letters. Vicentina was the mother of everyone, a professor's professor. She was worshipped. She asked Marta to formally take over the courses. Marta protested that she would continue to be diligent, but as a volunteer. But Vicentina wanted staff she could count on, not a volunteer who might one day begin to come and go at will. Finally Marta decided that she did need the money, for she was getting married. She became a paid instructor at the university, but she kept her job at JUCEPLAN. Like so many other people who were working two and three jobs, she was highly committed to long days at multiple constructive endeavors.

Some of Marta's old professors were still there, although not the one who had steered her into librarianship (and into her exchange year in the United States), Herminio Portell Vilá. He had fled to Miami, becoming an anti-Fidel radio personage, speaker, and pamphleteer. National Library director María Teresa Freyre de Andrade, who had refused to hire her at the National Library alongside her classmates, was there. For the rest of them, Marta was a dear. They liked her.

Other graduates from Marta's time at the university were tapped to join the university faculty as well.[86] And of course, there were also what Marta remembered later as the old games of race and prejudice and cliquish elitism. But in the main, these professors had been watching Marta since she began her university studies in 1948, and they trusted

---

(Dominic Mulgrew, "Cuba: A Beacon of Hope for Disability Rights," *Rock Around the Blockade News Blog*, n.d.).

86. Several are still teaching, among them Roberto Fernández Retamar, María Elena Jubrias, and Graziella Pogolotti.

her. She began to teach on her own as adjunct, keeping her day job and her other involvements in the high-energy style of the period.

Before long, Marta also led the way in restructuring the original 1950s library course into the start of a library studies department. The librarians and faculty who had first organized Cuba's formal library trainings in the 1950s had left the country. Marta could see the need for reorganizing or reestablishing the library education program after so many retirements and departures—and so much transformation. Cuba was redefining what a university career was all about, Marta recalls. Against her will, she ended up being the organizer of the new department of Library Studies. She got the faculty together to decide what to teach and in what sequence of courses. They were not alone—every discipline was rebuilding and reorganizing itself.

Marta did not enjoy the struggles in the new department, or in the mature department decades later. In the library the challenges were material: Could the users get what they wanted? Could the librarians find what was sought? But modernizing the university was an abstraction, removed from the real world of library practice. It wasn't her thing. In the 1960s enthusiasm and idealism were widespread. That drew everyone into the learning process. But things began to be normal, as Marta put it. People's energy for solving problems waned. Librarianship did not have high status, so it did not attract the most hardworking and ambitious students. Not all library and information science professors understood professional library work or its actual challenges. Marta saw many of them as up in the skies when librarianship was on terra firma. In fact, this gap between library (or information) practice on the one hand and research and education on the other is mirrored in struggles continuing today in universities around the world.

So how did Marta teach? How did she win her students over to hard work and learning? Marta's basic orientation as a teacher was to convey to students the experience and knowledge in her mind that could help them do as she did, or to do better than she did. The difficulty was that they were invariably younger and brought different experiences to the situation. So how to overcome this and really communicate, really teach? Marta had five particular approaches or techniques among many in her arsenal.

One aspect of Marta's teaching was that she used the tools of the moment and enlisted help, just as Olinta had done. In the early days she and her husband made a big wall poster, a flowchart of the reference process, based on the work of the US library and information science scholar William Katz. The department always marveled: her husband even helped! Later it was transparencies, and eventually PowerPoint slides. No matter how basic the technology—for sometimes the slides were simply shown on a computer screen turned around to face the class—these helped command people's respect and convey the key ideas. This was also true when she and others pioneered the use of email for organizing IFLA in Cuba.

Another aspect of her teaching she had learned in Denmark in 1968. As part of the IFLA training program, a professor of teaching methods conducted a session. He said that a professor has a lot in common with an actor since both are always performing. So Marta developed and applied her acting skills to succeed in the classroom.

Marta also adopted the attitude of Professor Herminio Portell Vilá, who had been at University of Havana. He taught in a classroom where the professor sat or stood on a slightly elevated platform. He would tell the students, "This platform is not for you to see me, it's for me to see you!" It became second nature for her to observe if those she was talking with were paying attention and understanding—and to adjust as needed.

More than watching, she trained herself to look into her students' eyes to gauge their understanding. This was rooted in her experience as a twelve-year-old in high school—the first student allowed to study with teenagers and even adults at that age—when Marta encountered the challenge of mathematics. She already had a mental block about math, even though her husband later protested, "But you're so logical, surely you could do mathematics?" The first year in high school #1, she failed a math exam. She was miserable, but she had a conversation with the math teacher that stayed with her. He was an older man, an engineer or mathematician himself. And he had never had a girl student. But not only did he tell her that she had failed, he said, "I knew this was going to happen. When I teach, I always look into my students' eyes and so I knew when you were paying attention and when you understood. Or not!"

A final aspect of Marta's pedagogy was evaluation. At the University of Havana this evolved from a classical style more common before 1959. Early on, students wrote an essay at the end of the term to demonstrate what they had learned and retained. As Marta tells it, this was a time when professors did what they wanted to as far as evaluation.

As the Ministry of Education and the university itself assumed responsibility for educating greater and greater numbers of people of all ages, they also took into account international advances in this area. For the first time in the history of Cuban educational policy, national development was the explicit and actual goal. A strategy was promoted—in fact, required: professors had to evaluate along the way. Marta would give tests 20% of the way through the term, then 40%, and so on until the end. When the classes were small, these tests were essays. When enrollment surged and courses met day and night, she turned to multiple-choice questions, a format she herself had experienced at the State Teachers College at New Paltz.

According to Marta's students, her tests were famous. This was partly because Marta was always looking to see if an answer was correct, although different from the way she wanted students to answer. Innovation was prized and promoted. As one former student, now in her 40s and a colleague, explained:

> So many of us remember Professor Marta Terry. But what is more, she remembers so many of us. This is a sign of a good teacher, because she made such an effort to teach the particular students she found in her classes. And she always told us, "You think my tests are tough? Consider life itself!" I always say that to myself when my life presents me with big challenges.[87]

---

87. María Aurora Soto Balbón, speaking in a group discussion with the authors, March 2014.

For some years Marta was assigned to teach History of Books and Libraries. This course was very close to her own university studies: it covered the intellectual study of language and literature in historical context. It considered the library as a social artifact. But she soon shifted to teaching Reference Work. This course reflected—and benefited from—Marta's maturing identity as a working librarian, sensitive to the growing need in Cuba for professionally trained librarians ready to hit the ground running. One of the most important ways that a library serves its patrons is via reference—in other words, librarians encouraging and responding to any patron question, helping them find their way in the library's collection. This was, in fact, her favorite activity as a librarian. And as things happen in life, it was also the specialty of María Teresa Freyre de Andrade (head of the National Library, 1959-1967), who had directed the university library's reference department and taught reference as a professor in the 1950s.

Not only did the new course more closely reflect her librarianship, it was part of an important turn in library studies around the world, away from the book and the collection and towards the patron. This turn was labeled a shift from system-centered to user-centered library theory and practice. In many ways the turn was actually a return, a rediscovery of first principles. Modern librarianship emphasizes use over preservation, for the modern library has a raison d'être: the advancement and even the liberation of people. Whether they use special libraries, public libraries, school libraries, or university libraries, people rely on libraries for their own cultural, social, academic, and economic advancement.

As a collection, a library, or a system of libraries grows in size and complexity, as new formats and technologies challenge staff to rethink and reorganize, this reality is sometimes obscured. But a library that is not used is a library that is endangered. It ceases to be a social priority and its materials become at risk of decay and loss.

Successful reference work entails a deep understanding of the library collection: how it is organized, what books are on the shelves, and how they can be used. All that is background to the process of the reference interview. This is a short or long conversation wherein a patron with a purpose and a librarian (who knows what can be found and where) find an answer together. Even a patron who knows how to use the collection will need to upgrade that knowledge by further learning—often from a reference librarian. And the reference librarians, being in continuous conversation with patrons, learn what they and the community are doing and how the library should respond. So reference librarianship, the work of reference, is a key component of a useful library.

For Marta the path of librarianship, its object, is universal understanding. This means a universal language. She always teaches this. And for her, reference work stands explicitly on cataloguing and other questions of technical librarianship, in which she has also engaged. One way she practices this is to search for and examine, in each library she visits, the catalogue entry for the *Complete Works of José Martí*. Most often, she finds it starts with "Martí, José (1853–1895)." The infrastructure that enables people to locate information and culture becomes ever more universal. She always shares that lifelong search—and her findings—with her students.

In addition to teaching classes, Marta was also sought out as a thesis advisor. She was good at helping students. She applied herself to the task when others didn't. Students whom other professors had turned away would find their way to her. Other professors would look for Marta and say, "Please help this student; you can do it." In her view, many professors just didn't care about the students. So the students were lost in the woods. She put them back on track towards coherent and useful research.

In the 1980s, the University of Havana directed its faculty to write textbooks for their courses, and the university began to publish them. The result was an outpouring of hundreds of textbooks. Up to this point, Marta had been designing her courses around her own experience and the work of other scholars. Over time she created or helped to create five textbooks: *Reference Exercises* in 1982, *Reference I* and *Reference II* in 1984, *Reference: Selected Readings* in 2003, and *Servicios Comunitarios* in 2005.[88]

---

88. Marta Terry González, *Referencia: Ejercicios* (Ciudad de La Habana, Cuba:

Her volumes make reference to scholars in Cuba and those associated with UNESCO. but also others in Argentina, Britain, France, Mexico, Spain, the Soviet Union, and the United States. Years later, she would recall her favorite international sources as William Katz in the United States, Denis Grogan in the United Kingdom, Alexander Ivanovich Mikhaĭlov in the Soviet Union, and several Argentinian library scholars, including Josefa Emilia Sabor.

A. I. Mikhaĭlov was an information scientist concerned with organizing the Soviet bloc countries, particularly the Soviet Union, for the most efficient use of scientific and technical information from within the Eastern bloc and beyond. This included a massive and speedy abstracting service and a reorganization of science and technology information institutions; placing information scientists closer to and even within the process of scientific research itself; and translating Western science writing, especially from the United States and Germany. He embraced librarianship and librarians as linked to this process, but cared more about understanding, facilitating, and improving the information practices of scientists and technologists outside of libraries, or as he called the field, informatics.

Although he also wrote about information service to scientists, Denis Grogan is the British author of a widely used handbook on reference work as well as several volumes of case studies. He believed that the way to really learn this work was to do it as well as reflect on it, so his case studies aimed at bridging students from the classroom to the library. His handbook synthesized a century of Anglo-American theorizing by

Universidad de la Habana Facultad de Artes y Letras, 1982); Pilar Grafton Horta and Marta Terry González, *Referencia I* (Ciudad de La Habana, Cuba: Universidad de la Habana Facultad de Artes y Letras Departamento de Información Científico Técnico y Bibliotecología, 1984); Pilar Grafton Horta and Marta Terry González, *Referencia II* (Ciudad de La Habana, Cuba: Universidad de la Habana Facultad de Artes y Letras Departamento de Información Científico Técnico y Bibliotecología, 1984); Marta Terry González and Isabel Portales Tamayo, *Referencia: Selección De Lecturas* (Ciudad de La Habana, Cuba: Editorial Félix Varela, 2003); Marta Terry González, ed. *Servicios Comunitarios: Selección De Textos* (Ciudad de la Habana: Editorial Félix Varela, 2005, reprinted 2009).

library and information science practitioners, scholars, and others, for to him (borrowing from Alfred North Whitehead) a profession is activity that is "subject to theoretical analysis and ... modified by theoretical conclusions derived from that analysis."[89] He commented on one hundred years of contention within the field over whether librarians should help patrons at all (he said yes) and whether a librarian should teach or do for a patron (he recommended both). He envisioned how computers could help but not replace reference service; the many formats of information that were joining paper and text in the library; reference work outside the library, in the patron's own field of activity; and the many other tasks of a reference librarian besides reference service per se. But the handbook really focuses on the process of reference work, that is, the "drama for two characters," wherein the patron asks a question, two parties clarify and contextualize, the librarian shares (or steers to) one or more possible answers, and the two parties conclude by evaluating the results.

William Katz was the American author of a two-volume textbook on reference work that was first published in 1969 and reappeared in an eighth edition as recently as 2002.[90] Marta used several editions. Katz's books explained a wide range of reference service as well as the reference interview, and considered the types of information sources thought of as "reference works." From the very first edition, Katz devotes at least a chapter to the role of computers in libraries. Marta also cited a North American academic librarian's early comparison of reference services using print versus online databases.[91] Marta also relied on her

89. Denis Grogan, *Practical Reference Work* (London: Clive Bingley Ltd, 1979), 7.

90. William A. Katz, *Introduction to Reference Work: Volume 1, Basic Information Sources* (New York: McGraw Hill, Inc., 1969); William A. Katz, *Introduction to Reference Work: Volume 2, Reference Services* (New York: McGraw Hill, Inc., 1969).

91. Bruce D. Bonta, "Online Searching in the Reference Room," *Library Trends* 31, no. 3 (1983).

2009 edition of Cassell and Hiremath's reference textbook to update these others; Cassell was an IFLA friend of hers.[92]

Josefa Emilia Sabor contributed to librarianship and library education for several decades from Argentina.[93] Internationally active herself, she asserted that poor countries could not simply adopt library theory and practices from rich countries—for Latin America she pointed especially to the United States, as influential as it was—and expect to fit those ideas usefully into terribly restricted budgets. Instead, she argued, different paths to library development were needed. Reflecting this in her writing about teaching librarianship, she documented and made space for a multiplicity of approaches. Among these was the workplace training program, as long as they incorporated (and perhaps even developed) library theory as well as practical techniques.

Marta was thus able to juxtapose involvement in library (and computer) innovations in Cuba itself with the reflections of a number of international scholars, who were themselves in touch with each other.[94] This was only a continuation of her 1952–1953 training at the university where her instructors were themselves part of the global discourse on libraries, her 1954 library internship in Washington, D.C., and her many IFLA meetings and trainings.

Historically, Latin American librarianship, including Cuba, was American Library Association (ALA) librarianship. This was for two reasons:

92. Kay Ann Cassell and Uma Hiremath, *Reference and Information Services in the 21st Century: An Introduction*, Second ed. (New York: Neal-Schuman Publishers, 2009).

93. Susana Romanos de Tiratel, "El Legado Bibliográfico-Bibliotecológico De Josefa Emilia Sabor (1916-2012)," *Información, Cultura y Sociedad*, no. 27 (2012); Josefa Emilia Sabor and Ricardo Nassif, *Methods of Teaching Librarianship* (Paris: United Nations Educational, Scientific, and Cultural Organization, 1969).

94. In turn, younger Cuban scholars of library and information science cite Marta's work and continue to compare and reflect critically on various countries' library development paths. For example, see: Miguel Viciedo Valdés, "Biblioteca Pública: Algunos Paradigmas En El Mundo Y Sus Puntos De Contacto Con El Paradigma Cubano," *Bibliotecas*, no. 1-2 (2001-2003); Miguel Viciedo Valdés, *Biblioteca Pública Y Revolución: Su Desarrollo De 1959 a 1989* (Ciudad de la Habana: Ediciones Extramuros, 2009).

the compelling results of North American librarianship, and even more, the relentless power of decades or even centuries of empire.

Marta's view, based on her engaging with European and Russian librarianship for three decades via IFLA and via Soviet advisors to Cuba, is that this strong kinship between Cuban librarianship and US librarianship is still true. She also sees a Spanish influence, because of that former empire, the language Cuba inherited, and because in recent decades Spanish economic and social power has been active in Cuba. And she is guardedly optimistic about the Internet, because it provides all kinds of library guidance that is helpful or not, depending on the expertise of the searcher. She herself has been embedded in virtual communities of librarians since she and others in IFLA steered both IFLA and Cuba's library community into broad reliance on email communication for the 1994 annual meeting in Havana. It is a fact that library theory and practice are continuing to become global. This fits with Marta's own vision.

Marta's position in the world's library networks reflects her origins and her experience. Apart from the scholars mentioned above, her authoritative foreign library sources over the years have been the American Library Association, the New York Public Library, the British Library and the British Council, and certainly the Scandinavians, among others.

The fundamental influence on Marta's curriculum was library practice in revolutionary Cuba. As she put it, "We had two equivalent goals: to change! And to do it better than before." So her curriculum was very practical. She always maintained that service was the first principle of librarianship: teaching the user, finding the right answer to the user's question. As new methods and new technologies emerged, often dazzling and distracting the profession, she asserted this principle again and again.

For some years, a student seeking admission to the library studies program was required to pass through an interview with a three-person admissions committee. Marta served for several years on this committee. The question was: "Who are we accepting, and then considering the curriculum, who will they be when they graduate? What will they know?"

Marta carried out her own tests to take a measure of her enrolled students, asking them why they wanted to study librarianship. She heard two kinds of answers. One kind of answer was focused on self, as in, "I like books," or "I like to read." The other kind of answer—which roused Marta's enthusiasm—focused on others, as in, "I want to serve the community" or "Because the library is an important institution to advance our country." Both types of students were important; everyone's contribution was needed. But Marta put a higher value on the student who had already made their own turn to the patron, the community, or the country. Usually students didn't yet know a thing about service. They would say, "I had to choose three fields so I chose medicine, law, and librarianship." Or, "I wanted to get into the University of Havana so I said 'librarianship' because it's not popular." After a certain point, students reported their first choices were foreign languages—good for the tourism jobs that had emerged. One year a popular telenovela featured an architect. Architecture suddenly became a popular first choice—without any student knowing of the historic architect-innovators of Havana. In the new university, high marks earned you your first choice, which was rarely library studies. But where does Cuba need students? How can university students be guided more carefully into fields where they are needed?

Another of Marta's personal tests for new students or staff was to hand them a book and ask them to open it. She would watch to see whether they would turn the pages carefully, at the edge, or near the spine where the page is likely to tear. She was feared and even hated for using this test to select her students. But under the circumstances, Marta could not assemble a team or build a profession from scratch; she chose to build on this basic familiarity and respect for the book.

As a teacher of librarians, Marta can be known by her students. Many of them never took her classes at the university. She trained them in JUCEPLAN, Casa de las Américas, the National Library, or the libraries she has worked at since. But her university students have become her colleagues as well as her admirers. Many of them are successful both in and beyond Cuba. As a patriot, Marta gets angry at those who leave

Cuba with the education the country has provided them. But she also sees it as demonstrating that people who study there learn a lot and can use that training somewhere else. This brain drain represents a crisis for Cuba, its educators such as Marta, and its highly educated emigrants: many leave and few find professional work abroad.

At IFLA 2011 in Puerto Rico, Marta found herself among librarians from that island, including a favorite former student who was also a one-time National Library staff member. There were also other former and favored students and colleagues from various countries. After decades of derision towards those who leave, and the pain of losing the investment that she and Cuba had made in them—for the Cuban word for such people was *gusano*, that is, worm, maggot—Marta asked herself: "What do I do now with all these exclamations of 'Prof, so glad to see you?'"

Several of her former students—who were eagerly awaiting her arrival, as it turned out— immediately began taking care of her, bringing treats and necessities, in essence hosting her in their adopted home. One of them had become the head of health information for the Puerto Rican Ministry of Health. Finally, as Marta put it, "I had to say yes. I had to accept that reality. These professionals were no longer in Cuba, but they were not delinquents either. They were making a professional and a personal contribution." The old feeling of an embattled Cuba, deserted by counterrevolutionaries and those who might be pressured to become such, was now linked with a curious feeling of pride in the young people's achievements.

One of Marta's best students ended up in Germany. He invited her to come and work there. But Marta felt that whatever library and information possibilities existed in Germany, they have to be developed in Cuba. And that continued to be her life work. After all this, though, she could no longer say that everyone who left was doing evil.

The students who stay in Cuba and build libraries for the country they know best are far more numerous. Marta remembers them and sees them across the island.

Marta taught and demonstrated that a librarian has to be a professional: she or he needs a high level of skill, strong values, and commitment

to library work. One student, then age twenty-one and now in his thir-
ties, was looking for a professor to advise him on a complicated thesis
topic: the creation of a digital repository for medical reference. He had
some bad experiences with other professors, and Marta agreed. Unlike
the other professors, Marta rolled up her sleeves to teach him what he
needed to complete. They met anywhere necessary on campus; at his
house; at Marta's house. Marta made an agreement with the student and
his family to make sure he would get serious and do all that was needed
to bring his work up to standard. Part of this was him rehearsing his
thesis presentation until the day of the oral defense. The student was
so anxious that he insisted that his mother not attend his thesis defense.
Once he got started, he set aside all his notes and suddenly, he was bril-
liant! He had been headed for a mediocre rating but the presentation
received the highest possible mark and he graduated with distinction.
He is now a medical librarian, and relates how recently two people tried
to pay him for teaching them how to use the computer for research.
"No way," he told them, "This is just what librarians do!"

A librarian now in her seventies, who worked with Marta in many set-
tings after graduating, remembers Marta's insistence on high standards:
"As a young girl I would cry when she rejected my work and said, 'Do
it over.' As I grew up in the profession, I would struggle with her. But
everything she had taught in classes—and I kept and often consulted
my class notes—was applicable to real library work. It was always about
how to make sure the library really serves its patrons--and seeks out
new patrons in the community, to raise the demand for library services."

In a 2014 discussion, her students maintained that the librarian has
to be at the front. This was not where Marta found herself over many
decades. The pearl, not the diamond. The professional staff, not the
leading intellectual cadre. As elsewhere, Cuban librarians were accorded
second-class status among cultural workers. Her students are pushing
past this, and they have to master and invent twenty-first-century librarianship to do so. Libraries are where patrons create information, not just
use it, and we have to adapt and be ready for that in all formats, they said.

Having participated in computerization efforts since JUCEPLAN in the 1960s, Marta knows that her "open this book" test for her students may be insufficient in the digital age. "Can you handle a mouse? A browser? A tablet? A mobile phone? Can you distinguish between useful and trivial on the Net?" She sees an educational crisis underway, as the technicalities of librarianship threaten to drown the broad cultural vision that she taught and practiced. As she puts it, she dealt with the 300s (social science) at JUCEPLAN, the 800s (literature) at Casa, and so on. But how does one deal with the Internet? Others see this crisis as well: a rethinking of education at all levels is underway across the island.

Just as the information world has changed, so have the generations. Marta and her peer faculty are not Herminio Portell Vilá or Vicentina Antuña. Today's students are not the young Cuban library students of the 1960s and 1970s. For one thing, they are no longer a middle-class elite, raised up by their families. They are poorer and more from the working class or off the farm, because Cuba has so effectively democratized higher education. Yet they are several generations removed from the privation and brutality of colonial or neocolonial Cuba. In many ways they are less well informed, because the world's information flows—media and culture of all kinds—are closed to Cuba, thanks to either the US blockade or astronomical costs. As above, updating Cuban education is underway to help overcome this.

Marta is sometimes uncertain how to teach or what to teach this new generation of future librarians. How to translate her broad cultural vision for libraries to work in the coming decades of the twenty-first century? How to contribute as she ages, yet wants to stay on point? One way is to continually pass on news and ideas from her worldwide electronic network of IFLA colleagues to her university and library colleagues.

But her core idea is to take inspiration from Armando Hart's current practice of dialoguing across the generations. Hart's vision came to life in a highly personal way when her brother Héctor was invited to a high school to speak about his experiences in the urban struggles of the 1950s. As he arrived at the high school, he realized it was the former Police Station #8 where he had been held and tortured in 1957-1958. He felt faint as he entered. What to say to these young people? He began to tell his story. They did not even know it had been a torture center. Disbelief turned to deep interest. Frustration over ignorance and lost history turned to mutual respect and honest talk. It was hard but not impossible to build a conceptual bridge in that prison-turned-public school.

# Chapter 10

## INTERNATIONAL FEDERATION OF LIBRARY ASSOCIATIONS AND INSTITUTIONS

The Cuban library experience is part of the global library experience. Its emergence in this global context is part of the history of the International Federation of Library Associations and Institutions (IFLA). Marta played a key role for Cuba in first learning from IFLA and later in representing the Cuban library experience and defending the national integrity of Cuba against attacks. This is a story—spanning more than four decades—of international and diplomatic significance in the library world and beyond.

IFLA was established in 1927 out of activity in the League of Nations on the one hand, and European and American professional development and international linkages on the other. As a measure of how intertwined professional activities and politics can be, its first official conference was held in 1929 in Italy and was opened by the fascist dictator Benito Mussolini, who received praise from the first IFLA president Isak Collijn.[95] IFLA was led solely by librarians and scholars from Western (and more particularly Northern) Europe and the United States for many decades. For instance, the Chinese Library Association was a founding member, but IFLA did not hold a meeting in China until 1996. That meeting was much helped by Marta's consulting and sharing her experience.

---

95. Al Kagan, "An Alternative View on IFLA, Human Rights, and the Social Responsibility of International Librarianship," *IFLA Journal* 34, no. 3 (2008): 231.

From 1927 through 1959, annual meetings included fewer than 150 people, except for the three larger IFLA World Council meetings held in 1929 (1500 people attending), 1935 (550), and 1955 (1200). During these years only three meetings were held outside Western Europe, despite a request for the 1936 meeting from the Chinese and Indian library associations.[96] The three held outside Western Europe were Chicago (1933), Zagreb, Yugoslavia (1955), and Warsaw (1959). Meetings were not held during World War II; IFLA leaders were keenly aware of the challenges and opportunities for professionals in the face of international political polarization. This was reflected in a 1939 speech by then-president Marcel Godet, remembered later in a history of IFLA:

> Pointing to the [Nazi] corruption of all library tasks which ought to be undertaken in the service of freedom and human decency, Godet raised the question of the purpose and possibility of any further cooperation, pointing to the love of the book shared by all, to IFLA's achievements and to the activities of its Sections and Committees that had proven their capability to surmount all barriers.[97]

The organization grew at a faster pace in the 1960s and 1970s, with meetings attracting as many as 1021, not including the 1977 World Council meeting (1700 people). Of the twenty meetings during this time, four were held in the Soviet Union or Eastern Europe and one in Toronto.

As this makes clear, there was a shift after World War II during which time IFLA opened its membership to the countries of Eastern Europe and the Soviet Union. However, this was still an international organization of Europe, the old colonial and imperialist bloc now joined by the socialist bloc. But IFLA continued to struggle over opening up to the poor countries as they built libraries. The influential Indian librarian and scholar S. R. Ranganathan commented on this in 1954:

---

96. Joachim Wieder, "IFLA's First Fifty Years: A Reprise. Extracts from 'An Outline of IFLA's History', by Joachim Wieder, Selected and Edited by Harry Campbell," *IFLA Journal* 28, no. 3 (2002): 109. The Chinese Library Association was in fact a founding member of IFLA in 1927.

97. Wieder, "IFLA's First Fifty Years," 110.

[W]hat the West achieved in library matters in a century, the newly awakened people are bound to achieve within one generation. The present occupants of the IFLA do not all realise this. Since 1948, I have attended several meetings of the IFLA. They have been all courtesy. But in their proposals and action, the old view that "international" in IFLA is exhausted by Western Europe and Northern America persists. It may be unconscious and even unmeant on their part. But to us outsiders, it is as clear as daylight in the tropics.[98]

By the 1970s IFLA had resolved to reach out to the developing world. More countries were forming national library associations that could join IFLA. Air travel and communications had become more affordable. As a result, in the 1980s participation grew at a quicker pace, with meetings as large as three thousand people. Several of these meetings took place in entirely new regions: Manila, Nairobi, Tokyo, and Sydney. Almost ninety years after its founding, IFLA has grown from a small club to a multifaceted international nongovernmental organization. But IFLA resources are tight and poor-country resources even tighter. In the 1980s, UNESCO funding to IFLA for outreach and support, notably for the library associations in the Global South, ended; Scandinavian librarians managed to find new support for the Advancement of Librarianship Program, but the general picture was less help for developing countries. So most countries continue to find it tough to organize their own library associations (required for IFLA membership), travel to meetings, and thus to assume leadership roles.

As it became more inclusive, IFLA faced the problems of the new global information crisis that focused on the production and distribution of artifacts of knowledge, books, and journals. The polarity of wealth and the destructive character of development under colonization meant that libraries outside the rich countries—particularly public libraries—were not stable and well-funded institutions, if they existed. Recall the story from chapter 5 of Cuba's national library being parceled out for

98. S. R. Ranganathan, "IFLA: What It Should Be and Do," Libri: *International Library Review* 5, no. 2 (1954): 183.

shipment to Spain, packed away repeatedly until it was partly lost to fire, and without government funding until the 1950s. Furthermore, as library systems were built, they faced the application of inadequate Eurocentric frameworks and standards to each of their national contexts. There was also the issue of professional training and the needed translation of global resources into local languages. The global organization of libraries is not a simple task, but the main context for this process has been IFLA because this is where the world's librarians, including its powerful librarians, gather.

The importance of IFLA was brought to the attention of Cuban librarians by many sources. In 1968, when Marta was at Casa and Haydée sent her to an IFLA training event in Copenhagen, she passed through Paris. There she met her former professor Carlos Victor Penna, who was still active in international librarianship. He advised her that Cuba should begin planning to join IFLA. Shortly after this, Ekaterina Furtseva, the Soviet Minister of Culture, visited Cuba and Casa de las Américas. She met with staff, and one of the points she made to Marta and others was that IFLA would be an important organization for Cuba to join, both a resource and a space for learning and sharing.

Cuban participation in IFLA began in 1980 when Olinta Ariosa attended IFLA in Manila as a representative of the Ministry of Culture. Marta was also asked to go but could not. Olinta came back a strong advocate for Cuba to pursue membership. But there was one major hurdle to overcome: Cuba could only join IFLA through a national professional librarians' organization. There were already five mass organizations that functioned by neighborhoods and workplaces: the Public Administration Workers Union, which was the labor union for the employees of the libraries; the Cuban Communist Party, which provided political guidance; the Committees for the Defense of the Revolution (CDR), for addressing the role of the library in the local community; the Federation of Cuban Women, since the librarian profession was dominated by women; and the National Revolutionary Militia, which was concerned with the security of the country. But a national movement was also underway to form professional associations for highly skilled occupations like doctors, engineers, and now librarians.

There had been two different organizations of librarians before 1959: Asociación de Bibliotecarios Cubanos and Collegio de Bibliotecarios. Both disbanded by 1959, one because of its ties to the Batista regime and the other because its members rejected the coming revolutionary transformation and departed for the capitalist world, mainly the United States. By 1980 it was time to start over. Within a year's time, Olinta and Marta had reestablished the Asociación de Bibliotecarios Cubanos. As always sharing and balancing responsibilities with Olinta, Marta also became a leader in this new group.

They organized the required documents to apply for legal status from the government, finding ways to set up a bank account and have formal legal and postal representation. They had to have branches in every province. In this process, Blanca Mercedes Mesa provided strong support, including devising a modern post-Batista name for the association: the acronym ASCUBI. The organizing committee was able to hold a founding congress attended by about fifty librarians, many of them former students of either Olinta, Marta, or both. By the 1981 IFLA meeting in Leipzig, the two were prepared to participate as members representing ASCUBI.

In 1981, as the sole English speaker of the two, Marta managed the documents ASCUBI had to prepare to join IFLA. Upon arrival in Leipzig, Germany, she handed them across the registration desk to the IFLA Secretary General Margreet Wijnstroom of the Netherlands. Margreet asked, "Are you a librarian?" "Yes," Marta answered, "Why do you ask?" "Because of your handwriting," Margreet answered. Marta had learned library hand—a style of writing once mandated for creating library catalog cards—in her year of library education at the University of Havana. Marta felt welcomed as she and Olinta Ariosa entered the first session of the day. A paper by the Indian librarian and scholar P. N. Kaula about librarianship in the Global South was the topic, and he had worked in the library of Havana's eminent engineering university, the José Antonio Echeverría Polytechnic University. In those days IFLA

provided copies of the papers in the back of the room. Marta scanned
the paper's appendix listing underdeveloped countries and their libraries.
No Cuba. She scanned again, wondering if it was possible that Indians
ordered the alphabet differently. Finally she raised her hand, anxious but
angry: "Perhaps I have some reading problem, but I cannot find Cuba
in this appendix here. Mr. Kaula has visited our country as a UNESCO
expert, and knows our libraries well. You understand—if a country is
removed from a list, it can also be removed from the map." A murmur
passed across the room. The session chair, the renowned French children's librarian Geneviève Patte, smiled sardonically and gently asked
her to share her name and her nationality. The Cubans had arrived. For
her second IFLA annual meeting in 1982, Marta had a paper accepted,
which she presented along with others from Latin America and the
Global South. And thirty-two years later, Patte herself sought Marta
out to participate in the Havana meeting of the International Board on
Books for Young People, a Swiss NGO. The two world library leaders
met and remembered that early moment and the unforgettable marvel
of IFLA Havana in 1994, and laughed.

This pattern became the rhythm of Marta's IFLA work: being welcomed in, meeting with resistance to her perspective, but finally earning
acknowledgement, respect, and allies. As third-world librarians in particular found each other, respect came more quickly, then admiration,
exchanges, and cooperation. The way to librarianship and professional
exchange was actually through the political thicket. So from the start,
Marta Terry the librarian had to push back. Her very first IFLA workshop in 1968 was not an annual meeting, but a training to which Cuba
had specifically been invited. But once seated in the meeting in Denmark,
she had to recover from surprise when some colleagues tried to shut
her out. She found her voice, telling them: "I am not a Soviet tank!"
For her travel came soon after two international events. On October
9, 1967, Che Guevara had been assassinated by the CIA in Bolivia. He
had become a global icon. And on August 20, 1968, the USSR and
its Warsaw Pact allies had invaded Czechoslovakia. Marta's comment
prompted various reactions: solidified opposition, embarrassment, and

a definite measure of admiration for the willowy thirty-seven-year-old who could turn a phrase in several languages. Higinia Terry, who swept her family out of Madruga to escape concubinage, and Marta O'Farrill of the elegant hand gestures who outlived slavery—her grandmother and great-grandmother were both with her that day.

From 1981 on, Marta Terry began to participate in IFLA annual meetings and more, missing only three for the next thirty years. When she began to serve on IFLA committees, she traveled to headquarters in The Hague, Netherlands. Her travel has always been problematic because of the US blockade, the lack of financial resources, and the demands of her local responsibilities in Cuba. Almost every year she managed to pull together the resources and get the official visas necessary for her international travel. For IFLA Nairobi in 1984, Kenyan visas did not arrive, but the trio of Marta, Olinta, and Miriam Martinez—for many years Cuba's IFLA team—traveled on. They were detained and interrogated at the airport until an IFLA representative arrived to reason with the police. For IFLA Sydney in 1988, she spent money to get to Mexico for a visa, but the Australian embassy turned her down. For IFLA Boston in 2001, the United States issued her visa only in time for her to arrive on the last day of the conference—too late to defend Cuba, as we will see below.

Leaders in the Cuban Revolution, whether world famous or known only to a few, have had to make great sacrifices, often placing their political and social responsibility above their personal and family lives. This is also true for anyone who works as a professional, adhering to high ethical standards. In 1987, Marta attended IFLA Brighton four months after her husband had passed away, her emotions and life in an uproar. She remembered that meeting only as a very hard one.

There have been three interrelated ways that Marta has played an important role in IFLA. First, she was the official representative of Cuban librarians. This entailed carrying lessons from Cuba to IFLA and the reverse, and spreading the word beyond the actual meetings. It entailed connecting people to each other and to new ideas and experience. Key here was making Cuba's national leadership outside libraries—the intelligentsia and the political leaders—take notice of libraries and what they were accomplishing for Cuba. Second, from the 1968 moment in Copenhagen, she carried out a global defense of Cuban libraries—and thus Cuba—against US State Department offensives. Third, she was a leader of third-world librarians in international discourse, helping others also transform the theory and practice of librarianship. As part of this she persuaded Latin American and Caribbean colleagues to become more active in IFLA. All three of these aspects of her work made libraries more effective and better supported in Cuba. The stories that follow illustrate these three aspects of Marta's international work.

IFLA Chicago in 1985 was characteristic of the duality Marta experienced in the international library world. In the international library world, Marta was usually a target for both hostility and solidarity towards Cuba. She was always searching for how to traverse the minefields and strengthen professional friendships. First, there was longtime IFLA member and ally Guust van Wesemael, who always managed to involve Marta in a preseminar.[99] He had put her in charge of the team making the pre-session summary report to the final plenary session of the annual meeting. In those days, the summary was written and then read out loud. Time began to lapse and the rest of the writing team had vanished, refusing to work with any Cuban librarian. Colombian librarian Miriam Mejía came to her concerned: "Listen, Marta, that report team is not going to help you." Marta hadn't eaten since her usual lunch of a hard-boiled egg. That was the lunch of choice for IFLA participants without funds. The president of IFLA's Latin American section (also a library school professor at Venezuela's Simón Bolívar University) Rosario Gassol de Horowitz brought her some grapes and asked, "What are

---

99. IFLA staffperson Van Wesemael was characterized as a "truly international librarian" in a 1991 tribute; this was in part for his organizing many effective IFLA preseminars but also for his hard work with and for librarians and libraries in the Global South, before and after the launch of the Advancement of Librarianship Program. ALP became one of IFLA's core activities. An IFLA prize in his name focuses on literacy and the Global South. Russell Bowden and Paul Nauta, "Guust Van Wesemael: A Tribute," *IFLA Journal* 17, no. 3 (1991): 226.

you going to do?" Marta answered: "What do you want, an Academy of Sciences report or a Committee for the Defense of the Revolution report? Should I finish the report with a 'Thank you very much' or a 'Patria o muerte?' How about this: when I'm holding that microphone tomorrow, I will do whatever seems best to me!"

Rosario laughed in approval and handed over all the grapes, which Marta had adored ever since she was a girl and they were a special treat, only for when she was sick. And so it was a writing marathon that lasted until she was standing at the microphone in the morning, reading the report. It ended with a thank-you. A Cuban foreign relations ministry staffer—for then there was money to send such people to IFLA—came to her afterwards with words of encouragement: "You know, people in the back of the room were saying, 'Well, Cuba is definitely here for good!'" There was more to follow: after the conference Marta led the entire Cuban delegation in a visit to the offices of the American Library Association, hosted by their director Robert Wedgeworth.

A curious incident occurred at IFLA Tokyo in 1986, foreshadowing future events. A librarian representing a Japanese medical school library approached her to spin tales about what she could do if she left Cuba. She felt that she was in the presence of a sinister force, larger than any single library. She left the conversation speechless. Three years later, he appeared in Paris only to tell her, "You have won." No one ever saw him at IFLA again.

By the time of IFLA Paris in 1989, Cuban and other third-world activity had turned the IFLA climate a little warmer. For one thing, that year Spanish (a native language for 7% of humanity, spoken in 31 countries) became the fifth official language of IFLA, along with English, German, French, and Russian (10% of humanity and in 99, 18, 51, and 16 countries respectively). Only Chinese (19% of humanity and in 33 countries) would have embraced more of the world's population. This new policy favored the rising Latin Americans. Today Chinese and Arabic, a native language for 4% of humanity and spoken in 26 countries,

are also among IFLA's official languages, in line with the languages of
the United Nations.[100]

An experienced and well-known library administrator from the United
States, Robert Wedgeworth, had just been elected to the board of IFLA.
That week he arranged a bilateral discussion between ASCUBI and
the American Library Association. The purpose of the meeting was
for Marta to present the Cuban library experience and the merits of
holding an IFLA annual meeting in Havana. The Paris session, which
opened the door towards IFLA Havana in 1994, also launched a long
collaboration between Wedgeworth and Marta Terry González.

Robert Wedgeworth was then Dean of the School of Library Service
at Columbia University, after serving as Executive Director of the ALA
from 1972 to 1985. He was also the first African American to hold that
ALA position. Elected president of IFLA in 1991, Wedgeworth was
the first non-European to hold that position, only the second from the
United States; he served two terms until 1997. He had come up through
the professional ranks in the United States, working at public and academic libraries, and specializing in the application of new information
technologies. A news item from Rutgers University, where he earned a
PhD, tells a characteristic story about him:

> In 1962, while a cataloger at the public library in Kansas City, he was
> picked to demonstrate the library of the future at the American Library
> Association's booth at the World's Fair in Seattle. "We had a Xerox copier
> there, and copiers were rare then," he said. "We had a Univac solid-state
> computer that would give you a computer printout and lots of lights
> flashing and disks whirring. Our booth was really popular."[101]

Wedgeworth was more than aware of equity issues in US librarianship. He had also been active internationally since the 1960s, and was

---

100. "Summary by Language Size," Ethnologue: Languages of the World,
http://www.ethnologue.com/statistics/size.

101. Ken Branson, "Forty Years Later, Doctoral Candidate Returns
to Rutgers to Defend His Ph.D. Dissertation and Earn Degree,"
*Rutgers Today*, http://news.rutgers.edu/issue.2012-12-20.2609038638/arti-
cle.2013-01-11.6369588550#.U5YGDSh3cQp.

committed to IFLA becoming more global, working for some years as an IFLA governing board member alongside Marta. The two librarians—Cuban and US—shared common interests in both equity and technology.

IFLA's 1991 annual meeting took place in Moscow. Wedgeworth was elected President and Marta Vice President. Marta was the first Latin American IFLA officer, and only the third woman. This was quite a meeting, taking place in an unstable power void. Yeltsin was seizing power and the streets were full of political protests, not to mention rumor. Marta was so determined to witness whatever was afoot—she said it felt like "the sinking of something very big"—that she left the conference building, passing a colleague who declared, "Marta Terry skipping a board session? This is a first!"

She found her way to Red Square and its phantasmagoric St. Basil's Cathedral. The multicolored onion domes rose from a stepped portico. Knowing porticos well from Cardenas Street, Marta sat there watching people, protestors, and police forces come and go—around the occasional curtained Zil or Chaika sedan. But how to understand it? Was the government actually imploding? Back in her hotel room, she got an unexpected call. It was none other than Pancho—Francisco García Valls from the University of Havana in the Batista days, from JUCEPLAN, and now from the Council of Mutual Economic Assistance. CMEA was meeting that same week in Moscow. "It's going to end," he told her. "A lot's going to change."

But Marta, newly elected IFLA vice president, saw something different in IFLA Moscow. Whatever was happening outside, the world's librarians—especially from the Global South—had spent hard money to get there to meet and share. The hosting librarians were in attendance despite their personal and family anxieties. Members from the West were slipping away with their luggage, able to negotiate new airline tickets and depart hastily. A murmur began about closing the meeting early, but dozens of participants had not yet made their presentations. This might be their first IFLA, or their last. Marta raised her voice to carry on with the meeting. "Whatever happens, we are the world's librarians and we cannot be afraid," she argued. Wedgeworth agreed, and their unique partnership was further solidified: a unity of opposites in the highest offices, an African American from the United States as president and an Afro-Cuban woman as Vice President. This strong collaboration was a counterweight to the crisis that began to engulf Cuban society as its largest trading partner collapsed, causing economic activity on the island to drop by one-third within a few weeks. It was the beginning of the Special Period in Time of Peace, in which Cuba had to reinvent itself in order to survive.

Marta experienced IFLA Barcelona in 1993 as the very best on account of the respect and friendship expressed between professionals from many countries, especially the Spanish-speaking diaspora and the developing countries. At the same time, one matter in particular arose for the first time. From the rich countries—some thought it emanated from the American Library Association, which has a similar unit—there came a proposal for an IFLA committee to assess and evaluate the world's libraries—and countries—on measures, not yet identified, of free access to information and freedom of expression. Marta expressed her concern that this committee would reprimand only the vulnerable or less-developed-library countries and interfere with international library cooperation and trust. It would talk without listening. She and others succeeded in tabling the proposal. The broad participation of local Spanish librarians made for a very festive concluding party. The hosting committee had recruited musicians to play habaneras as an acknowledge-ment of and introduction to next year's meeting in Havana. Born in Cuba and renamed in Spain, the habanera builds on a particular African rhythm, the same one as Marta's father's *danzón*. It was hugely popular in 1800s Cuba, then traveled to Spain, where it soon surfaced in one of the most famous of opera melodies, an aria from Bizet's *Carmen*.

Over the next year, Marta and Wedgeworth worked closely towards a successful IFLA Havana; Marta as head of the hosting committee, and Wedgeworth as IFLA president. The ongoing activity of IFLA and contributions from member countries (and more) had to be encouraged and organized. The hosting committee had to develop and implement a plan, and that was Marta's expertise. Apart from nailing down every detail with flair—her old Casa colleague and noted graphic artist Umberto Peña pitched in with a logo—she focused on mobilizing Cuban librarians to attend and speak. She wanted them to learn and measure themselves by global standards. They would advance where needed as they listened to librarians from elsewhere. They would draw strength from their own achievements as they explained them to the visitors. And all this would further awaken the international community to the strength of libraries in the context of the Cuban Revolution, Latin America and the entire Global South. It would also awaken the Cuban government to the importance of libraries for national development—including in the Special Period. Cuba was just three years into the economic crisis kicked off by the sudden collapse of the Soviet Union—a crisis which shrunk the island's economy by one-third from 1990 to 1993.[102] (It is interesting to note that the Russians attending IFLA Havana, led by Ekaterina Genieva, constituted their first big delegation to an IFLA annual meeting).

One particular aspect of the organizing work was centered on technology—where Marta and Wedgeworth found common cause. His vision was IFLANET—a "virtual IFLA" that would involve individuals and groups who could not attend annual meetings.[103] It was clear that some colleagues saw that as another barrier for poorer countries with less computer infrastructure. Marta's vision was putting Cuba's own strengths in a global context for all to see—with regard to its technological resourcefulness as well as its libraries. The first step was to connect IFLA leadership on several continents, in and out of Cuba. Canadians were the early hosts of this service. Marta persuaded key Cuban agencies to provide more computers and phone lines to Cuban

---

102. Measured as GDP per person. For this and more see Emily Morris, "Unexpected Cuba," *New Left Review*, no. 88 (2014).

103. Robert Wedgeworth, "The Virtual IFLA: Moving Knowledge through Time and Space" (paper presented at the 60th Annual Meeting of the International Federation of Library Associations and Institutions, Havana, August 21-27 1994).

libraries so that they could help organize the meeting. She mobilized Cuban libraries to use the fledgling IFLANET.

As the date for the meeting approached, librarians from more and more countries connected. They got onto email, many for the first time, to make inquiries and register. When they arrived at the conference, each one received the IFLA conference papers on a CD that could be shared through each nation's more or less developed computer infrastructure. By the following year, ninety countries were represented on IFLANET, many of them following Marta's example to make the case to their own governments for the practical necessity of expanded technological resources for librarians. As email continued to be adopted, delegates from Eastern Europe and the Global South who had never attended began to participate in IFLA, reading conference papers and attending meetings. All of this was launched as a result of the partnership between Cuba, the US, and IFLA headquarters in Western Europe—in spite of the US blockade. What had appeared to many as an exclusionary move was in fact including more librarians from the Global South.

Apart from hosting the meeting in the first place, one particular highlight of IFLA Havana was Cuban librarians demonstrating their high standards for service to the blind. A seminar was organized between the IFLA Libraries for the Blind Section and Cuba's national organization of blind and visually impaired people, ANCI (Asociación Nacional del Ciego; National Association for the Blind). This work is still bearing fruit in Cuba today. Another highlight was the networking at all levels with librarians from Africa and Latin America.

Finally, the meeting succeeded through a very short and sudden crisis of emigration to the United States—by any means possible. Why? The Cuban population became polarized in the early days of the Special Period over departing for the United States or defending and rebuilding Cuba. People had come to deadly blows in at least one case. In early August, just days before IFLA was to convene, the US government's Radio Martí broadcast that friendly boats would be coming to illegally ferry Cubans to a new life in Florida. In the austere economy, plenty of people were lured. They climbed onto boats and rafts, patched together or stolen. But the promised boats did not come, until the US Coast Guard activated its fleet and moved more than 32,000 Cubans to US detention camps in Guantanamo. After one week, trapped in brinksmanship by the US radio message, Cuba set a new policy: sail to the United States or anywhere if you choose, it's now legal to leave. The tables were turned, and Miami's Cuban community began to reverse course, warning, "Don't risk it!" The next week the United States proposed making legal a limited flow of immigration. The agreement was signed by both governments in September. This murderous drama—for people totally unprepared for the open sea were drowning—played out during IFLA Havana, and yet the session was a success down to the last strains of music for the participants. Marta and her committee had decided months before that one thing that Cubans could share, could use to resist such bad times, was their music. And while the hosting committee had no control over the major events of the day, it was appreciated. On a professional level, Havana marked a high point as well: Marta and her hosting committee had mobilized Cuban librarians to participate in every session. This broad contact between Cuban professionals and their global counterparts was a tremendous blockade-breaker and stimulus for the professionals on the island.

Included in this was the involvement of librarians from the US. Before the meeting, the American Library Association was caught up in discussions: Could US librarians legally go? Debate was high over interpreting the US Treasury Department's travel limitations. Should US librarians go? And as the meeting got underway, the plane carrying ALA president Betty Turock received a bomb threat and was turned back. The top US library representative did not get to IFLA Havana.

Even with those disruptions, the US delegation was 75 strong, including public librarians, school librarians, academic librarians, LIS faculty, and others. All 75 of them were moved by what they called their "productive participation" in the meeting to sign a "Statement of Librarians from the United States and Puerto Rico on US-Cuba Relations." This statement called on the US to normalize relations with Cuba and end the blockade. It noted that trade in food and medicine would stem the current exodus from Cuba. It noted that US travel restrictions were contrary to library principles of intellectual freedom and the right to know. And it acknowledged the hosting activities of "hundreds of dedicated Cuban librarians from all types of libraries throughout the island."[104]

After the success of Havana, IFLA asked Marta to advise other host countries to help make meetings in new locales a success. Again using email before any other tool, she took the responsibility to advise Turkish librarians and then Chinese librarians, as they prepared to host their first IFLA annual meetings, in 1995 and 1996 respectively. And she helped them in person. Her advice was always: mobilize your own librarians to participate and show off your country's culture as best you can. For she and ASCUBI had indeed galvanized librarians and impressed others. IFLA Havana was a high point for many Cubans, the crest of a wave of innovation that libraries rode for many years. Even in 2014, an IFLA-ASCUBI discussion continues—via (of course) an island-wide LISTSERV, that is, an electronic discussion list operated by the foreign relations department of the national library. Marta's comment regarding any IFLA annual meeting that did not recruit local librarians to attend in force was: "Boring!"

By IFLA Copenhagen in 1997, Marta was chairing a preseminar for librarians from developing countries as part of IFLA's Advancement of Librarianship Program, later the Action for Development through Libraries program, funded primarily by public and private funds from Scandinavia. She had been serving as a regular advisor and trainer for this program to advance librarianship in the Global South.

When Robert Wedgeworth became president of IFLA (1991-1997), he felt that IFLA needed to engage in work on two issues: copyright and intellectual freedom. These became a focus for his last two years. In 1995, at IFLA Istanbul's council meeting, eight library associations from Finland, Norway, and Sweden proposed a motion, which passed,

---

104. The document has been reproduced numerous times, for example as: "Statement of Librarians from the United States and Puerto Rico on US-Cuba Relations, Havana, 1994," *Library Juice* 3, no. 38 Supplement "Good Stuff on Cuba" (2000).

in general support of Article 19 of the 1948 Universal Declaration of Human Rights. The declaration was a cold-war-era statement of principles adopted by the United Nations.[105]

The IFLA Executive Board then established an ad hoc Committee on Access to Information and Free Expression (CAIFE) and arranged for the American librarian Marianna Tax Choldin to address the IFLA Beijing annual meeting in 1995. In her talk (later published by IFLA) she laid out three assumptions. First, that librarians as a profession are committed to the fundamental principle of access to information and freedom of expression. Second, that "every country—no exceptions whatever—has problems with access to information and freedom of expression." Finally, that:

> people within a country know their own situation better than anyone outside possibly can, and are therefore in the best position to suggest strategies and solutions for improving access and achieving freedom of expression in their own country. This assumption has a very important corollary, of which I remind myself frequently, and I will take the liberty now of reminding you: outsiders cannot solve this kind of problem; only people who live inside a country can do it. There are certainly useful things outsiders can do, but preaching, pointing fingers, and inciting to action while safely on the other side of the fence are rarely, in my view, among them. [106]

CAIFE was led by British library professor A. J. Evans, who relied on a de facto executive group of Marianna; another American, Robert Doyle; an Australian member of the IFLA executive board, member and treasurer Warren Horton; as well as a committee of thirty-some librarians from around the world. In discussions during 1996 and 1997, different viewpoints surfaced: a German librarian called for forceful

---

105. Article 19 reads as follows: "Everyone has the right to freedom of opinion and expression; this right includes freedom to hold opinions without interference and to seek, receive and impart information and ideas through any media and regardless of frontiers." The United Nations voted on and adopted the declaration in 1948; the Soviet bloc and Saudi Arabia abstained.

106. Marianna Tax Choldin, "Beginning a Conversation on Access to Information and Freedom of Expression," *IFLA Journal* 22, no. 4 (1996): 281-82.

action and a British member argued that impatience should trump diplomacy. A member from the US commented, "IFLA needs a platform to 'bark' from." [107] On the other hand, a Chinese librarian asserted that cultural differences must be respected. Marta urged courage, patience, and diplomacy. She was supportive of the initiative but determined that it avoid becoming a way for the rich and powerful nations to beat on the poor and less powerful. One can sum this up as the search for universal standards that can only be applied in a very polarized and stratified world. As a result, controversy is inevitable. By 1997, CAIFE had become a permanent IFLA initiative called the Committee on Freedom of Access to Information and Freedom of Expression (FAIFE). A process of information gathering from the countries of IFLA was underway.

While this was unfolding, the US was taking further steps against Cuba as it experienced the extreme austerity of the Special Period. The US hardened its embargo with the 1992 Torricelli Act and the 1996 Helms-Burton Act. These turned the blockade from a US policy into a US law. Helms-Burton aimed explicitly at "international sanctions against the Castro government in Cuba [and] to plan for support of a transition government leading to a democratically elected government in Cuba." [108] Among other measures, it authorized funds to support democracy and human rights groups in Cuba. This act made official and public what had been decades of secret US subversion in Cuba. Cuba's response was to pass a law making it illegal to distribute or accept Helms-Burton funds.

In 1998, two dissidents in Cuba announced that their home book collection was an "independent library" and a handful of other dissidents followed suit. A US librarian, Robert Kent, and a Cuban emigré hired by organizations funded by the US government, formed the Friends of Cuban Libraries and began advocating for these so-called libraries on US library listservs, at American Library Association meetings, and to the US media. Making several trips to Cuba and giving out money,

---

107. Alex Byrne, *The Politics of Promoting Freedom of Information and Expression in International Librarianship* (Lanham, MD: Scarecrow Press, 2007), 60-61.

108. Helms-Burton is formally the Cuban Liberty and Democratic Solidarity (Libertad) Act 22 § 6021-6091 (1996)

medical supplies, and books to US AID funded groups and others, Kent was deported from Cuba in February 1999.[109]

Kent was also communicating with the FAIFE Committee itself. In September 1999, based primarily on Kent's information as well as phone contact with some of the "independent librarians" in Cuba, the chair of FAIFE (the Australian librarian Alex Byrne) and IFLA staff in The Hague decided to issue a report critical of Cuba and send a letter to Fidel Castro.

IFLA's August 2000 annual meeting was held in Jerusalem during heightened battles with Palestine. This was a polarizing venue: the host committee had excluded Palestinian librarians and thus the Arab librarians boycotted and held a separate meeting elsewhere. An Israeli official opened the conference by explicitly contradicting IFLA's promises of maintaining an open conference.[110] Marta was among a number of librarian-delegates from the Global South who were swept into lengthy and frightening interrogations either upon arrival or departure at the airport. She was traveling alone without a hotel reservation or any local friends. But she pursued her objective: to defend and advance what she was starting to call the "dependent libraries" of Cuba and elsewhere, those that rely on a mass base of patrons, stable funding, and their own country's publishing sector as the basis for collections and programs of all kinds. The FAIFE chair remembered well one particular word she used for the FAIFE actions of the previous season: Slander![111] As the committee's discussion unfolded, IFLA President Wedgeworth characterized it as the coming of age of FAIFE.

---

109. Ann Sparanese, "Statement to the ALA International Relations Committee's Subcommittee on Latin America and the Caribbean, January 8, 2001," *Library Juice* 4, no. 9 Supplement (2001).

110. Al Kagan, "IFLA and Social Responsibility: A Core Value of Librarianship," in *Libraries, National Security, Freedom of Information Laws and Social Responsibilities: IFLA/FAIFE World Report*, ed. Susanne Seidelin and Stuart Hamilton (The Hague: International Federation of Library Associations and Institutions, 2005), 40.

111. Byrne, *The Politics of Promoting Freedom of Information and Expression in International Librarianship*, 101.

The barrage of commentary in favor of the "independent library" was also meeting resistance outside of FAIFE. North American and other librarians traveled to Cuba and reported back in print. IFLA and the American Library Association each sent an investigative team of librarians to Cuba in 2001. They found book collections, not independent libraries; political activists, not librarians; government action against those activists, but not against libraries or books. Welcomed by Marta and others, they visited Cuba's extensive library infrastructure and talked with librarians.[112] They found many so-called banned books—in the collections of the national library and various public libraries. Over this same time period, Marta and other Cuban librarians came to ALA meetings to describe the reality of libraries in Cuba.

ALA Council adopted a resolution that called on both the US government and IFLA to improve access to books on all topics. Ultimately, both ALA and IFLA got the facts and understood that they and their profession were being used by the US government in a sustained attack on Cuba, spelled out in the language of Helms-Burton. The international library community had realized that a trick was being played on them. Although every US librarian attending IFLA Havana had signed the post-conference letter urging an end to the blockade for reasons of intellectual freedom and the right to know, IFLA had taken no action on the matter after 1994.[113] Instead, as Wedgeworth explained, "After the formal adoption of the FAIFE program, Robert Kent and others tried to hijack the program."[114]

But by partnering with librarians inside Cuba, both the ALA and IFLA were able to obtain and disseminate information that unmasked the dishonest "independent libraries" campaign. This was done through

---

112. For a brief and clear history of the recent stages of Cuban library development, see John Pateman, "The Development of Public Libraries in Cuba since 1959," *Library History* 17 (2001). The author was also very active at the time in helping dispel confusion and misinformation.

113. Kagan, "IFLA and Social Responsibility: A Core Value of Librarianship," 39.

114. Robert Wedgeworth, personal communication to the authors, July 2014.

people-to-people contact and through official research. The ALA even filed Freedom of Information Act requests that went unanswered—but still they pieced together the facts regarding US sponsorship of the "independent libraries." A summary ALA statement in 2008 explicated how US government funds were channeled through multiple organizations in order to sponsor and promote the "independent libraries."[115] In the end, even librarians with no prior knowledge of Cuba could see that they were phony.

Through all of this, Marta was the representative of Cuba and its actual libraries. She became a personal target of the attack on Cuba. But her decades of leadership in Cuba and in IFLA; her base among librarians of the Global South; and her continuous diplomacy and non-confrontational style, honed in the libraries of Revolutionary Cuba, saw Cuba through this attack. As a postscript to this prolonged battle for Cuba's right to self-determination, she won FAIFE support to organize librarians to tackle access to *basic* information regarding health and safety. The goal was practical and exemplary projects providing intellectual freedom and access to information. They produced materials for training African librarians, most of whom work without access to library education. In these documents, Marta refers to "international consensus on these matters" and explains:

> So what is intellectual freedom? As we see it, it [is] an individual's capacity for expressing his or her ideas. Those ideas come out of previous information, previous knowledge that has become his or her interpretation of reality.... When a librarian feels free to give any information requested by a user, that librarian is also using that sovereign right. The manifestation of intellectual freedom may be determined by religion, culture, ideology, and national social heritage.[116]

---

115. Michael Dowling, "Cuba Update for ALA 2008 Annual Conference," (Washington, DC: American Library Association, 2008.

116. From a draft of IFLA-FAIFE PAHI (Public Access to Health Information) 2009 workshop materials, provided to the authors by Marta Terry González.

Marta remembers IFLA Seoul in 2006 as the peak of the battle: a whispering campaign against her and against Cuba, and even a painful— and dangerous at age seventy-five—tumble over a chair. But she was vindicated that same year: IFLA named her an Honorary Fellow. This award is only given to those with decades of service and leadership to IFLA. She was then the twenty-first person so recognized over eighty years of IFLA; the third woman; and the first from outside Europe or North America. She had made many varied contributions advancing librarianship worldwide, and this was widely acknowledged. After so many campaigns, struggles, and victories, she felt that it was an award both to her and to Cuba. In the end, IFLA was arming her to better defend and advance libraries in Cuba and elsewhere.

# *Chapter 11*

## FURTHER CONTRIBUTIONS

One of the most interesting questions for the life cycle of people in every society is what constitutes the working life, or when does one retire. In fact, we can even ask the question of what retirement means. On a personal family level it often means more time to spend with one's grandchildren, and more time to seek whatever rapprochement is needed with one's siblings, children, and friends. On a professional and political level it often means focusing on finishing projects and finding a way to join in the generational effort of handing off the task to those who will continue the journey. As a member of the Centennial generation in Cuba, Marta was facing all of that while continuing to hold down one job after another.

In 1997, as part of this process of change, the newly appointed Minister of Culture Abel Prieto named Eliades Acosta Matos the new director of the National Library. Each of these men was born in the 1950s; their ascendancy reflected a generational passing of the baton from the Centennial Generation that seized power one hundred years after the birth of José Martí. As a result, at the age of sixty-six, Marta moved from the National Library to the Cuban Book Institute.

She joined the Book Institute, which oversees the island's publishing houses, while continuing her roles in IFLA, ASCUBI, and the university. Her first project there was to develop a reading promotion program. That proposal did not go forward, but as one might expect, her focus turned to building another library. That proposal did go forward, and it became the Arca de Papel, a small library that gathered together foreign books —particularly philosophy, literature, and social analysis, in English as well as Spanish—from the collections of writers and editors, as well as other sources. These books were made available to writers and others working with the Book Institute. Marta envisioned others following the path that had been such a success for her: engage in global discourse, take what is useful for Cuban reality, build upon it, and in that way talk back to the world.

At the same time, she found herself repeating her path at the National Library. She joined the party organization in the Cuban Book Institute and helped that group grow and better connect the institute to its tasks in relation to national priorities. They discovered she was a good organizer of people, and she earned a place on the Executive Committee of the Institute, just as she had at Casa. The constant struggle was to avoid the pitfall of pragmatism, that is, following one's nose without looking up to strategize, just doing what is practical or easy. In the world of books, this would lead to an elitist posture, and Marta was having none of that. She contributed to keeping Cuba's book industry focused, cultured, and serving the people.

She was asked to study and help improve the institute's long-standing and popular International Book Fair. It was moving from the Havana Convention Center to a larger venue at the Morro Castle (as well as other sites across the island), and her work on that expansion spanned several years. She brought twenty of her university students to experience the fair for themselves and carry out a broad survey of attendees and participants. Planning this survey was a class assignment. Again, she was implementing what had worked for her and her generation: being part of actual practice as well as classroom learning. As a student, Marta helped build and operate libraries; now her students were learning firsthand how Cubans relate to books. Her study pointed to the need to reach out to various organizations to make sure that there was always a broad distribution of books. This had implications for the layout of the displays, the organization of panel discussions, and the participation of a wide diversity of Cuban authors and artists.

In 2004 the Book Institute asked her to organize the library at the Dulce María Loynaz Cultural Center, which they were opening in cooperation with the government of Andalusia, Spain. Loynaz was herself a Cuban aristocrat married to an Andalusian, a daughter of a Cuban independence general. She had lived in Havana her entire life, writing poetry until 1959, and then retiring from most literary activities only to be rediscovered and reemerge in the 1980s. Seven years after her death in 1997, her mansion was to become a cultural center. Marta designed the library as a place for students and other readers to gather, an outreach post of the Cuban Book Institute. It became a site for one of the hundreds of writers' groups that blossomed in Cuba in the first decade of this century. This work brought her into a neighborhood setting for the first time in decades, and recalled for Marta an earlier policy from Armando Hart's time as Culture Minister (1976–1997). His policies—among them the 1977 policy to create or support "Ten Basic Cultural Institutions" for each of 169 municipalities—aimed at bringing cultural resources close to where people lived.[117] Once again she brought her university students into fieldwork at the library so that they could learn by doing. And once again, she was organizing the party in the Loynaz Center and thus the center itself; as a leading staff person, she was helping the center find and achieve its purpose.

In 2010 Marta retired again, and she made plans to ease out of IFLA duties and teaching. She realized that for her, retirement meant keeping involved in what she knew best, and so she contacted her old boss Armando Hart. Now bookending her career, he immediately brought her into his current project, the Office of Martí Studies, particularly his Crónicas (Chronicles) project. Crónicas is a part of the national archives pertaining to his own work since before 1959, and it is also a publishing project. Just like the university dean Vicentina Atuña, he wanted Marta as paid staff, not coming and going as a volunteer. So, as she put it: "It became a serious job." To start, Marta organized Crónicas'

---

117. These ten institutions were a bookstore, library, drama troupe, community chorus, band, museum, movie house, art gallery, handicraft shop, and cultural center.

eight thousand books, moving them onto shelves and processing them according to Dewey with her Cuban adjustments. She found herself doing it completely from memory.

She also found herself teaching: a young man not sixteen years old was assigned to work with her. One day he asked her, "Was Batista really so bad? What did he do exactly?" The question stunned Marta. And it illustrates the quandary of the Centennial Generation: they learned things from older generations, then they made their own path, which included overthrowing Batista, taking power, and building a new Cuba. As Marta puts it, she is not like her professors' generation. And her students are not like her own. How to prepare today's sixteen-year-old Cubans, or twenty-somethings such as in her university classes, for what they are going to face? Hart's approach is to foster dialogues of all sorts, informal and formal, so that the old can learn to talk with the young and vice versa. This is the content of the book fair, with its readings and panels—chances to talk with the authors but also with other readers. And so Marta's work is participating in and supporting dialogues across the generations.

Upon the publication of some of Hart's collected writings, Marta traveled to talk about the volume to librarians. She found herself explaining the usefulness of the book for a reference librarian, since she was teaching reference to the young librarians gathered that day. Her talk was basic, but it was welcome, and even reprinted by a Mexican newspaper. Hart's aim coincides with this biography itself: to connect the ideas and experience of his and Marta's generation with the generations who are rising and ruling today in Cuba and elsewhere.

In June 2012, Marta gave a keynote speech at an ASCUBI meeting in Havana Province, held at the Ruben Martínez Villena Public Library. Her talk was titled "Reading Promotion: Reflections and Annotation." Marta is a living library for Cuban librarians and librarians all over the Global South. Drawing from the Santeria pantheon, Marta is also a daughter of Yemayá. She has a role to play as a model for young Afro-Cubans, and in this way for all Cubans. She continues to care for those coming after her as her generational children.

With all of the great advances that Cuba has made, the struggle continues to be a difficult and challenging path. Ration cards have been a part of Marta's life since they were implemented in the early 1960s. With these Marta gets her daily bread: a round bun roughly six inches across. Her brother Héctor tells her that these buns provide the basic minimum daily nutritional requirements—as far as vitamins and minerals are concerned—which have been hard to meet in Cuba for many years. Other foodstuffs are rationed on a weekly or monthly basis: rice, beans, oil, etc. This is the great impact of Cuba being victimized by global forces, the demonic blockade by the United States and the betrayal of international solidarity by Russia. It is also a legacy left by the revolutionary or Centennial Generation that is one of the greatest challenges facing the generations yet to come: the survival of Cuba as a sovereign country able to feed and protect itself with a rising standard of living.

The genius of Cuban leadership has been to make sure that each generation of Cubans has its own revolutionary experience, both within Cuba and as part of Cuba's international solidarity with other people, mainly in Latin American, the Caribbean, and Africa. There is a global trend for former socialist countries to backslide into new forms of capitalist accumulation based on exploitation of labor and natural resources. In each case, the old-timers have helped slow this process down, and so it goes in Cuba. No one can claim to know the future, but thanks to Marta and her generation of librarians we can know the past, and because of that the next generation can try to avoid repeating past mistakes.

One of the interesting developments of the revolution was that it led to a complete reinvention of the personal library. Before 1959, a personal library was the possession of an elite class requiring literacy, education, and a disposable income to invest in expensive hardback books and space to store them. The Cuban Revolution popularized the process that led to a personal library being common in the homes of workers who became educated and whose children had more and more access to a free university education. Books were printed on newsprint and distributed very cheaply. The first two generations after 1959 embraced this reading culture and became grounded in Cuban history and culture, as well as the culture and politics of world revolution. The crisis today is how to keep this going.

# Rethinking the Revolution in the Revolution

The military phase of the Cuban Revolution began in the Moncada attack and the guerilla war waged out of the Sierra Maestra Mountains. It moved through the seizure of power in 1959 and has been institutionalized in national policy, institutional development, and structural realignments providing for the security and well-being of the total population. Within this macroapproach to revolution there are the microrealities of how all of this is internalized in the life of every family, every person. In this sense there are unlimited revolutions in the revolution. Every story of transformation needs to be told.

We have organized this book about Marta Terry González in two parts. The roots of Marta have been her family anchored in the Afro-Cuban experience, her female self, her educational experiences, and her peer group networks. The flowers of Marta have been her many, many library projects that have served Cuba in local educational institutions, in regional institutions of UNESCO and the Cuban Revolution (Casa de las Americas), in national institutions (JUCEPLAN and the José Martí National Library), and at the international level through IFLA, including her time as its Vice President. Indeed, roots and flowers abound in the magical life of this very wise and hardworking Cuban librarian.

In concluding this review of her life and its context we need to address the question of what we have learned that can be generalized for Cuba, and what we have learned that can be used in comparison to other countries, especially the United States. No one person represents everything about a country, and no one country represents the entire world. On the other hand, every universal has its origin in a particularity. That is the task of logic and theory building, to grasp the relationship

185

between the particular and the universal. The life of Marta Terry has been so rich and full that, by focusing on her, we have a starting point for examining the Cuban experience over the last 150 years.

The roots and flowers of Marta Terry can be conceptualized into content and process. As content we can identify class, color, culture, consciousness, and gender. As process we can use the concept of social networks to map the dynamic motion that propelled her through life. From the family to the university campus to the party to her profession, Marta's life has been successful because she was nurtured and valued by the strong ties she developed in these four institutional contexts.

Her foundation was her family. The matriarchal structure helped her defy the norm by being a strong and attractive mulata who escaped racist victimization as a sex object. Her grandmother and aunts instilled in her the oft-repeated ambition to be "the best of the best." She lived what they wanted by moving beyond their experience to dance in the narratives of their dreams. This is the story of upward mobility: from slavery to freedom, from the rural area to the urban big city, from education with little job advancement to education resulting in professional job status, from informal family ties to sustainable two-parent households.

Her university experience connected her with peers living at the heart of the 1959 revolutionary generation in Cuba. They anticipated their future by defying the oppressive neocolonial hegemony of the 1950s, by embracing global culture, cutting-edge ideas, and the discourse of their own political culture, and having various ways of being in sync with all forms of revolutionary action. This was a generation of people who joined the Cuban revolutionary process and went on to play leading roles in the institutions of their chosen profession, including the military, government, culture, science, health, education, and libraries.

The Cuban Communist Party has been the critical institution for educating and mobilizing the masses of people. Clearly the US government is only ninety miles away and maintains a military base inside Cuba as well (Guantanamo). For the last fifty years the US has imposed a blockade against the Cuban people that has severely limited trade and access to the global economy. Also, the United States has attacked and spread disinformation about Cuba, both in general, as part of its anticommunist mania and specifically, since Cuba has been the main instance of self-determination against the US imperial policy of Monroe Doctrine. Marta joined Cuban patriots in the party and its mass organizations, both the Federation of Cuban Women and the neighborhood-based Committees for the Defense of the Revolution (CDR). Particularly in her library work, the political orientation of the party was essential in transforming the library profession from one of serving elites to one of serving the masses of workers and farmers.

The library profession in every country has the responsibility for contributing to national identity by preserving and institutionalizing memory. There is also the task of providing access to information that impacts culture and insures that an enlightened community drives civil society and political discourse. Marta's experience reflects her professional struggles to meet these two responsibilities.

It is hard to compare the Cuban experience with the US, first because of size. Cuba can be compared to New York City in terms of population – in 1960 there were 7 million people in Cuba and 7.8 million people in New York City. Networks of like-minded people and people who came through the only national university made Marta's networks and her experience possible. Even in large countries like the United States, when a movement emerges (like in the 1960s) activists have to get to know each other to work together. We live and flourish in such networks.

This again speaks to Marta Terry's experience from 1960 through today. Such times to live in: a revolution, an explosion of struggle and transformation of national liberation struggles in Asia, Africa, and  Latin America, and the restructuring of global politics. Cuba needed its Martas just as they needed their beloved country to become closer to the ideals of José Martí and Antonio Maceo. Big bricks in any structure  need mortar and tuck-pointing to hold things together.

The legacy of class exploitation and racism has not been completely eliminated as a result of any twentieth-century revolution, including the  one in Cuba. However, in Cuba the social transformation since 1959 has pushed back hard against these social evils, making Cuba the best case for envisioning a future without these barbaric practices, no matter how subtle or hidden they are in beliefs or in blatant overt practices. If, however, there should be a counterrevolution that returns Cuba to its former life as a cauldron of class exploitation and racist oppression, a new revolutionary generation will be born. We can look to cadres of the revolution like Marta Terry as an inspiration in any case. What we know for sure is that the future will require militant activists who can learn from the life of Marta Terry.

Part of the crisis of the 1959 generation is that they are facing the final days of their contribution to their revolution. This is symbolized by the Castro brothers, Fidel and Raúl. But this is a generational experience. Growing old and facing the future with less and less power to impose your will on how things will turn out is a great reality check. Parents have to face their children as they choose their own paths, sometimes as the parents would wish but most often with the innovation of who they are and will become. This is not unlike revolutionaries who begin to see the generations coming behind them make decisions and choices of their own, taking the country forward and at times backward.

Imagine how Marta has had to deal with the librarians she helped to train who have fled to the United States, turning their backs on revolutionary Cuba. And yet she and her peers have soldiered on, creating an amazing trail of success when all odds were against them. Were they a shooting star or a glacier, a one-time event or a fundamental transformation? As Marta and Haydée debated about the library, is the Cuban revolution a diamond or a pearl? Or both? This determination will be made by the generations to come, but one thing is for sure, they will do it because Cuba has good libraries because of librarians like Marta Terry.

Our study of Marta Terry has been a way of discussing the Cuban Revolution. As people from the United States, one of us an activist in the Black Liberation Movement, and both of us activists for social justice, we have felt a special responsibility to present this study to demonstrate that everyone in the United States is not blinded by the anticommunist hysteria of the political and economic establishment. We are among those who uphold the Cuban Revolution as an advance for humanity, to discover what is possible when we evolve into a political culture based on social justice. Cuba is no utopia, but it is a giant step towards the future. Please think about this book with a critical frame of mind. Investigate these arguments with further research and speak about what you find. Criticize this book when necessary and help all of us get closer to the truth that can be a consensus for the future we all so desperately need.

Each generation has their own experiences and then faces the challenge of passing along the lessons learned, especially when the reality of life has changed. The Centennial Generation connected sacrifice to a revolutionary morality, a necessary denial of some material things for a greater social good. This is not unlike Europeans who experienced World War II and understood the need for rationing, or Americans who lived through the Depression. When the temperature dropped in 2014, Marta went to her closet and pulled out clothes from her 1953–1954 year in the United States—that's a sixty-year yank back! And furthermore they fit.

Part of this is that a generation can find comfort in being relied upon and having the chance to grow old together. Marta's Committee for the Defense of the Revolution still calls on veterans such as herself and she finds that fulfilling. And that local CDR is a source of well-being, reuniting her with comrade veterans of the party who share their memories and experiences in the final years of their lives, being in their eighties and nineties. Marta often jokes that every time she retires she looks for  a new job. Well, maybe that is how every revolutionary lives out her or his life, always looking for new ways to contribute, new lessons to learn, new people to teach.

What Marta says about life is tied to her generational experience—whether it's being an Afro-Cuban, a woman, a librarian, a mother, or any other identity, the key is whether you are a revolutionary, whether you can transcend your particularity and thrust yourself into the general  struggle for the emancipation of everyone. Marta constantly demonstrates that she is eighty-some years young.

# APPENDICES

# *Appendix 1.* **Family Tree.**

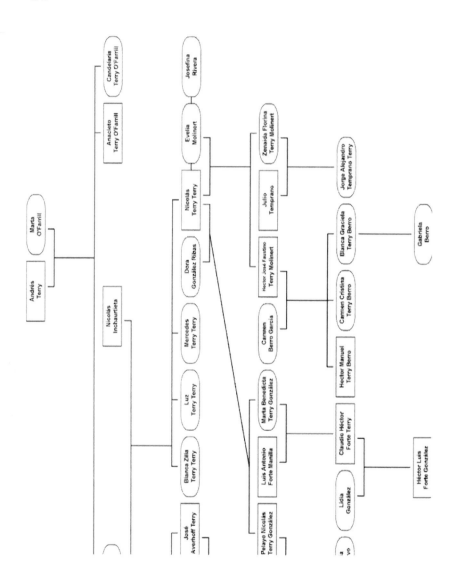

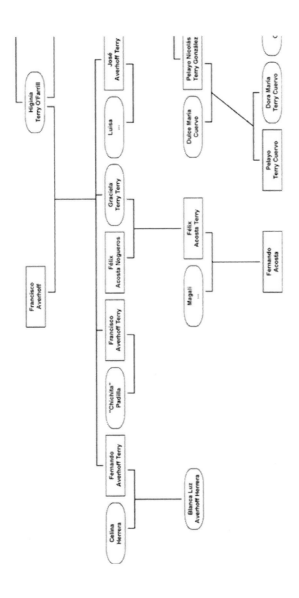

# *Appendix 2.*

## "MARTA TERRY OF CUBA HERE 'TO SEE US FOR MYSELF'" FROM THE CHICAGO [DAILY] DEFENDER (NATIONAL EDITION) JULY 17, 1954[118]

Washington—Marta Terry, a 23-year-old beauty from Havana, Cuba who is here as a foreign exchange student, thinks that the only way to get the proper impression of the United States is to see it for yourself.

"You cannot tell," she said in liquid English accompanied by Latin gestures, "about this place from what visitors say. Some say it is beautiful and wonderful. Some say it is bad. I want to know this country so I come to see it for myself, to feel it, to know the people, then I can say I know America."

Marta majored in social sciences and got her master's degree from the University of Havana. She is now working for her Ph.D. and is particularly interested in Negro problems and history.

Her thesis for her master's degree was "The Impact of Slavery on White Society in the South up to 1860."

The Cuban last year spent a year at a state teacher's college in New York State under the P-6 program. At present she is working at the Pan American Union in Washington.

Next month she will go on a scholarship by the American Friends Service Committee to a seminar on "Roots of Freedom" at Orcas Island off the coast of Seattle.

---

118. Reproduced with permission of the *Chicago Defender.*

Marta says she plans to either teach or work in a library when she returns to Havana. She is the daughter of Nicholas J. Terry, and [has] two brothers, Pilajo a technological student, and Hector, a medical student, and a younger sister Zenaida.

Her mother died when she was quite young and she and her brothers and sister were reared by aunts who teach school in Havana.

Marta says that although there is some discrimination in Cuba, the American brand puzzles her.

She says that she went with a French girl, also an exchange student, to a restaurant in Maryland. At first she was refused service, but when the proprietor found out that she was a foreigner, she was quickly served.

 Cubans, she said, are so mixed up that none can tell who is Negro and who is not, but she said it is estimated that 25 percent of the people are Negro. They are not referred to as Negro, but as "people of color."

# *Appendix 3.*

## Tentative plan for the services of the library of JUCEPLAN, the Junta Central de Planificación, Cuba's Central Planning Board, August 14, 1961[119]

| | |
|---|---|
| Date: | 14 August 1961, Year of Education |
| To: | Dr. Regino G. Boti, Technical Secretary |
| From: | Marta Terry, Librarian |
| via: | Administrative channels |
| Re: | A tentative plan for JUCEPLAN Library services. |

The attached plan is proposed with the objective of serving as the base upon which adequate library services can be built. The Plan is subject, naturally, to variations that will be suggested about the use to be made of those services, the Board's own work trends, etc.

It must be borne in mind, moreover, that the classification into stages is in no way rigid, but is rather a means by which the Plan will develop, with goals incorporated to be completed as circumstances dictate.

It is hoped that the Technical Secretary and Directors, especially the constituents of the Library Commission, will see fit to suggest changes, additions, restrictions, etc., that they think advisable, in order to assure the greatest success of the work carried out hereafter at the JUCEPLAN library.

---

119. Reproduced with the permission of Marta Terry González. Translated by Laura K. Aase.

Best regards,
We will win
MT/ach.

cc:    Central Director
        Administrative Director
        Director of Assessment
        Director of Industry
        Director of Agriculture
        Archive
        Library Archive

## Tentative plan for JUCEPLAN library services

Given the specific needs that the library of a specialized agency like
JUCEPLAN has to satisfy, its work methods, organization, and services
have, perforce, to be different from those of more general libraries.

The function of the library in an agency like this has to be, principally,
documentation and reference; that is to say, working through queries,
locating data, selecting bibliographies, preparing indexes, reviewing
books, etc., which not only serves to help the technical workers at any
given time in the process of their work, but to keep them abreast and
up to date on all matters within their areas of expertise or interest.

To that end, the job of the library should not be limited to the acquisition and administration of publications that add to or form its holdings;
instead, the library should also plan its work so as to get material to
those who must use it, including anticipating information requests or
demands. Thus, instead of being a traditional department, the library
would become an information and reference center. That is to say, it
will provide the most modern and effective ways of disseminating the
technical knowledge contained in various materials that are organized by
contemporary special libraries, in order to serve the needs of the users.

To provide these services, which are the end goal of the library, work
must be completed which can be divided into three stages.

### First stage

The work of reorganizing the library's holdings, the acquisition of new bibliographic material, and the physical location of the library constitute the first stage.

Reorganization includes: weeding the collection, reorganizing the loan system, checking up on loaned materials before beginning the new system, re-cataloging and re-classifying books and periodical publications and inventory, and networking with international information centers on matters of concern to the Board.

Acquisition includes selecting bibliographic material, preparing lists, and performing other procedures necessary for purchasing these materials.

The physical location of the library depends on the general conditions of the location of JUCEPLAN. Although it would be ideal to be able to count on having adequate space for the library from the start (which is why it is included in the first stage), we will not insist upon this point. Physical location includes the acquisition of furniture and all necessary equipment. It should be clarified now that this does not preclude the removal of furniture and library equipment, and an enlarging of absolutely inadequate premises.

### Second stage

The second stage would include receiving, cataloging, classifying, and distributing acquired materials.

Distribution would comprise circulating review sheets of acquired and recently received books, circulating journals and periodicals, preparing analytical indices of periodicals, and so on.

The review sheets of acquired and recently received books, the bibliographic list, etc., would appear not on a fixed schedule, but according to the arrival and quality of bibliographic materials. Those loose sheets could be called "News" or "New Acquisitions" or whatever was decided;

they could be collected quarterly in a Bulletin of the JUCEPLAN Library. This Bulletin would also include all other informational material considered appropriate.

## Third stage

The trend of economic and social development in Cuba, the general development of the sciences, and the establishment of relations with socialist countries that use languages other than those traditionally known by Cuban technical and professional workers, means that much of the material the library holds will be written in languages such as Czech, Russian, Polish, etc., which are not easily understood by our technical staff. For these reasons it is necessary to provide a service for identifying and translating the most important materials these publications cover, so that our technicians do not miss data, information, and details that may be of great use for the better performance of their jobs, and, most important, to keep them up to date with what is published in those languages for their respective fields.

To implement this stage, in addition to the administrative task of circulating such materials (which is not appropriate to describe here), the library will have to rely on a technical translation service. These translators moreover must be able to suggest and identify those materials (journal articles, book chapters, bibliographic lists, etc.) that may be of use for the previously mentioned purposes.

Since a technician cannot depend exclusively on translations and book reviews, it is recommended that such services be supplemented by language training for those officials who want it or whose work and time commitments permit. To that end, we recommend the organization of language classes among small groups of technical workers. In these classes the most emphasis would be placed on reading knowledge and technical vocabulary of the language rather than on acquiring speaking knowledge. These classes could be organized as part of the library's outreach activities to be scheduled later.

With those two systems--translation and language training—a better and more suitable use of the library's collected bibliographic material would be guaranteed.

## Staffing requirements

To start enacting the work proposed in this tentative Plan, a minimum staff of four librarians, two typists, and one custodian would be required.

Currently the staff includes two professional librarians and two typists, which means it would be necessary to hire two more librarians and a custodian. Not included here is the translation staff.

## Librarian duties

Reorganization of loan system.

Formalization of acquisitions lists.

Inventory.

Re-cataloging and re-classification of existing library holdings.

Cataloging and classification of newly acquired books.

Book reviews.

Preparation of leaflets listing newly accessioned library materials.

Organization of a consultation and reference service.

Preparation of the Bulletin.

Library loan services.

## Typist duties

Reproduction and duplication of records.

Library archive services.

Preparation of letters, forms, circulars, etc.

## Custodian duties

Special care in cleaning the library.

Handling packages and transferring books, etc.

Internal messages, circulation of different materials to departments and people, checking on materials loaned, etc.

## Schedule

Once the library is adequately installed, that is to say, when it has a dedicated reading room and a suitable loan and circulation system, an extension of library hours would be appropriate. The goal of such a proposition is the facilitation of library reference services outside of regularly scheduled work hours. Therefore we recommend keeping the library open and providing services in the morning until noon, after work until 11:00 p.m., and all day Saturdays. With this system, officials would be able to take full advantage of the services the library plans to offer. Of course, when discussing the adoption of this measure, the reorganization and extension of library staff schedules would have to be taken into account.

## Technical advice

In order to guide library policy in all its current aspects we will rely upon advice from the Directors of Assessment, Industry, and Agriculture, who form the Library Commission (which has already begun to act) and with whom this Plan will be discussed in detail in meetings that will be set for that purpose. However, we will always require the help of every official who, through his specialized field, job, etc., may, at any given moment, guide and cooperate with the library regarding questions of acquisition, adoption of classifications and subject headings, etc.

Havana, 14 August 1961, Year of Education

# Appendix 4.

## Twenty Years of the José A. Echeverría Library of Casa de las Américas (1980)[120]

The José A. Echeverria Library of Casa de las Américas was founded on December 7, 1959. We received a small legacy collection from a society of Latin American authors that existed in the building we occupy.

It is through the library that Casa meets the growing demand from researchers and students for information concerning our county's culture. It is the section of Casa that works most directly within the county.

### Collection

The collection consists of 77,000 volumes of books and 5,000 periodical titles. Most of the books, as well as the magazines, cover the field of Latin American culture in the broadest sense. That is to say, they cover a range of subjects including literature, linguistics, art, sociology, folklore, history, economics, and music, in all their different forms of expression, and more.

Among its resources is a collection of Chilean books, acquired over the course of many years through intense exchange with Chilean institutions. This was done in spite of the blockade and during the reign of the Popular Unity government. These works have acquired an inestimable

---

120. First presented to the Encuentro Científico Bibliotecológico (Scientific Conference on Library Studies), Havana, 1980. Reproduced with the permission of Marta Terry González. Translated by Alison M. Lewis.

bibliographic value because of the situation that fascism has brought about in that country.

## Technical and Administrative Organization

The library is divided into three work areas: technical processing, including cataloging and classification of materials; information services and newspaper archive; and user services.

## Staff

There are fourteen staff members, all of whom have some degree of qualification in information science and are also currently continuing their studies at the appropriate level. Three are pursuing their professional studies in Information Science and the others are taking internal continuing education courses to stay on top of the most modern methods of dealing with information.

Since the University of Havana's work-study plan started, the library has taken on student interns. At this time, we have two student interns who are working on a course project consisting of compiling a bibliography of all of the Chilean books in major libraries in this country.

## Services

Those who have priority use of the various library services are writers, students, and professionals, as well as foreign researchers whose field of study has an impact on understanding the problems and the culture of Latin America.

The library boasts 4,500 registered users, of which 2,862 are worker-students and the rest are students.

Between 1968 and 1976, 98,289 readers have been assisted and 120,000 books have been provided.

Moreover, due to the large number of books that are received, those that do not fall within our collection development profile are sent elsewhere, where they may be of better use. Donations have been made to the libraries and archives of agencies such as the Psychiatric Hospital, Ministry of Justice, School of Journalism, the National Library, and others.

Casa's different departments (Visual Arts, Music, History, Theater, and the Center for Literary Research) are given full support in their work to actively investigate and recover Latin American treasures.

Another of the services provided is the publication of works about Latin American countries and issues, which are of great interest to students and researchers looking for this information. We have edited works on the following nations: Argentina, Brazil, Chile, Peru, Puerto Rico, Uruguay, and the West Indies.

## Perspective on Future Developments

From the technical point of view, we are planning the compilation of a thesaurus, which will serve to systematize the indexing of materials that meet the collecting profile of the library, that is, those covering Latin American culture. In this work we can bring together all the experience accumulated during our information processing in recent years.

On the other hand we want to widen and deepen relations with libraries and documentation centers in Latin American and Caribbean countries.

## Personal Information

My name is Marta Terry and I have 20 years of practice in the profession. I graduated in 1953 in philosophy and letters. in 1954 with credentials to be a librarian, and earned a doctorate, each from the University of Havana. In 1962, I started teaching in the professional program in the School of Library Science at the University of Havana. Today the school has developed and become the Department of Library and Information Science within the Faculty of Philosophy at the same university. I qualified as an Auxiliary Assistant Professor a few days ago.

In 1959 I started working as a librarian in the Centre of Pedagogical Documentation at the Regional Center of UNESCO. In 1961 I transferred to direct the JUCEPLAN library and have been there until 1967, the year I moved to Casa de las Américas. And here I am.

# Appendix 5.

ENCYCLOPEDIA ENTRY ON CUBA'S LIBRARIES AND INFORMATION SERVICES, 1993[121]

The Republic of Cuba occupies the largest island in the Greater Antilles. The Cuban archipelago consists of several thousand small islands, islets, and cays. Population (1990 est.) 10,609,000; area 110,861 sq. km, including the Cuban archipelago. The official language is Spanish.

**History**. The Biblioteca de la Sociedad Económica de Amigos del País (Library of the Economic Society of the Friends of the Country) was founded in 1793 to "contribute to the promotion of the moral and economic interests of Cuba and to stimulate culture and popular instruction in all their manifestations." The library has the most important collection of Cuban books and periodicals. The Real y Pontificia Universidad de San Jerónimo was created on January 5, 1728, by Pope Innocent XIII with provision for a library, though it took many years for the library to work as such.

The Constitution of the Republic issued in 1940 called for a public library in each municipality, but the law needed to enforce that obligation was never passed. A Decree of 1954 created the Organización Nacional de Bibliotecas Ambulantes (ONBAP) with the goal of founding fifty small public libraries; each library was to have a collection of

121. First published as Marta Terry González, "Cuba." In *World Encyclopedia of Library and Information Services*, edited by Robert Wedgeworth, 234-38. Chicago: American Library Association, 1993. Reprinted with permission of the author and the American Library Association.

approximately one thousand volumes; by 1958, twenty-one of those libraries were created with modest monthly allocations. In 1958, out of a population of 6,700,000, a million were illiterate, 600,000 children had no opportunities to obtain any kind of education, and 10,000 teachers were jobless. In 1959 there were about thirty public libraries; by 1983 there were more than three hundred. But those [first 30] libraries did not provide any of the features nor meet the standards of service that make an adequate modern public library. Only two of those libraries could be counted as such—the Lyceum Lawn Tennis Club Public Library and the Sociedad de Amigos del País Public Library.

The Lyceum Lawn Tennis Club was a women's liberal and cultural society whose public library made contributions toward shaping the literary taste of the generations of the 1930s through the 1950s. It also supported interest in librarianship.

During the nineteenth century and the first half of the twentieth, some academic libraries were founded, such as those of the Academy of Sciences, Academy of Arts, and Academy of History. Some professional societies, such as the Engineers Society and the Architects Society, also founded important libraries. The sugar industry has been the main economic resource of Cuba, and one of the first research libraries of the country was that of the industry's Asociación de Técnicos Azucareros.

**National Library**. In 1901, by a military order during the United States occupation of Cuba, a director to the National Library was appointed. In 1936 the Cuban writer and historian Emilio Roig de Leuchsenring, Historian of the City of Havana, denounced the poor condition of the National Library through his articles in the weekly magazine *Carteles* and called urgently for improvement. The Asociación de Amigos de la Biblioteca Nacional (Association of Friends of the National Library) was founded. Many distinguished writers and historians were members, with Emilio Roig de Leuchsenring as president.

In 1935 the Foreign Policy Association, based in New York, published a report entitled "Problems of the New Cuba," which cited the National Library's "shameful conditions. Its shelves were drawn off during the President Machado administration and the books were packed into boxes and stored in a facility belonging to a state prison, and even though they have already been returned to the library, the deplorable state of the building and the shelves made possible the unpacking [of only] a few volumes; in addition a fire took place in the building and a great deal of books were burned to ashes."

In 1938 the government decided to move the library to the Castillo de la Fuerza and to tear down the building that housed it and build a police station instead. The books were packed again with haste and transferred to their new place.

The lack of resources and qualified personnel led to deteriorating conditions that became so obvious that the government appointed a Cuban writer and diplomat, José Antonio Ramos, as the library technical adviser, giving him power over cataloguing and classification. Ramos implemented a system of classification on his own, based on the Universal Decimal System and adapted to Cuban needs. His was undoubtedly the most significant attempt to organize the bibliographic resources of the institution up to that time. After struggling to improve the National Library, Ramos resigned in 1946, shortly before his death.

In 1941 the government imposed a one-half cent tax on each 325-pound sugar bag in order to raise funds to build a National Library. Construction of the National Library's new building began in 1952. It was named after José Martí (1853–95), the Cuban national hero who was a poet, a thinker, a warrior, and a "symbol of the National Liberation against colonialism and imperialism."

After the Cuban Revolution of 1959, sweeping changes took place in the library as well as in the rest of the country. María Teresa Freyre de Andrade, Cuban librarian and long a fighter for the development of librarianship in Cuba, was appointed director of the institution. She started intense efforts to move the National Library toward modern goals and to make libraries reach everyone. She also encouraged the reform of library science studies at both university and technical levels.

The government resolved that all books that belonged to the dictator Fulgencio Batista (1901–1973), to his associates, and to people leaving the country should be transferred to the National Library. These "rescued libraries" played an important role in filling out the collections of the National Library and in starting collections in the new libraries in various parts of the country.

Because of the shortage of libraries, the National Library has served as a public library. Its Department of Bibliographic Research created a Union Catalogue of Scientific and Technological Periodicals and a Union Catalogue of Social Sciences and Humanities. A special service of the National Library is the Children and Young Adult Department. Its activities, including storytelling, painting, literature, philately, and others, have been the model for other children's and juvenile libraries in the country. At the international level, the National Library has an information exchange agreement with the Centro de Información Científica Técnica Humanística (CICH) of the Universidad Nacional Autónoma de México. It coordinates the cultural information exchange work of several cultural institutions in Cuba.

In 1989, as part of a restructuring of the Ministry of Culture, the Biblioteca Nacional José Martí became the National Methodological Center for the Public Library Network, head of a network for culture and arts information with its main focus the present and prospective condition of public libraries in the country. It became responsible for promoting reading among adults and children through the Programa Nacional de la Lectura. It also assumed responsibility for collecting the official documents of the Ministry of Culture into the Archivo General de Cultura and for organizing the Biblioteca Memorial Juan Marinello, honoring a Cuban leader who bequeathed his library to the National Library.

*National Bibliography.* In the nineteenth century the Cuban scholar Antonio Bachiller y Montes published his *Apuntes para la Historia de las Letras y la Instrucción Pública en Cuba.* The second volume of that work includes the first account of periodicals edited in Cuba; the third makes the most important contribution to the field of bibliography of that time. It was titled *Catálogo de Libros y Folletos Publicados en Cuba desde la Introducción de la Imprenta hasta 1840.*

Some Cuban and foreign authors worked to compile the national bibliography during the first half of the twentieth century. Carlos M. Trelles was the most important of the group, because of the completeness and accuracy of his *Bibliografía Cubana del Siglo XX*, published in 1917. From 1937 to 1958 the *Anuario Bibliográfico Cubano*, compiled and edited by Fermín Peraza, tried to continue the work of Trelles.

In 1959 the National Library was appointed to compile and publish the Cuban National Bibliography. It published the bibliographies for the following years: 1917 to 1920 (published 1960); 1921 to 1936 (1979); 1959 to 1962 (1968); 1963 and 1964 (1967); and yearly from 1965.

*National Archives*. The Archivo General de la Isla de Cuba was founded by an order of the Queen of Spain in 1840. In 1888 the Captain General of the Island, by order of the Madrid government, sent to Spain 2,300 documents of great historical value. An official decree of December 20, 1904, established the island institution as the National Archives.

From 1921 to 1956 an outstanding Cuban historian, Joaquín Llaverías y Martínez, was its director. He had "a constant preoccupation [with] the search for and conservation of valuable documents that are in the collection of the institution." From 1945 to 1958 it published the periodical *Memorias*. In 1963 the National Archives was attached to the Academia de Ciencias de Cuba. It succeeded in forming a network of provincial and regional archives.

**Academic Libraries**. The history of the Library of the University of Havana reflects the history of the main institution, which had scant resources until the late 1930s, when a new building was constructed and a new organization was established as a result of the revolutionary movement of that time. After 1959, the University of Havana Library evolved toward the concept of a Biblioteca Central (Central Library), providing the conditions for better development of the particular libraries of the university faculties.

The Central Library of the University of Havana was named after Rubén Martínez Villena, a revolutionary leader of the 1930s. The complete holdings of the Central Library total 150,500 volumes, with a reference collection of 10,200 volumes and a natural sciences periodical collection of 10,800 titles.

Higher education was expanded in order to reach more people and improve its overall quality. In 1976 a scientific and technical information network for higher education was organized to serve the universities and research centers attached to the Ministry of Higher Education. The system includes nineteen scientific and technical information centers and forty-six libraries. The network provides a system of storage and retrieval for unpublished documents such as theses and papers (*informe de investigación*), and a printed union catalogue of scientific and technical periodicals in the network.

**Public Libraries**. In 1961 the Dirección General de Bibliotecas (General Library Board) was created as part of the National Council for Culture with the task of establishing a national network of public libraries under the technical guidance of the National Library. In 1977 the Ministry of Culture was established, and within it was created the Dirección de Bibliotecas with the aim of continuing and broadening public libraries' work. There are almost 375 libraries of this kind in all parts of the country. The system is organized with the National Library at the head, main libraries in the provinces, and libraries and branch libraries in the municipalities.

By the early 1990s, there were 13 main libraries in the provinces, one for each, except for the City of Havana province, which does not have its own provincial library; more than 200 municipal libraries in the main towns; and more than 150 municipal branch libraries, 65 of them in sugar mill areas and 12 in new rural communities. The system also has 6 bookmobiles that make almost 300 stops in rural communities without libraries and about 1,500 minilibraries in factories, mass organization offices, hospitals, and other institutions.

**School Libraries**. There are no available statistical data on school libraries prior to the Revolution in 1959. A statute issued on July 6, 1960, mandated that a school library service was to be organized. It was the first official step toward reaching the goal of having a library in every primary and secondary school. UNESCO had helped in the late 1950s with technical assistance through a School Library Pilot Project. After that experience was adapted to the new and growing demands of Cuban society, the school library system started to work.

The main objectives of the school library are to contribute to the formation of "a scientific conception of the world and a communist morale" in the students through "systematic reading of socio-political as well as scientific and recreational literature linked to the curricula." The school libraries have circulation and reference services.

**Special Libraries**. Each of the central administrative bodies of the government, research institutes in the various branches of the economy, and the services has its own information center or special library. Among them are the ministries of the Sugar Industry, Foreign Commerce, Public Health, Agriculture, and Construction, the Central Planning Board, and many others.

The National Information Center for Medical Sciences, founded in 1965, is the main body for the scientific information system in the field of public health in Cuba. The system is structured into a network formed by the national center and other health centers. The National Center provides services for administrative and technical leaders and for scientists and research personnel in the medical disciplines. It also serves as the National Medical Library for physicians, students, and other users.

Personnel requirements for the various levels of medical libraries are as follows: for minilibraries at the "bookcase" level, nontechnically qualified employees with minimum training; at the hospital library level, graduates of the Medium Technical Medical Librarianship School; and at the provincial centers, Medium technical graduates and university graduates. At the National Center librarians must have university degrees not only in librarianship but also in medical specialty fields.

The José A. Echeverría Library is part of the Casa de las Américas, an institution set up "to put into practice measures and initiatives which would contribute to cultural unity among the Latin American and Caribbean countries, as well as situating these regional cultural expressions in the context of universal culture." This institution was guided and directed until her death in 1980 by Haydée Santamaría, one of the two women who participated in the attack on Moncada Barracks (July 26, 1953), later a member of the Central Committee of the Cuban Communist Party and the country's Council of State. The library serves all those interested in Latin American culture, history, and sociology. It houses almost 100,000 volumes and more than 6,000 periodical titles.

The Pedagogic Documentation Centers form a network founded in 1960. It is composed of the Centro Nacional de Documentación e Información Pedagógicas, 162 centers, and 15 Provincial Departments of Research, Documentation, and Pedagogic Information.

The Junta Central de Planificación (Central Planning Board), the Cuban government institution that deals with the main economic affairs of the country, has a Scientific and Technical Information Center. At the first experts' meeting held at Havana in 1979 under the auspices of the Comité de Desarrollo y Cooperación del Caribe (CDCC; Caribbean Committee on Development and Cooperation), planners agreed to establish an information network whose coordinating center would be the Centro de Documentación del Caribe (CDC). The International Development Research Center (IDRC) of Canada granted financial aid for the project. The Scientific and Technical Information Center of the Junta Central de Planificación coordinates the work of the economic institutions of the country as participants. Among those institutions are the Banco Nacional de Cuba, Comité Estatal de Estadística, Comité Estatal de Finanzas, Instituto de Investigaciones Económicas, Ministeria de Comercio Exterior, and Oficina Nacional de Diseño Industrial. Among the main accomplishments were advances in bibliographic indexing and abstracting, the use of a thesaurus for economic information indexing, and the definition of the kinds of documents the system should process.

**The Profession.** Many attempts were made to establish the study of library science in Cuba prior to 1960. The most significant was the foundation in 1950 of the Escuela de Bibliotecarios (Library School) in the Faculty of Philosophy and Letters of the University of Havana. Many librarians holding leading positions in Cuba in the 1980s and 1990s were graduated from that center. From an enrollment of about ten students with five professors in 1956, the school had grown to seven-hundred students and more than twenty professors by the early 1990s.

The Department of Scientific and Technical Information at the University of Havana was created in 1970 by the Ministry of Higher Education as a part of new approaches to university studies. Subjects added to the curriculum included computing, bibliographic research, information storage retrieval systems, and organizing and managing information institutions. This department played an important role in fostering scientific research and in publishing textbooks written by Cuban authors.

After passing the five-year university course, a graduate receives the degree of Licenciado. A university graduate may obtain the Doctor in Library Science degree. For library technicians, undergraduate programs are conducted at the Escuela de Técnicos Medios under the Ministry of Culture. By examination, graduates may enroll as students in the evening courses offered by the University of Havana.

# *Appendix 6.*

## REMARKS TO THE OPENING SESSION OF IFLA'S ANNUAL MEETING IN HAVANA, AUGUST 22, 1994[122]

Dear Colleagues:

In 1980 the first two Cuban librarians to attend an IFLA conference took part in the fifty-sixth conference held in Manila. I would like to take this opportunity to pay tribute to a person who was not only a pioneer of Cuban representation at IFLA, but was also responsible for many other achievements in Cuban bibliology,[123] which you will be able to see for yourselves during these days. She is Dr. Olinta Ariosa who, although unable to attend, is present here in heart and spirit. We send her greetings and our warmest regards.

On the occasion of the 1985 IFLA Conference in Chicago, ASCUBI held its first talks, through us, with Else Granheim and Margreet Wijnstroom, then IFLA chair and secretary general, respectively, who offered their support, advice, and warmth. At that time we discussed the possibility of holding an IFLA conference in our country, since this event had never been hosted by any Latin American country. This was in itself

---

122. First published as Marta Terry González, "Address by Dr. Marta Terry to the Opening Session of the 60th General Conference of IFLA, August 21-27, 1994. Conference Programme and Proceedings," International Federation of Library Associations and Institutions, http://archive.ifla.org/IV/ifla60/60-terry.htm. Reprinted with permission of Marta Terry González and the International Federation of Library Associations and Institutions.

123. The word bibliology is not often used in English, but in Spanish the words bibliología, bibliografía, biblioteconomía, and bibliotecología (each with its own etymology) refer to knowledge about books, libraries, and information, sometimes emphasizing different aspects.

an important motivation for them and it was also the desire of Cuban librarians to share our experiences with IFLA representatives, our colleagues from all over the world, and to show them the results of our professional work. In this context, it must be recalled that in the 30s librarians such as María Villar Buceta and later on María Teresa Freyre de Andrade, Blanca Bahamonde, Maruja Iglesias, Blanca Mercedes Mesa, and many others, with the support of the country's best writers and intellectuals, stressed the need for the training of librarians and the creation of libraries as part of a drive to enhance our people's cultural and educational standards. While they were publicly striving for these goals they were also, at times secretly and other times openly, battling for the necessary political and social transformations which could allow the realization of those seemingly unattainable ideals which have been translated into our modest but firm reality of today.

Such motivations were also understood by the next IFLA Chair and Secretary, Hans Peter Geh and Paul Nauta. It was during their term of office that Cuba was granted the venue of the Sixtieth Conference.

And here we are at last, meeting on this day of 22 August, 1994, opening the Sixtieth General Conference of IFLA in this room in the Havana Convention Center, which has hosted so many important meetings in the history of our country and the development of Cuban arts and sciences and the promotion of solidarity with Cuba.

We would also like to avail ourselves of this occasion to recognize the importance to the Cuban library community of our relations with IFLA. IFLA has made it possible for Cuba to become professionally a part of contemporary bibliology. IFLA has opened the world to us by facilitating bilateral links with libraries from all countries and serving as a vehicle for the mutual exchange of information, knowledge, and experience. In short, IFLA has brought about tangible improvement in Cuban bibliology.

And that is not all; through IFLA we have received a great deal of material and professional assistance, contributed to our country as solidarity aid by libraries from a number of countries.

In summary, we can safely state that the benefits obtained by Cuba through IFLA have in fact been tantamount to breaking the blockade in our professional field.

The Sixtieth General Conference of IFLA has been both an honor and a challenge for Cuba. This conference is an event of major importance for all Cuban librarians as well as for the Cuban Ministry of Culture, our government and party.

Each library in every community and every province, each documentation center and special library in the country has in one way or another contributed to ensuring the successful outcome of this conference, and each one of them sends you all its warmest greetings. On their behalf and indeed on my own behalf I extend to you our cordial welcome and a hearty embrace from all Cubans.

Thank you.

# Appendix 7.

## REMARKS TO THE AMERICAN LIBRARY ASSOCIATION, JUNE 2001[124]

*The Social Responsibilities Round Table of the American Library Association organized a panel for their 2001 annual meeting in San Francisco in order to educate ALA members about Cuban libraries. Although the US government never responded to Marta's visa application, her written remarks were read at the conference session by an American colleague.*

Dear colleagues:

I have come here at the invitation of a group of American librarians headed by Ann Sparanese, as well as the ALA Executive group, to share with you some common professional worries and preoccupations, but, above all, as a way to help to break the information blockade that my country is suffering from, among other aspects of the economic blockade that my country is subject to.

I come to tell you about the worries and preoccupations of us, the Cuban dependent[125] librarians. I also come to speak about their successes and their aspirations. I come to speak about their uneasiness in relation to the misinformation some, or perhaps many, of our American colleagues may have about our libraries, our country, and our way of

---

124. Reprinted with permission of Marta Terry González.

125. Marta refers to the country's networks of public, school, academic, and special libraries as dependent libraries as a way of commenting on the so-called independent libraries promoted by US government funds and agents. See next page.

living, and their concern that all that disinformation will deepen still more the already-deep waters of the Florida Strait that separates our two countries

I come to share the voices of solidarity of those Cuban librarians with all of you who have refused to believe those absurd campaigns of disinformation about our professional practice and our beliefs, and have decided to go and see for yourselves and draw your own conclusions, and then come back and talk loudly and fight hard about what you consider to be truthful and honest.

I also come to thank you all for your interest in my country and my profession and to try to increase that interest that is giving birth to a new pattern of relations between the American library community and the Cuban library community. Until very recent times relations between Cuban and American librarians have been scarce and sporadic, being based on personal contacts among a few of us. Nowadays it is perfectly clear that a different approach has been initiated, precisely an approach marked by more understanding, collaboration, cooperation, and mutual professional respect.

I said, at the beginning of this small dissertation, that I had come to tell you about the worries and preoccupations of the Cuban dependent librarians. It is not a question of my poor English. You have understood quite well. I mean it. I mean that I have come to talk (allow me to repeat it) on behalf of the Cuban dependent librarians.

Because we are and represent those librarians who live in Cuba depending (shall I say defending, too?) on our socialist society, simple, honest, egalitarian, that society we build every day with our work ...

We are those librarians who depend on a child's smile of satisfaction after having read a book of stories (sometimes all worn out because of so much use and very little possibility of replacement) and we depend upon the child saying to us, "Is it there another one to be read? I liked that story so much..." We also depend upon the thanks the old retired laborer gives us when he has just finished reading, for the third time, the biography of Napoleon or Abraham Lincoln, or Lenin, or Antonio Maceo because he has already read the Martí biography more than five times ... and then the old man tells us, "You see, compañera, what I like to know is how things were before, I like to know how those great men were, I like to know all they had to do to build their world."

And how much we depend on the new and young writer who is entering his or her first book in the competition for the David Prize[126] and who has consulted us a thousand times about the sound or the correct spelling of some very important phrase in his or her work!

We depend on the bus that takes such a long time to arrive—because of the shortage of buses and fuel—so that we can get to our library on time, one of the 390 public libraries (at least 1 in each municipality and 1 in each province) the more than 3,000 school libraries, the more than 50 university libraries, and the scientific and technological units of the scientific poles along the country.

Sometimes transportation is not the bus or the guagua [that is, a minibus]—to be more clear, it might also be a bicycle or catching a ride with some unknown compañero or compañera who has a car and so we depend on them to be able to get to our job: the library.

We also have depended on—that is to say, we have adjusted to—the lack of electricity or lightbulbs to be able to maintain library services, and when it happens we have to change the positions of chairs and tables and put them near doors and windows to use the sun's natural light. Or else we have been obliged to break the unwritten rule of not circulating out of the library any one-copy titles, because that particular title is needed by someone who has to study or read that book to pass an examination or finish a term paper. And so we give the book on loan so that person will be able to study it when the electricity is back on but the library has closed. And we cross our fingers that the book will make it back to our stacks because it might be impossible to replace it if it gets lost.

---

126. The David Award is literary prize for young writers sponsored by the Cuban Union of Writers and Artists.

I have chosen a few examples out of hundreds that happen in our daily work as Cuban librarians. We depend on the satisfaction of our users to feel we and our profession are useful and needed to our society.

But I am sure that if we take out the peculiar and difficult conditions under which we live in Cuba that make our work so much different (sometimes full of anguish) compared to other places, many of you—if you are real librarians, and I think you are—you will find those human-contact (librarian–user) stories are not so strange and alien to you.

There are still more circumstances we must mention that are not as pressing for you as they are for us: the lack of a title or even worse the lack of the information our users may need.

Sometimes a user is looking for a title he or she is interested in or he or she has heard of. It may happen that the book is on loan. Well! The user gets frustrated because someone else has what he needs and we only have two or three copies for circulation. But it might also be the case that the book is not in our collections or that the desired item is not a book of fiction to be read for recreation in your free or spare time! Sometimes what is needed is a scientific or technical book, or a book of essays for a student or a professor or an engineer, and the book is not there. This happens because we have very few titles and copies—because of all the circumstances of the blockade of your government of my country.

The colleagues who have made their presentations before me have mentioned other details and so I do not think I should take up those themes again.

But in the midst of all these arguments and discussions it seems we are taking for granted that the books our people need to read are just novels and books on politics and we are forgetting in the newly born twenty-first century information is the most crucial resource and that libraries are centers for information and formation and the first one is an essential part of the second.

Have we asked how many copies of the latest edition of *Encyclopedia Britannica* can be found in the main Cuban libraries? Or how many copies of the latest edition of *Diccionario de la Real Academia Española?* How many libraries have been able to acquire the Nobel Prize collections that are so needed by literature students and professors, as well as the general public? How many books of world-renowned art reproductions published in the 90s can be found in the public or university libraries in Cuba?

Or, let's be more modern: How many CD-ROMs? Has somebody asked himself or herself how do we acquire CD-ROM information? Has anybody sought out the reference collections our students have in the librarianship study centers in Cuba? Has anyone seen the latest editions of *The World of Learning* or the *International Who's Who* in any Cuban public or even any university library? Does anyone remember the reason we launched the Ediciones R collection?

We are not trying to arouse your sympathy. We are just opening a small window on the so-scarce freedom to acquire information abroad that the dependent Cuban librarians experience. Money, as is well-known, is difficult to get, but sometimes we do have the money. But we do not have a way to acquire items directly from the publishing houses, and the already high prices continue to go up, so nothing can be done.

On the other hand, to say "We have been through," is quite an euphemism because no matter the achievements we have made during the last two or three years, in terms of the quality of life and the economy of our country, and no matter that the special period is starting to pass, the blockade is as firmly in place as when it was first instituted, and is even more restrictive with the most recent laws and bills that have been passed by the US Congress. I am afraid that if I were to write to the editors of *Fortune* magazine as I did when I worked at the Junta Central de Planificación in 1964, they will answer with the same line: "We are sorry but we cannot accept subscriptions from your country."

You may ask: How come you are still there and you are able to speak about having overcome illiteracy and having hundreds of medical doctors and trying to be a most cultured people, if you do not have the facilities to acquire the books you need for all that?

That is the Cuban big question: How is it possible?

Well, first of all, because the immense capacity for sacrifice on the part of each of us as individuals as well as the social resistance of the Cuban people. Our daily work of building and rebuilding, of believing in the justice of our cause.

And also because of the solidarity of many people in many parts of the world. Just to mention library educators: professors of librarianship and information science at the University of Havana are able to navigate the Internet because we have a fairly well-equipped laboratory to work in. We can find resources there, but we cannot acquire the many articles in the commercial and noncommercial databases that require subscriptions. A full-text offering is still very rare. We have found, though, that some authors are generous enough to send us a copy themselves when we approach them just by simple email.

I mentioned that, at this moment, a slow but sure economic recuperation is taking place as a result of the tremendous effort the country is making. We are able to start to replace some titles in our collections due to the gradual recovery of our publishing industry. Some of the very deteriorated public libraries buildings are being reconstructed. The electricity cutbacks have diminished by almost 95%, so they are not a daily problem and the libraries' evening hours are being restored. Three years ago the launching of the Programa de la Lectura was made with the same old books and with the new editions that have started to be published by the Instituto Cubano del Libro. In that way we started the fight for the recovery of the reading habits of our population that the long night of the special period was about to make disappear. New ideas were a real contribution, such as the Minerva Club program, which allows patrons access to some of the main works of world literature for a very small membership fee.

The successful battle for the returning home of Elián González, in which the American people were so instrumental, demonstrated the excellent state of the artistic and political culture of our people attained by forty years of revolutionary struggle. We have started a new fight to keep that going. We call it the battle of ideas. That battle has a lot of different fronts and only one objective: to make our people more culturally

literate and well-informed so that they will go on being unbeatable, or
to put it in better words, much more unbeatable still.

Among those fronts the schools for art instructors that were responsible in the 1970s for the great amateur artists' movement have been
reestablished. Music, dance, drama, and the visual arts are being promoted in a big community-based movement. Opportunities for university
careers in education, humanities, and social sciences have been increased.
Computers for primary and secondary schools are being acquired so that
in a short period all the young people of the country may have access
to these technologies, just like the youngsters of what is called the first
world and the information society. Televised courses on University for
All (in English, literature, and art history) are new ways to reach everyone who is interested. And what has become more interesting for us
librarians: the library work of the country is being renewed.

Easing the blockade? Does that mean that we would have more
opportunities to buy the books we need (Shall I add "the medicines"?)
than we had, let's say, two or three months or three years ago? Does it
mean that we could buy directly from McGraw-Hill or Macmillan or the
University of Chicago Press? Does it mean that we could click on the
website of Barnes & Noble and get the titles we need? Does it mean
that we would have all the money needed to acquire the copyright of
the works of the best foreign authors to publish them in Cuba, so as
to publish them in Cuba at very low prices and in such large quantities
as we used to do, even though the number of copies will never be as
many as before the hardening of the blockade and the establishment
of the special period?

By no means. It is only that we advance inch by inch in our revolutionary struggle.

Up to this point we have tried to show a panorama of our difficulties,
our realities, and our new achievements in fields that may be near to
your professional interest as well as your human and solidarity feelings.
It is not our objective to relate the history of Cuban Revolution in such
a small space of time. What we want is to for us together to open an
understanding panorama based in the unprejudiced comprehension

arising from a professional and human exchange based on truth, the rule of law, and the respect for the right of each country to live and to defend the project of the society their individuals chose to live in.

We, Cuban librarians and in particular those members of the Cuban Association of Librarians (Asociación Cubana de Bibliotecarios— ASCUBI), would very much like it if it were possible to launch a program that would allow American librarians to have access to our literature, to our authors, both the established as well as the youngest, those of the nineteenth century as well as those of the twentieth and the upsurge in the twenty-first. We would like to know what is read about Cuba in American libraries, how many times the computers of American libraries get in contact to our sites to know our own versions of our reality, our opinions, our success in sports, our doctors saving lives in Central America and Africa and Haiti and our people demonstrating from the Plaza de la Revolución to the whole world. We would like to find ways to go into many small and humble American libraries like ours or the immense ones that we would like to have, and examine the catalogues and find there the Cuban editions of the works of Ché, the speeches of Fidel, the poems of Guillén, Retamar, Fina, Cintio, Pablo Armando, las décimas de Waldo Leyva or of Alexis Pimienta, the short stories of Heras León, or the essays of Graziella Pogolotti.

We would like to find in your children's collections copies of *El Cochero Azul* or *El Caballo de Coral* for your children to know, as ours know about Huckleberry Finn.

We would like to find in our catalogues and stacks the novels of Toni Morrison or Gore Vidal or William Kennedy and replacements for the lost copies of Ralph Ellison's *The Invisible Man,* just the same way we find Walt Whitman's *Leaves of Grass*, the anthologies of American short stories published in the 1960s, or some of the works of Dreiser.

Martin Luther King said he had a dream. That dream meant equality, solidarity, understanding, peace. The Cuban librarians share that dream and we make it ours.

Cuban librarians depend on our collections, on our readers, on the honesty and passion we put in our work. We do not tell our readers,

Believe. We tell them, Read. That was Fidel's thought many years ago—
¡No creer, leer!—and we practice the word and the spirit of it. We also
depend on the solidarity with and understanding of our colleagues
everywhere in the world. We need allies in our battle of ideas.

# *Appendix 8.*

## OLINTA ARIOSA MORALES, 1921–1999 (2003)[127]

Olinta Ariosa Morales. Photo courtesy of Marta Terry González

Olinta Ariosa Morales was born in 1921 in Zulueta, in the municipality of Remedios in the former province of Las Villas. Her mother was a teacher; her father ran the old San Agustín sugar mill. She attended elementary school in her hometown, and received her bachillerato from the Institute of Secondary Education in Remedios. During the 1940s, she studied at the School of Philosophy and Letters at the University of Havana, majoring in language and literary studies.

In 1952, "looking for work and new horizons," she returned to Havana, where she enrolled in the School of Library Science, which,

127. First published as Marta Terry González, "The Pioneers: Olinta Ariosa Morales (1921-1999)," *World Libraries* 13, no. 1/2 (2003). Reprinted with permission of the Marta Terry González and the editors of *World Libraries*.

at that time, operated as an adjunct school to the University's humanities division. She received her library degree in 1953.

However, the unfavorable political, social, and economic situation of the times, and the lack of libraries, meant that even with her new degree, Olinta still found herself "looking for work," although, given the potential in the library profession for personal and social development, "new horizons" certainly did open up to satisfy her intellectual and professional restlessness.

Olinta, along with other classmates from school, began her professional life as a volunteer, under the direction of the well-known Argentine librarian and UNESCO expert on libraries, Carlos Victor Penna, who at that time was living in Havana. Their hard work established a library for Elementary School No. 2 in the Marianao district, one of the very first in Cuba to provide services to schoolchildren.

Always in search of new opportunities to create a better world, Olinta, like many young people of her generation, took part in revolutionary activities, for which she was imprisoned in 1955 by the Batista regime.

With the victory in 1959 of the Cuban Revolution, Olinta began to work on organizing and putting into operation the Municipal Library of Marianao, and in 1962, she was appointed head of the Department of School Libraries within the Ministry of Education.

Here she performed ground-breaking work to advance the condition of school library services in Cuba, both in administrative and scientific and technological areas. Surrounded by a circle of young professionals, she became a teacher and team organizer, something quite different from the activities which would define the rest of her professional life. During this period, she also began teaching classes in librarianship at the Library School of the University of Havana, which she continued doing until 1965.

In 1972, she was named to the executive board of the Instituto de Documentación e Información Científica at the Cuban Academy of Sciences. Her outstanding accomplishments there laid the foundation for the modernization of information services in Cuba, by introducing instruction in the new techniques of data processing and programming languages, the publication of texts, and the first exchanges with librarians from other countries.

When the Ministry of Culture was created in 1976, Olinta was chosen to head the Library Division, whose objective was the scientific and methodological development of Cuba's public libraries. She provided a systemwide focus for this task, improved the administrative structure of the division, and concentrated efforts on library processing, and library services, including the use of "mini-libraries" to reach people. She initiated research into new aspects of librarianship, and strengthened sponsorship of professional meetings, conferences, and workshops.

Olinta promoted literacy programs in Braille for the visually handicapped by creating special reading rooms for them and offering them specialized services. She introduced the concept of the ten cultural institutions of every town in the country, among which the library was viewed as the most important and the most basic; and established a strong international and professional network for the exchange of library ideas and personnel. During this period, she also served as director of the José Martí National Library.

Olinta was deeply committed to and very involved in the founding of ASCUBI, the Cuban Association of Librarians, and as its first president, she organized and oversaw the attendance of a group of Cuban librarians at the 1980 International Federation of Library Associations and Institutions (IFLA) conference in Manila.

Her dedication, hard work, and achievements have been recognized with many honors and distinctions, such as the Bachiller y Morales Medal (el Sello Bachiller y Morales), awarded by the Cuban Association of Librarians; and the Cuban Culture Award (Distinción por la Cultura Cubana), presented by the Ministry of Culture.

# *Appendix 9.*

## SPECIAL LIBRARIES AND OTHER INFORMATION PROVIDERS IN CUBA, 2003[128]

*An earlier version of this paper was presented to the American Library Association/Canadian Library Association joint annual meeting in June 2003. This was the first ALA meeting Marta succeeded in attending—because she did not need a US government visa.*

### Introduction

Although there has been much discussion recently about Cuban libraries, it is quite likely that only a few of the participants have any real knowledge of the subject beyond a passing familiarity with the public libraries they may have encountered during sightseeing tours in Havana, or hasty excursions into the provinces. But the world of information science and librarianship is not limited to this single aspect of library activity. Special libraries, teaching libraries, information centers, and the professionals who staff them are essential components of the professional life of our country, and important providers of information for the scientific, technical, and cultural development of Cuba.

Even under the colonial rule of Spain during the eighteenth, nineteenth, and twentieth centuries, Cuba began to see the formation of

128. First published as Marta Terry González, "Special Libraries and Other Information Institutions in Cuba," *World Libraries* 13, no. 1/2 (Spring and Fall 2003). Reprinted with permission of Marta Terry González and the editors of *World Libraries*.

institutions which, in one way or another, were concerned with education and learning.

The dominant social class, the *criollos*, had access to important institutions such as the University of Havana, the Sociedad Económica de Amigos del País, the National Archives, and the Academies of Science, Liberal Arts, and History, and were able to use the information these institutions provided to help shape the era, to put down roots, and to establish a tradition of improving Cuban society through knowledge and education.

One can name hundreds of illustrious physicians, engineers, architects, writers, and artists whose work helped shape the Cuban national character and identity, in which science, technology, and intellectual curiosity and creativity all play an important role.

Early Sources of Information

During the pre-Revolutionary era, the Lyceum Lawn Tennis Club, a well-known and prestigious women's cultural society with an advanced social agenda, was a pioneering institution in the field of library studies in Cuba, and virtually the only public library in our country at that time which made use of modern technical and professional advances.

The professional Colleges of Medicine, Engineering, and Architecture provided their students, faculties, and educational affiliates with access to information resources, in one form or another. The thirteen schools within the University of Havana had their own bibliographic resources, some organized as traditional library collections, others accessed by students and teachers in different ways. The University's Central Library became the home of the first university-level library school in Cuba.

In other areas, the Association of Cuban Sugar Workers (Asociación de Técnicos Azucareros de Cuba) maintained an excellent library which specialized in resources dealing with the sugar industry. Although the library's fine collection of journals on the subject was particularly noteworthy, its professional library staff was inadequate.

From its founding in 1902, the National Library of Cuba began its fifty-six-year-long pilgrimage in search of a home through garrisons and barracks.

The second half of the twentieth century saw the founding of universities in Oriente Province, with a main campus in
Santiago de Cuba; and the Central University of Santa Clara
(now called Villa Clara), each with its respective libraries organized by well-trained and respected professionals of that era.

## The Revolutionary Period

Revolutionary activity affected all aspects of Cuba's social, economic,
and scientific life, producing profound changes, and in some cases, a
sudden new birth. The outcome was the reorganization and growth of
the national government bureaucracy, and an expansion of its functions.

In order to provide each sector of social, economic, and political
activity with the necessary attention, the government institutions, organizations, and ministries of state responsible for implementing the
policies and programs outlined in such fundamental documents of the
Revolution as "History will absolve me" were either newly established,
or restructured.[129]

In order to implement the vast political, social, and cultural movement
authorized by the Agrarian Reform Law (Ley de Reforma Agraria), the
National Institute for Agrarian Reform (INRA) was formed. The creation of the National Institute for Urban Reform (Instituto Nacional de
la Reforma Urbana) resulted from the need to confront new challenges
and changes in housing. In order to deal with changes in, and to implement new directions for, the economy, the Central Planning Council
(Junta Central de Planificación or JUCEPLAN) was established, as well
as the National Bank of Cuba (today known as the Central Bank of the
Republic of Cuba), the Ministry of Finance (Ministerio de Hacienda),
and the newly formed Ministry of Industry. The need for hydraulic

129. Note by the editors of *World Libraries*: "History Will Absolve Me" is a
transcription of Fidel Castro's defense speech, dated October 16, 1953, at the
trial after his unsuccessful attack on the Moncada barracks in Santiago del
Cuba on July 26th of that year, three years before the revolution. It became
one of the central documents justifying the revolution. Fidel Castro, "History
Will Absolve Me," *Castro Internet Archive*, http://www.marxists.org/history/
cuba/archive/castro/1953/10/16.htm (accessed March 9, 2005).

development gave rise to the National Institute for Hydraulic Resources (Instituto Nacional de los Recursos Hidráulicos).

The former Ministry of Health (Ministerio de Salubridad) became the new Ministry of Public Health (Ministerio de la Salud Pública), organized around an entirely different concept, ideology, and agenda, in order to comply with the mandate of Moncada[130] to make the health of the nation a top priority.

Educational reform on all levels of instruction, including the literacy campaign of 1961, became the responsibility of a totally restructured Ministry of Education, a government department whose reputation under the former "pseudo-republic" had been completely eroded, and whose effectiveness had ultimately been weakened by the loss of status and respect. Some years later, the Ministry of Higher Education was organized to deal with the growth, development, and specific needs of the university educational system, all of which resulted from the greatly increased access of the public to the universities, and from all of the scientific, technical, and cultural development they were producing.

Radio and television would take a new direction under the aegis of the Cuban Institute for Radio and Television (ICRT), while the almost nonexistent production of Cuban cinema was addressed by the Cuban Institute for the Cinematic Arts and Industry (ICAIC).

The need to provide recreation and entertainment for the general public through sports, and to channel the abilities of numerous men and women athletes (who performed in many cases under all types of pressures, and without any official sponsorship during the "pseudo-republic") led to the creation of INDER, the National Institute of Sports and Recreation; while the National Institute of Tourism (formerly INIT, now INTUR) began to focus on national tourism for the Cuban people,

---

130. Note by the editors of *World Libraries*: The "mandate of Moncada" is a reference to the attack on the Moncada barracks. Among the motives that were cited for the attack in the subsequent trial were health and access to health care. See Antonio Maria de Gordon, "Health and Health Care in Cuba: The Transition from Socialism to the Future," Finlay Medical Society website, http://www.finlay-online.com/finlayinstitute/healthandhealth.htm (accessed March 9, 2005).

and then turned its attention to developing international tourism, some of the earliest clients of which were Canadian visitors.

The guardianship and development of the country's cultural values were the responsibilities of the National Culture Council, which, due to a sharp increase in, and broadening of, its functions, was reorganized as the Ministry of Culture in 1977. At this time, the groundwork was laid for the establishment of various councils and institutes that currently nurture and promote the coordinated development of artistic expression in the country.

Very soon it became apparent that in order to realize these transformations, it was necessary to have access to information and a knowledge of the rhythm and level of development in the areas of science, technology, and culture in the modern world. In other words, along with all of this political change arose the need and the quest for information.

In their need to implement all of the aforementioned changes, to carry out founding decrees, organizational regulations, and calculations of staff and office space, those institutions—which today are Cuban state institutions—were pulling books off the shelves of refurbished libraries, searching for bibliographies, titles of books and journals, and of course, new forms of processing and acquisition.

The fervor of all the revolutionary changes that were occurring also brought about the establishment of the JUCEPLAN Library; the Center for Agricultural Information (Centro de Documentación e Información para la Agricultura, or CIDA); the library of the Ministry of Foreign Trade (Ministerio del Comercio Exterior, or MINCEX); the library of the National Bank of Cuba; the Information Services Center for Medicine; the library of the Public Works Ministry (known at that time as the Ministry of Construction); the information center for the Ministry of Foreign Relations (Ministerio de Relaciones Exteriores, or MINREX); the INIT ( National Institute of Tourism, now INTUR) Information Center; the INRA library; and the library of the Ministry of Industry. The latter enjoyed the support of one of the figures of the Cuban Revolution most concerned with the value of the book as a source of information, and with the library as a center of scientific and technical study and discovery, namely Commander Ernesto "Che" Guevara.

For the first time, we librarians could sit down around a table to analyze the concrete reality of the need for development by trained experts, for the development of library collections, construction of shelving, placement of lights and location of storerooms, and a new emphasis on the formation of trained staff in terms of quality as well as quantity.

Quickly we realized the need to systematize all of these independently conceived efforts and projects, and to coordinate them, in order to achieve our proposed objectives.

## Science and Technology: IDICT

On April 19, 1963, by the authority of Law No. 1107 of the Council of Ministries, the Institute for Scientific and Technical Information— IDICT—was created as a subsidiary of the Cuban Academy of Sciences, which had celebrated its fortieth anniversary, just a few weeks earlier. This legislation called for an Advisory Council made up of representatives of the libraries and information centers of many of the organizations previously mentioned: The José Martí National Library; JUCEPLAN; the Ministries of Industry, Public Works, Public Health, Foreign Trade, and Transportation; and INRA. Other libraries and information centers were added to the initial membership throughout the formative stage of this project.

Among the earliest advisory reports on developing scientific information in Cuba were those of the Indian professor, Pitiri Kawla, who consulted with the Central Library of the José Antonio Echeverría University City (CUJAE), today called the José Antonio Echeverría Polytechnic Institute (IPSJAE), and the Soviet specialist from UNESCO, Mijail Kiyaev. We began to hear a completely different language. We were introduced to the idea that scientific and technical publications were considered obsolete five years after publication. These new standards for scientific information were a bit strange to us, having at that point already been mired in the underdevelopment produced by the embargo, where it often took us five years to find out that a certain book even existed, to seek funds with which to purchase it, and then to request that someone agree to sell it to us.

In the early years of the creation of IDICT, there was little or no expertise in Cuba on scientific information resources and delivery systems, regulations, and objectives; and even less on issues in the information world's ongoing debate about methodology and the handling of documents, given the overwhelmingly rapid discoveries and developments that had been taking place since the early 1950s.

The efforts of IDICT were very decisive in synthesizing foreign advisory reports, most of which originated in Eastern European countries, principally the Soviet bloc. These evaluations introduced new ideas on information processing, such as the use of the Dewey Decimal Classification system, consecutive order for shelving books; making a distinction between "documents" and "books"; and the use of abstracts as preliminary sources of information for specialists, among others.

Through agreements established between IDICT and VINITI, we were able to receive abstracts of hundreds of journal articles published all over the world to which we had no direct access due to the limitations imposed by the embargo.

"Since our creation, and for almost three decades, we [IDICT] maintained close ties of cooperation and collaboration with many important information organizations in Eastern Europe, who facilitated our access to the most important human, information, and technical resources of the world at that time."

Perhaps IDICT's most impressive achievement of that era was the way in which it became, practically speaking, a clearinghouse for professional information, and a source of information for our country on all the latest information technology.

In 1976, following the principle that even the most remote corners of the country should benefit from the successes and victories of the Revolution, branch centers, known as Multisector Centers for Scientific and Technical Information (CMICT), today called Centers for Technical Information and Management (CIGET), were established in other provinces.

In 1982, for the first time in Cuba, IDICT began using an XT micro-computer for information services, and in 1983, in collaboration with CIICT, initiated dial-up access to databases located in Europe.

By virtue of Resolution No. 16/84 passed by the Cuban Academy of Sciences, IDICT was designated a member center of the National System of Scientific and Technical Information (SNICT), and shortly thereafter, of the National Center for the Automated Exchange of Scientific-Technical Information.

The National Scientific and Technical Library was inaugurated in 1988, with a modern focus on giving its scientific and technical patrons better and more direct access to specialized information in their respective fields through automation.

IDICT is now the headquarters for the INFO Congresses, recognized as the most important event in the field of information science in Latin America and the Caribbean, attended by colleagues from all over the world. The 1990 Congress coincided with the meeting of the Forty-fifth FID Congress and Conference in Havana. That year, the institutional name of IDICT became Institute of Scientific and Technical Information, although the acronym IDICT is still used.

Once Cuba gained access to the Internet in 1996, IDICT became the organization that introduced, supplied, evaluated, and popularized this technology throughout the country.

### Culture: José Martí National Library

While the creation of IDICT was aimed at developing science and technology, the National Library turned its attention to rescuing the national bibliographic patrimony and to developing culture for the enormous numbers of people who, through the literacy campaign, were acquiring the ability to read, and to recognize the cultural values of the nation.

To elaborate a bit on the National Library's project of recovering the national bibliographic patrimony, a retrospective edition was prepared, in order to gather together bibliographic information from those years during which the bibliography had not been published.

The foundations for what is today the National Library System were established with the creation of a library in each province that would function as the central organizing agent for the growing number of municipal libraries which were springing up. The first reading-incentive programs were initiated, and the novel concept of the "mini-library" was introduced as a means of bringing books and information resources to many different sectors of the population.

Under its strong influence, the Library Technical Assistants School was founded, which produced mid-rank library professionals with solid training, on whose shoulders rested the better part of the Cuban library system. In addition, the National Library played a key role in the reorganization of library studies at the university level.

Library service for children and young people began with the children's room of the Lyceum Lawn Tennis Club, but it was not until the creation of the José Martí National Library that such services were formally instituted and made accessible to all children.

When the Ministry of Culture was set up in 1977, the National Office of Libraries was created, which assumed responsibility for the development of public libraries. At the same time, the office also recommended the creation of ten basic community cultural institutions for each municipality: library, drama troupe, community chorus, band, film, theater, cultural museum, art gallery, and cultural centers as a means of making cultural events accessible to the greatest number of people. Although from the perspective of the public libraries, it seemed that much progress had already been made, this initiative helped to strengthen and complete that which we have now: a public library in each city and territory. In particular, it introduced library organization as described in the Minaz-Cultura agreement, which defined a very special sui generis type of public library.

During the 1970s, work on Cuban libraries was expanded, scientific and technical collaborations with library systems of the socialist countries were set up, and Cuban professionals participated in various groups set up for designing and implementing political strategies for the scientific and technical development of the library profession in those countries.

In 1981, the Cuban Association of Librarians (ASCUBI) was organized with the participation of distinguished librarians from all systems, and soon became part of the International Federation of Library Associations and Institutions (IFLA), whose Sixtieth Conference was held in Havana in 1994.

During this period, Cuban libraries began providing library services for the blind and visually handicapped; initiated library and information science research; and pursued new methodologies for scientific and technical development of the Public Library System, which are still in operation today.

In 1987, the transfer of responsibility for the development of public libraries in Cuba to the José Martí National Library brought with it a higher profile for the library, and an organizational restructuring. The first library research department was added, which has carried out important research work on socio-historical and cultural subjects, and has served as the center for methodology and library development throughout all of Cuba.

New means of automation and transmission of information were introduced, and there was a renewed interest in the study of preservation and conservation concepts, and in the practical applications of these ideas to the collections. A national bibliography was compiled, as well as specialized bibliographies on outstanding figures and events in Cuban history and culture.

The library publication, *Revista de la Biblioteca Nacional*, was once again being published after a long hiatus during the Special Period.[131] Collections became increasingly specialized, and were made available exclusively to students and specialists. As a result of the decree of June 8, 2003, Eliades Acosta, director of the José Martí National Library since 1998,

---

131. Note by the editors of *World Libraries*: The term "Special Period" is used in Cuba to refer to the years after the collapse of the Soviet economy. See, for example, Cuba Heritage.com, History: Special Period and after (Post 1990), http://www.cubaheritage.com/subs.asp?sID=12 (accessed March 9, 2005).

ordered that all items acquired by the library must be catalogued elec-
tronically, as a first step towards the automation of the library's entire
catalog.

"Reading is an activity which expresses and sustains the culture of a
nation, its spiritual motivation, and its values, its ability to persevere and
develop." Guided by these principles, Cuba carried out an enormous program to promote reading, which culminated in the annual *"Leer a Martí"*
competitions, in which more than 500,000 children and young people
from all levels of education participated. At the present time, the system
maintains 392 libraries located in Cuba's provinces, districts, and towns.

### Education: School Libraries

In the last five years of the 1950s, with the establishment in Cuba
of the UNESCO Regional Center for the Western Hemisphere, a pilot
school library in the Teacher Training School in Havana was set up
for the dictatorship's Ministry of Education, under the administration
of UNESCO library specialist Carlos Víctor Penna. This pilot project
helped to spur the development in Cuba of school libraries, which are
so necessary for the complete education of children and young people.

At the same time, the Office of School Libraries was created within
the Ministry of Education. Dra. Olinta Ariosa, a pioneer in many areas
of Cuban post-Revolutionary librarianship, was selected, under Minister Dr. Armando Hart, to establish and direct the Cuban Network of
School Libraries, one of whose goals included the continuation of the
literacy campaign begun in 1961.

This network connects the Colleges of Medicine in each province of
the country, offering them e-mail services and access to other information services. INFOMED, the National Center for Medical Sciences
Information, and the National Library of Medicine form an information
network for public health in Cuba, which, for 40 years, has made information accessible to medical professionals, collaborated in the training
of doctors, and helped to further the study of medical sciences in Cuba.

## Other Institutions and Libraries

Between the earliest years, to which we referred at the beginning of this paper, and the present time, other powerful information institutions and libraries have arisen that form part of the spectrum of libraries and library services in Cuba.

The first library established in Cuba, the library of the Sociedad Económica de Amigos del País, second only to the José Martí National Library in its collections of the bibliographical patrimony, today operates under the aegis of the Ministry of Science and Technology, and is the central office of the Institute for Literature and Linguistics.

Casa de las Américas, a cultural institution which focuses on the study and dissemination of Latin American and Caribbean culture, has one of the most complete libraries in the area. The universities have tripled their offices, libraries, and information systems.

The huge strides of progress in scientific and technical research, which have determined the discoveries and advances made by our scientists in many areas, are greatly supported by the information centers of LABIOFAM, BIOMUNDI, and Polos Científicos, which provide information and consulting services.

Many of those early organizations to which we referred were developing excellent modern information centers, among which we would include the Center for Information in the Basic Construction Industry, mentioned earlier.

## Some Observations

In order to show points of development in the different information systems which comprise the National Information System, and to trace the evolution of Cuban library and information sciences, we have chosen to focus on just three of the greatest and oldest systems of the Revolution.

We should like to draw your attention to the fact that the systems represented in each of these three cases outlined today exist simultaneously in each province of Cuba, including the special town Isla de la Juventud. In each province there are as many school libraries as there are schools, as many university libraries as central university campuses, as many public libraries as towns, as many Teacher Training Information Centers as towns, including an Information Center (CIGET), and a Center for Medical Information.

What we have shown so far might lead one to think that the scientific development of library and information services in Cuba has been carried out in a coherent, sustained, and cooperative manner, without any great impediments.

However, all of this development has been marked by the unimaginable confrontation of and struggle against the economic and political blockade imposed by the United States government since January 1959, to which, hidden under the fig leaf of the term "embargo," Cuba has been forced to submit.

The formal imposition of the North American blockade took place February 3, 1962, the date on which the US president, John F. Kennedy, signed Executive Order 3447, which established, from that moment on, a complete embargo of all trade with Cuba.

The initial order was reinforced in 1988 by an amendment to the defense spending bill of 1992, introduced by Senator Torricelli, and in March 1996 by the Helms-Burton Bill. The collapse of the Soviet Union in 1990 made the situation even worse, when it deprived us of all material, financial, and commercial assistance. As a result of these developments, in 1992 the Revolutionary Government was forced to initiate the Special Period—el Período Especial—in our country.

Whenever concerned colleagues and visitors inquire about the effects of the embargo on information access and library services in Cuba, questions center on the acquisition of books and other materials in order to increase collections and develop services, and the ways in which the embargo might deprive the people of access to literature and information. But this is only one side of the issue.

Undoubtedly, there have been instances in which it has not been possible to obtain materials necessary for the continued development of these information institutions which we have described above, hindered as we have been by the many obstacles imposed on us by prevailing US legislation. We have been compelled to develop many different types of initiatives on our own: for example, Ediciones R, the immediate response to the abrupt cutoff of the supply of materials from the large specialized North American publishing houses, and/or from their subsidiaries in other countries, opened up a new phase of development for the government press, Imprenta Nacional.

The large printing runs demanded by the cultural and intellectual development of the country were initiated with Ediciones Huracán, and today are continued by the Biblioteca Familiar. Meanwhile, other editorial houses were established in Cuba to fill important gaps in publishing for the sciences, technology, and the humanities: Editorial Academia, for subjects of great scientific importance; Pueblo y Educación for school texts; and the publishing houses which comprise the Institute for the Book (Instituto del Libro), namely: Editorial Arte y Literatura, dedicated to the publication of the great works of world literature; Editorial Gente Nueva for children's books and young adult literature; Letras Cubanas for Cuban literature, both traditional and contemporary; Editorial Oriente for literature of the eastern provinces; Editorial José Martí for literary works in foreign languages; and Editorial Nuevo Milenio for works of social science and technology.

As an example of the publishing output of the ICL, in 2001 more than 5 million copies of books were produced, a figure which does not include the output of the other 136 existing publishing houses. This was how we dealt with the difficulties of buying books abroad: we created our own publishing industry. However, given the impenetrable nature of the embargo, we still faced many obstacles; we have to use all of our skill and cunning just to buy paper, ink, and printing equipment, and to keep up with advanced technologies.

Book fairs in Cuba were not held until the beginning of the 1980s, although there had been fairs, expositions, and book sales earlier at different points in Cuban history, in particular those organized in the 1940s and 1950s by intellectuals such as Raúl Roa García, later known as the Chancellor of Dignity (Canciller de la Dignidad), and other national cultural figures.

Those fairs officially known as the Havana International Book Fairs (Ferias Internacionales del Libro de La Habana) were inaugurated in 1982, exactly twenty-one years ago, when the first was held in the Fine Arts Palace (today, the Museum of Fine Arts), attended by a small sampling of Latin American publishing houses, and which featured the work of José Martí and Félix Varela and other outstanding intellectuals. Its slogan, "The book: bridge of friendship among the countries of the world," characterized the fair for many years thereafter.

The Ninth International Book Fair of 2000, with a new slogan, "To read is to grow," and dedicated to the famous Cuban poet and essayist, Cintio Vitier, winner of the National Prize for Literature, and to Italy, as an invited guest country, was held for the first time in San Carlos de La Cabaña, currently still the official site. Growing national and international participation, which accompanied a gradual recovery of the Cuban book, has prompted the fair to be held annually.

The most recent fair, the twelfth, was held in February of this year (2003), and was dedicated to the winner of the National Prize for Literature, Pablo Armando.

# *Appendix 10.*

## THE CUBAN BOOK FAIRS: A NEW FORM OF READING PROMOTION. A PAPER PRESENTED AT THE IFLA ANNUAL MEETING IN BUENOS AIRES, ARGENTINA, AUGUST 2004[132]

### Background

Among the principal aims of Cuba's 1959 Revolution were the nationalization of education, a literacy campaign, careful attention to education, and access to culture and information for the masses. In the Year of the Assault on the Moncada Barracks, 1953, with a population of 6.5 million inhabitants, there were in Cuba: more than half a million children not in school; more than a million illiterate people; a system of primary education that only served half of the school population; a secondary and higher education for the minority of the population, offered only in large urban centers; and 10,000 unemployed teachers.

In 1961, the Literacy Campaign was carried out. Of the 979,207 illiterate people identified, 707,212 gained basic literacy skills; residual illiteracy was reduced to 3.9% of the total estimated population in Cuba at that time.

At present (1999 data), Cuba's population is 11,170,000, which includes a large body of university professionals and people with associates' degrees. Education is compulsory through the ninth grade, i.e., upper primary, which implies one of the highest technical, professional, and intellectual levels in the continent.

---

132. Reprinted with permission of Marta Terry González and the International Federation of Library Associations and Institutions. Translated by Laura K. Aase.

After the Literacy Campaign came the Seguimiento (Follow-through) and Superación Obrera (Worker Improvement) programs, which covered the basic primary education cycle of first through sixth grades. With teaching methods and materials adapted for undereducated children and adults, the Battle for the Sixth Grade was developed in 1962 and used through the five-year period 1975-1980. The Battle for the Ninth Grade was developed in the same way, culminating in 1980-1985. Simultaneously, the Workers and Farmer Education program was developed, in which adults can acquire the equivalent of a 12th-grade education in order to continue with university studies or choose courses at the upper secondary level for technical qualifications.

Under the general designation of the Battle for Ideas, the country is currently carrying out the Municipalization of University Education program. The program consists of creating university centers in each municipality of the country, providing special programs of study for adults who had not been able to complete their education cycle. The objective is to allow those adults to complete prioritized career programs, including Library and Information Science.

The Cuban Revolution's implementation of the cultural education project set multiple programs in motion. The National Press was founded in 1962 and, because of the growth and development of publishing in the country, became the Cuban Book Institute in 1967. It created the Department of School Libraries, which made possible the National Library, which in turn established the national system of public libraries which launched the first plans for the formation of the habit of reading, among many other measures for the development of the library profession and libraries in Cuba.

It is not surprising, therefore that what was considered the First International Book Fair[133] took place in Havana in 1982. The cultural level of the people guaranteed attendance, and the maturity of the institutions involved and the economic

---

133. Jorge Luna Mendoza, "Las Ferias Cubanas," La Editorial Electrónica Cubaliteraria, Web Portal of the Cuban Book Institute, http://www.cubaliteraria.cu/evento/filh/2005/memorias3.htm.

development of the country at that time made the fair totally necessary.

## The Book Fairs

Book fairs are generally events designed for exhibition, hiring, and buying wholesale for libraries and publishers, as well as simple promotion or commercial dissemination of bibliographic products that have been created over a period of time, almost always one year. Some are big events where thousands of books are displayed and authors and titles are advertised; such fairs are meant to satisfy the demands of different types of users (booksellers; librarians; the public according to gender or age: seniors, teens, children; and according to professional, cultural, and intellectual levels). Among the best known are the Frankfurt and the Guadalajara Book Fairs. Frankfurt encompasses books of all sorts and includes the multimedia and communications industries. Guadalajara focuses on Spanish language materials and the products of Latin American publishers, and it is considered a place where "knowledge about new technologies in the book world is realized."

In Cuba, book fairs have had, from the beginning, a more popular character. The earliest fairs resembled the other connotations of the word "feria" in being more like bargain sales, liquidation or damaged goods sales, or discount sales. Books in those days were not in high demand, and the fairs became a way to redistribute volumes that had been well used by students and intellectuals but they had little or no impact on society in general. The first of those fairs was celebrated in May of 1927, but they never gained regularity in either time or space.

What was considered the real "First International Book Fair of Havana" took place in 1982 at the Museum of Fine Arts in Havana and continued biennially after that. From 1990 to 1998 they were held at the Exhibition Pavilion at the Conventions Palace, PABEXPO.

This was a period in which the Fair tried to demonstrate the character of Cuban editorial productions to both foreign and domestic publishers, and to promote transactions, sales, and subscriptions for all parties. At that stage, even though there wasn't a great deal of publicity, the Feria[134] was already an event for librarians, teachers at all levels, students, and the general public.

It could be said that the rising expectations and pressures of public attendance each year were factors that the organizers, the Cuban Book Institute and Cuban Chamber of Books, took into account before making their definitive move: transferring the Fair to the Fortress of San Carlos de la Cabaña, a former military building constructed by the colonial Spanish government, situated at the entrance of Havana Bay.

Its architectural style, the size of its facilities (which can accommodate thousands of people at a time), and its geographic location in relation to the city of Havana made the Fortress a fitting site. The change was very well received by the people of Havana, who appropriated the Fair and turned it into a massive event.

In 2000, the first Book Fair was held at the Fortress de la Cabaña, which presupposed a change both quantitative (more space, a larger number of stands, more publications, more book launches, a larger number of guests) and qualitative: a great interest was shown by all segments of the public, adults as well as children, writers, artists, teachers, and more.

The Fair continues to project a more popular character rather than being a mere commercial venue for books. Cultural activities are multiplying in such a way that it is necessary to prepare and establish various programs: the Literary Program, the Professional Program, the Artistic Program, and more collateral programming in cultural institutions in the city.

In the midst of all this activity, the annual publications awards are given, including the social sciences award, among others. The awarding of the National Prize for Literature constitutes a very special moment; among the award winners are eminent Cuban poets, novelists, and essayists. Each year the Fair is dedicated to one of those award winners.

---

134. This is how Cubans commonly refer to the Book Fair.

Last year's Fair was dedicated to the beloved and notable Cuban poet Carilda Oliver Labra.

Taking as a reference the catalog and general program of the last Fair celebrated this year (February 2004), one notes that 230 activities were programmed and carried out within the Literary Program, including book launches; panels and conferences with prestigious speakers, intellectuals, writers, professors, and critics (both Cuban and foreign); literary meetings; and poetry readings. Meanwhile, academic meetings included conferences and reflections on Cuban historiography and the German presence in Cuba since the 16th century, and the traditional publishers' meeting, among others. A total of 60% of those surveyed said they had also attended plays and concerts.

Despite the economic difficulties that the country suffers under the blockade or embargo imposed on Cuba by the government of the United States, during the Fair the number of books sold for the average price of $5.50 (Cuban national currency) multiplies.

All this coupled with the Battle for Ideas mentioned above led in 2002 to a consolidation of those qualitative and quantitative changes that had already begun to develop in the Fair. The most notable change is the extending of similar activities to 18 cities in other provinces of the country, which indicates that, in a strict sense, the Fair is no longer the Havana Fair, but that of the entire country. During the 2004 Fair, activities spread to 34 cities, including Santiago de Cuba, Matanzas, Pinar del Rio, Moron, Guantánamo, Baracoa, San Antonio de los Baños, Artemis, and Camaguey, among others.

In order to have objective information on the movement and opinions of the population in attendance, and more, groups of Library and Information Science students, led by specialist professors, took the first statistical samples in 2001.

Those statistics, just to cite one example, show that in that year, out of 2025 people surveyed, 92% had bought a book. This high purchase rate was maintained in 2003 and 2004.

Likewise for the size and the sampling, the same approval and demand of the people in attendance. And so also the festive atmosphere, where one sees families with children; young people looking for the latest novel by Chavarría or a book of poems by Tony Guerrero, one of our heroes unjustly imprisoned in the United States; sports lovers following the biographies of our most famous athletes; academics searching for books on science and philosophy; veteran fighters from the Cuban Revolution filling the room for the book launch by Armando Hart; children or their parents asking after stories of the Golden Age and the location of the Children's Pavilion; the best of the Cuban intelligentsia together with university students, treasuring Alice Walker's signature in her book Meridian. The author gave Cuba publishing rights for the Spanish edition—her dedication written in fine hand—"in peace." And likewise the hours of waiting in line in the sun in front of bookstores to get the desired book; the mass media attention on all this activity that for one month captures the attention of all Cuba.

All of that makes us say that the Cuban Book Fairs are an incalculably valuable and effective way of promoting reading, which we librarians should take more into account.

*The author is director of the library of the Dulce Maria Loynaz Cultural Center and is responsible for data collection and surveys during the book fairs in Havana.*

# *Appendix 11.*

## ACCEPTANCE SPEECH UPON BEING NAMED AN IFLA HONORARY FELLOW, SEOUL, KOREA, AUGUST 24, 2006[135]

In 1953 when I was studying organization and administration of libraries in the Library School of the University of Havana, I first heard the meaning of the IFLA acronym, which at that time was known in Spanish as REL, and learned about the work that the organization conducted to develop librarianship around the world.

Since 1959, with the triumph of the Cuban revolution, our country was seeded with new ideas, new ways of living, new schools, the literacy campaign, the founding of new universities, scaling up culture for everyone, and more. Soon we began to feel the effects of the blockade that formed around our country. The information highway was cut. So we were deprived of, among other things:

- knowledge about development trends of library science
- cataloguing rules of the ALA
- versions of the Dewey Decimal System
- new forms of bibliographic citation
- methods to make libraries more attractive and welcoming for children and youth
- pathways and requirements for developing library services for blind and visually impaired people

---

135. Translated from Spanish by Kate Williams and reprinted with permission of Marta Terry González.

• new ideas regarding the apparent dichotomy between librarianship and information science.

Looking at it another way, what did the library world know of Cuban
librarians: the challenges we faced, the discoveries we made? What was
known of the stressful circumstances in which we performed our work:
the invasion of the Bay of Pigs, the bombing of important centers of
the country, the murder of young literacy workers, our crops burned
and more? How could others know that while these things happened,
we Cuban librarians continued with our programs to develop the Cuban
library: mini-libraries, or reading promotion in remote communities in
the mountains, in prisons and with children on long hospital stays, and
many more?

At IFLA's 1981 annual meeting in Leipzig, Olinta Ariosa and I completed the registration form the Margreet Wijnstrom gave us to formalize
the participation of the Cuban library association in IFLA. A new era
opened for Cuban librarians. Under the auspices of IFLA and thanks to
IFLA, then happened friendship, sharing, tips, confrontations, discussion of scientific-technical, ideological, and political policies. Under the
auspices of IFLA and thanks to IFLA, librarians in Cuba and worldwide
have found and known each other and I think we have demonstrated
that coexistence based on mutual respect for our rights and beliefs is
possible. And that the goodwill of all the world's librarians is part of
realizing the ideal of all Cubans that a better world is possible.

# Appendix 12.

## THE BOOK FAIRS AND THE LIBRARIAN: A SPEECH TO THE BOOK FAIR IN ARTEMISA, CUBA, FEBRUARY 26, 2009[136]

In a few days, the parks and squares of the cities and towns where the Cuban book fairs have been held will return to their daily lives. Silence will return, the elderly sitting lonely on some benches; baseball fans screaming in excessive praise for the success of Team Cuba; children riding scooters, skateboards, some locked in their cars. As happens all over the world, some teenagers will be making trouble and others will be seeking love.

At Plaza de la Cabaña, those footsteps of the guards that remind us of colonial Spain will continue to resonate, warning residents of Havana that it is 9 pm as they have done since Spanish colonial times. But when they sound the cannon at 3 in the afternoon, there will no longer be kids and moms and dads and boys and girls running after them to see them, touch them and deliberately be frightened by the singular explosion.

The thousands of people who stroll around the parks during the fair, look at and touch the books, touch them and touch again and again, open, close, browse, flip through them, hesitating : "Do I buy it or don't I?" and the phrases that you hear, among many: "Look at this coloring book, it is the one I told you about," "Mom buy me this, this is what I want," "No, baby, that's for when you grow up," "But buy it for me now, I want it now!" All that will be gone. Now most of those who were talking like that are at home watching TV. A mom or dad is

---

136. Reprinted with permission of, and translated by, Marta Terry González.

reading to a child, or a child is reading some product of Gente Nueva Editorial, or else reading Little Red Riding Hood for the thousandth time.

Those who are not girls and boys any longer will open the pages of a Stephen King novel without knowing or caring who he is or how good he is. He is fashionable like a gold tooth cover you slide over your tooth. But as they are Cubans living here among us, we will not be so surprised by their possible disappointment or their saying, "It was not what I thought." And some others will let themselves be seduced.

Marta Rojas will slip among a few boys and girls with her eyewitness account of the immortal *Moncada Trial*. Other older boys or girls will read it for the second or third time. Uncles and aunts want to know well what Fidel said in the *Declaration of Havana*, or how he and Camilo went about the nationalization and what that was like. Is that in the book *25 Speeches of Fidel*? Some will go directly to his speech when the Cubana airplane was shot down and remember how people cried tears of indignation as he spoke.

Older people, contemporaries of all that, will retire to some corner and with a tear will recall the times of militia marches and the October Crisis and the voluntary work in tobacco or potato plantations: days of the sugar cane cutters.

Some others, be they teenagers or elders, will be delighted with the verses of Fina (nobody thinks to call her by her complete name Fina García Marruz). Others will seek out those verses of the semi-hidden poet known almost exclusively by his friends, Luis Marre, who was awarded the prize of prizes for Cuban writers, the National Literature Award, and some old friend will remember Ochún dancing "con sus aros de oro/with her gold bracelets" like no one has ever sung.

We are watching, or imagining we are watching, or imagining how to help, what happens after the book fair. Once someone asked me: Why do you you do this big book fair in February, when February is a month so close to December and so there is no money to buy more? And indeed there is no money, I answered.

Dozens of books, we could say hundreds, thousands of titles are taken home, as we have tried to point out, they are taken by children, students, teachers, retirees, workers.

They are taken home after the fatigue of long queues with joyful and triumphant smiles. "I caught one!" or "I got the last one!" or "I don't care, tomorrow morning they will be on sale again" or "I already have mine."

And that book of mine might be any of those already mentioned, or endless stories from Martí´s *La Edad de Oro*, or a new and rewarding collection of Cuban art, or an exotic small paper boat that is not our paper but is more like a children's boat, or Fidel Castro *La Paz en Colombia* or the surprising volume of verses by Silvio.[137] The title might be *Colección Historia de la Revolución* ("Youngsters are so grateful") or a novel by Chavarria[138] ("I found a gem") or the fine bindings of Ediciones Bologna. And what about Amaury Pérez as a novelist?[139]

After the mass phenomenon and the popular celebrations that our book fairs have become, recollection and silence must follow. That is the way to become an accomplice of the writer, to learn or to appropriate what the writer says, what he or she says to me alone. The author and me, we confront each other. He or she tries to invade me, to convince me, in fact Cortazar[140] would speak of the "male novel" that tries to conquer me the reader. But just novels? What about poetry and short stories and history? And what about the sports titles?

What I want to say is that after the big feast, you must read. *Read to grow.*[141] Read and understand the message. We must move from the invitation shaped by the book designer, or from the speech given by the book presenter, without any further ado, in order to capture the reality of

---

137. Silvio Rodríguez, the composer, guitarist, and singer who helped initiate a movement in Cuban music called Nueva Trova.

138. Daniel Chavarria is a Uruguayan writer living and working in Cuba for many years.

139. Amaury Perez, Nueva Trova composer and singer who published his first novel quite late in life.

140. The Argentinian novelist Julio Cortázar.

141. This is one of José Martí's sayings and also the slogan of the Book Fair.

the message the writer sends us and invites us (incites us). The message we have chosen in our long queues under sun and wind at La Cabaña.

At this time the cultural, intimate act materializes. We have passed from feast to reflection. Just like when the child chooses colors that will be used in a coloring book that mom and dad bought him or her, or when the adolescent dreams of Poem 20, there is no other Poem 20 throughout world literature except Pablo Neruda. And these days more than ever, days dedicated to Chile and its culture, we can afford the luxury of devoting ourselves to "Puedo escribir los versos más tristes esta noche." And the student of Martí, new or old, man or young woman, is determined to figure out why "el canario amarillo tiene el ojo tan negro / the yellow canary has such a black eye."

An old French friend named Marcel Proust, who wrote a monument that qualifies as a novel titled *Remembrance of Things Past*, wrote:

> once the novelist [the writer—MT] has brought us to that state, in which, as in all purely mental states, every emotion is multiplied ten-fold, into which his book comes to disturb us as might a dream, but a more lucid dream, and of a more lasting impression than those which come to us in sleep; why, then, for the space of an hour he sets free within us all the joys and sorrows. (From *Swann's Way*, Volume 2 of *Remembrance of Things Past*, by Marcel Proust, Project Gutenberg edition)

That is the act of reading which is performed once the book is acquired (something Proust also describes, a few lines above this quote). The confrontation occurs, and the reverie.

You could use many impressions or definitions or descriptions about reading books, but we stand by these somewhat incoherent definitions. We would just add that to reach that state of mind, a moment of concentration is needed. Sometimes the concept scares us, given the noisy life of our circumstances, but it can be achieved. Try to observe, in the midst of bustling squares people seated in reading groups, reviewing the newly acquired copy. That's concentration, or as we say "getting inside the book." And I think that popular Cuban expression deserves to be considered and raised up high.

In the long run, that is what scholars all over the world try to express.

It has been said that thousands of books were carried home during the book fair. Statistics show tens of thousands of people flocking to the streets and parks purchasing their titles. Someday we may know what percent of the population attends the book fairs. Whatever percent is a figure, a part. Not everyone can go or wants or needs to go to buy a book. The intent of reading or browsing through a book fair is not universal.

That's one thing. Once the books are acquired, they are left on shelves, chairs, tables, or inside boxes. Some are lent to friends and colleagues, who usually never return them. The ones they like the most are kept like holy relics. Many are lost.

But the mass media and the information media have been responsible during the whole time of promoting. Teachers and professors have taken notes. We talk over and over about Poema 20, but there are other poems in that book as good or better, and many people do not know them. Curiosity may arise but there is no more Feria until next year and it is difficult for bookstores to maintain enough stock for an entire year. Moreover Neruda not only wrote *20 Love Poems and a Song of Despair*. There are those other monuments such as *Canto General* and *Confieso que he Vivido* and many others. Nor did Marta Rojas stop writing with the epic of the Moncada trial. And Amaury Pérez has published a new novel launched at another book fair, and Chavarria has several new titles.

The fair will be over but the need for the act of reading does not end, once you have come to know its ritual. There will be many who did not have the will or interest or opportunity to purchase their book, yet they met a friend who told them about how interesting it was to read this book or that author.

Some would go to the fair because they already know authors and titles and wish to confirm their information or add to it.

Libraries have everything else, everything that is not the fair, but perhaps the fair drew our attention to the author or the subject, the period, or the era; to what the professor assigned as homework; to a small or large manual that answers a question at work. The smallest and unhappiest among all libraries will always have a bench or a chair, and its behavior policy will facilitate assembly, privacy, and answers to curiosity. We resent the loud whistle that quiets us when we walk happily into a library to undertake a search for the task the municipal university professor has assigned or to read Garcia Marquez, seeking that man who wrote love letters for pennies. When we are inside the small or large area and throw ourselves into the pages of *Love in the Time of Cholera*, we understand the value of the silence asked of us, and we understand that person who protects our space for concentration is actually taking care of us.

History tells that at the entrance to the library of an Egyptian temple it could be read on a stone something like "The Place That Cures Souls." Since that early time it was known that the library was a place for peace, introspection, and search for knowledge. And knowledge cannot easily be found within bustle and companionship. It is also said that the Egyptians kept in their libraries an entire wealth of information which helped them understand and make the most out of the Nile floods. Olinta Ariosa used to say that she considered the Egyptians as having founded the first documentation center.

The practical minded Romans found that several libraries scattered throughout the neighborhoods of the city could give the people more than bread and circuses, and they created something of a superintendent of public libraries to monitor them.

And Catholic monks, masters of the art of writing in the Middle Ages (or Dark Ages as some may say), knew they had to copy to keep for the future what had happened with the Greek and Roman past and what the founders thought and demanded of the new religion, in their desire to expand their faith. The beauty and richness of this work gave the book and the library in which they were kept an aura of a closed, exclusive, and treasured site, today perhaps archaic but not quite gone.

The driving need and search for information and knowledge, along with the development of technology and science that the Renaissance times proposed, led to the rise of printing. Universities proliferated and ruling classes sought them out. Books were needed to shape the emerging modernity and to master knowledge and information. To preserve information and its power, university libraries would chain the books to the shelves.

British workers who were protagonists of the Industrial Revolution discovered with Engels that to survive and respond to the demands of new emerging technologies, information and knowledge were needed and thus arises the subscription library. This library gave rise to the public library of our time.

UNESCO and other major international library associations and institutions ask libraries for more. In the turbulent and unequal world of today, they ask, How, why attend a library if you cannot read? So libraries are assigned the highest task of teaching the illiterate how to read. Afterwards we shall see if libraries win over the new literate to read something more than the literacy primer.

When our country's literacy campaign was conducted and the National Printing Office, Department of School Libraries and Public Libraries Network were created, large associations and UNESCO had not yet forseen this challenge. And still today they have not realized this: We do not live by bread alone, but you can't give an empty stomach a book.

That seemingly contradictory story I have told make libraries such as we have today.

Definitely libraries are gathering places giving peace and environmental possibility for reading and in some cases to calm down and rest, to surrender to the author and/or for the author to surrender to us. They are centers for conservation and preservation of the historical past and the coming future and for disseminating that richness. We have to chain the books, if not physically, then in records, papers or files, so as to makesure the information is there for everyone. Our virtual chains are the ghosts of those older chains.

In between the book fairs, some parks and squares in towns and villages continue to be popular, so librarians make their way to them loaded with some chosen titles (for adults, children, women) and read them and promote them and lend them during culture weeks or holidays or just as part of the reading campaigns each public library in Cuba carries out all year long.

In the past three years, Cuban librarians have presented in international library exhibitions and conferences more than twenty papers
showing the results of our our libraries' reading promotion. Those
presentations have been much praised. Yet praise has been attached
to amazement at the discovery of what we can achieve despite the
extraordinary circumstances of economic blockade we live in our country, which in turn produces the misinformation that exists about our
country among many of the world's professional gatherings.

But there is more. We should talk about the mission, vision, goals of
a library: reading and/or teaching reading; cherishing our bibliographic
heritage. For each village or community has poets, historians, essayists,
teachers, branches of the young artists' Hermanos Saíz Association and
the Writers and Artists Union.

Are we going to throw *Bohemia* magazine out of our public libraries because after all it's kept by the National Library? And how do we
educate a young person about Cuba's uniqueness in the entire world?
Should I do it with that impersonal digital tool, the Internet? Recall the
sign found in a US library: "Ask a librarian, not a machine."

At the same time we need to discuss the role of the library in promoting reading and deciding what is promoted. In this small essay, we have
been talking about literary and historical reading. Of course literature
and history define national culture. To quote: The Spanish librarian Ana
Teresa García Martínez in an article in *Puertas de la Lectura* magazine called
"Marco Jurídico de las Instituciones de lectura / A Legal Framework for
Reading Institutions" makes two interesting interventions. First she says:

> These days we often hear about the information society, referring to
> the time we are now entering, noted as an evolution of the complex
> contemporary social structures, with its raw material centering on infor-
> mation and leading to a telecommunications infrastructure to support
> their objectives.

Then she adds,

> We must highlight the role library has been playing as mediator in that

access to information. This institution so endearing to some has emerged as a bulwark, ensuring reading and access to culture for masses of people, satisfying their own human urge for independent learning.

This isn't entirely new, but it is an authoritative voice from abroad regarding the role of information. And if we add to information the concept of knowledge, that is, access to knowledge and information, we then complete the image of today´s library and its relationship with reading.

It remains true, more than ever before since we are dealing with a literate and educated people, that literary reading is a pleasure and a duty. Reading literature creates much knowledge and provides just as much information as a treatise on chemistry to a chemist. It's just that the treatise is aimed at chemists and literature is there to be read and enjoyed by all.

It is also true that our libraries have more literature, histories, sociologies, that is, the spirit of humanities, than they do science. But if we are in the era of information and knowledge and we affirm that knowledge is information and vice versa, our libraries must go beyond their eminently humanist tendencies and accept their new role in a society of men and women already used to seeing and explaining life's phenomena using a scientific approach.

The public library may be located in front of a square or a park, in the middle of a block or on a corner. The librarians will be highly sympathetic towards a novel of the twentieth century Latin American explosion, the exploits of *Huckleberry Finn* or *Uncle Tom's Cabin,* or the works of François Sagan. They will try to find on their shelves Brazilian novels published by Casa de las Américas to help explain what's unfolding on a Brazilian soap opera. They might search for texts needed by students and teachers for University courses. When the coaxial cable and communication satellites are ready and the communication band wider, Cuban librarians may find additional information in Wikipedia for term papers, final exams or a doctoral degree.

It will be as in Nineveh, Alexandria and Babylon: treasuring, processing, completing the dialectical contradiction: give/save, use/preserve.

All this for your user, your client, your reader, to read more, learn more, be better informed and hopefully more cultured and therefore more eager for the re-animation of the streets and parks of Cuba's cities and towns with the books and bustle of the next book fair, and next year's 3 p.m. cannon at La Cabaña.

# Appendix 13.

## DE RERUM BIBLIOTHECARII: THE ORIGINS, 2011[142]

De rerum bibliothecarii. When I wrote that phrase, the spell check on my computer put a wiggly red line under it. The program was not ready for a Latin phrase, much less for one invented by an 80-year-old "student." But in this case that phrase is my homage to, or my memento of, Vicentina Antuña, the magistra [teacher] who had so much to do with what happens in libraries today. Vicentina was my supportive precursor, active in the consolidation of library studies at the University of Havana. From our first high school classes and courses at the University Library to the founding and development of the Library Department at the Faculty of Letters. From the firm conviction that we were the PhDs in Philosophy and Literature best prepared to act as librarians. Such stories must be written and interpreted. Because Vicentina defended to the utmost the humanistic quality that should be the basis for the training and therefore the practice of the library profession. And she did so not only as an academic but also through the Cuban National Commission of UNESCO.

And in each one of her classes Vicentina would write a phrase taken from the fabulous Latin canon, so that we would become familiar with it, translate it, and apply it in our future professional life—that future which is now past.

---

142. Reprinted with permission of Marta Terry González. Translated by Laura K. Aase.

One day she touched on Lucretius and his De rerum natura. And how does that translate? Is it about the things of nature? About human things? About things of normal life?

The bad parody of Lucretius in my title serves to explain the unexplainable: what was I going to talk with you about today?

So I decided there was nothing else to do but talk about things related to librarians ([*bibliotecarios y bibliotecarias*, that is, both male and female in the original Spanish] to be current with the times).[143]

To begin we have to define for ourselves what it is to be a librarian; if we surveyed people on the street the way television journalists do, we would get various answers. A girl with sparkles in her hair would shrug her shoulders delightfully and smile; a guy with a babyish pompadour and a reggae rhythm to his speech would say, "Well, I…"; and the everlasting over-50 colleague, knowing that it pays to get her little white head shown on TV, would say, "Yes, of course, I have a [female] friend," or she might even say a [male] friend.

And from there we could go on. That friendship, on the other hand, has been much abused. The librarian is a friend to books…and the enemy of readers, as a user or reader (whichever word you like) from one of my libraries—those places I've worked I consider mine -- would say. He's now a famous artist, and the worst of it is he's absolutely right. That's one of those things. We'll come back to that.

I don't want to keep going off topic, but something happened to me a few days ago. A future colleague—that is, a library student in one of the country's universities—called and told me or informed me that he was writing or editing his final project to graduate as a licensed librarian, or whatever we're calling our field nowadays. His project was on a person he'd been told was very important in the history and development of libraries in Cuba, and this person was called Olinta Ariosa. What was he looking for, this graduating student to whom I refer? Information on the life and work of this colleague. I was happy and prepared to

---

143. Similar to other parts of the world, librarianship in Cuba became a female dominated profession as libraries became widespread in Cuba. The Spanish word for librarian remains a masculine noun in everyday usage.

cooperate. If anyone deserves a book or two or three, it's my late friend
Olinta. The young man told me that he had done some research and
had found very little data. We struck up a friendly conversation; I asked
how this topic had been proposed, and he recited all the steps one must
follow to present a preliminary project and then a capstone: the research
problem, the research question, the thesis…He told me that he lacked
much of a bibliography, the work Olinta had published, the places she
had worked. From memory, I gave him people's names, colleagues with
whom she had worked. Anything I knew, her family, her place of origin…
The young man insisted, Yes but her work, where she published, where
it appeared. By now I was beginning to lose the great patience that you
all know I have, and I tried to tell him, Look, Setién [Dr. Emilio Setién
Quesada], he knows everybody, Miriam Bendamio, Conchita, María
Esther, Aymé, Laura Rumbaud. In the life and work history of those
colleagues you'll find Olinta's achievements and characteristics…Write
it down, write it down, I said. And I was already prepared to look for
telephone numbers and addresses, when, somehow, all my patience
vanished and I said two things that bothered me when I realized I'd
said them: If that's how it is, if the method is more important than my
friend, that's not going to fly. Because where do we get the footnotes,
the op. cit., the Works Consulted, and the recommended bibliography?
Her work? What more work do you want than the University of Santa
Clara Library, the school library system, and the public library system? I
don't know, are those not enough of an endorsement to give her a grand
entrance into social networks or the Internet? Or in the history of the
achievements of the Cuban Revolution? Isn't that an admirable thing,
something of value? Isn't it something to remember when calculating
the cultural balance sheet of the Cuban people? What happened when
the Literacy Campaign ended? The Seguimiento, the Battle for the Sixth
Grade, school libraries, public libraries? Why have we forgotten these
associative links between the works of Olinta and María Teresa and
all their workers, who, more than that, were like their platoon soldiers,
partisans, comrades-in-arms in the great cultural work of the Cuban

Revolution? Is that not work, the reason for being...? The things of librarians with an @ sign.

But memories still remain, and some names remain that make students like the one in my story, and some professors like his teachers, worry about ensuring that Library Day (another thing that should concern us) is not Librarian Day. Big deal: there's the Day of the Doctor, but the days for hospitals and nurses are different celebrations. Do they suppose that Library Day will be the day of the library buildings? Or the day of the people who work, live, grow, and die within those walls, from the grayness and dust, according to some? The issue of dying, or at least getting sick, aside from being a rhetorical device, has an element of truth in some cases. Think of yellow mold, rhinitis, and asthma. But anyway, what is that thing of being a librarian with an @ sign?

To write that phrase or thought and, above all, repeat it, we should be very sure. If we concentrate on the library thing, we find ourselves inside the oikos, the edifice; if we concentrate on that which gives life, well, that's another thing to keep in mind, the human being we serve.

What can we say to the young man who wants to write his thesis, or to the girl who wants to choose this as her profession, or to the grandmother who shudders to know her granddaughter's choice, or the mother who sees her precious offspring, with her eternal Salbutamol inhaler, cloistered in the hidden dusty places without a prince to rescue her?

And now, one more thing. Where do we situate ourselves: in the past that some of us consider the present, or in the present that some of us ignore in order to think about the future?

It's a small thing. Etymologically, biblos, book, papyrus house. Thousands of years ago we said that, and even if it's a house or a building or a shelter or a construction with glass walls with a view of the River Thames, it continues to be a place where books are put, collected, kept, cared for, preserved. Some logical oddball whom I don't want to remember would say plainly, a storehouse of books. And thus we arrive at that other thing.

I could not resist the temptation (or simply the reflexive act) of exerting one aspect of the office of librarian, that of reference (which is also losing its significance, but that's not important now). I had to resort to that great Dictionary [Diccionario Usual de la Real Academia Española], which sparkles, flashes, and casts its brilliance upon us, and which I conjure up mysteriously by pushing a button or key on my computer. The dictionary says that a library is

(From the Latin bibliothēca, Greek βιβλιοθήκη). Noun. 1) An institution whose purpose consists in the acquisition, conservation, study, and exhibition of books and documents. 2) A place where a considerable number of books are organized for reading. 3) Furniture, shelving, etc., where books are located. 4) A set of these books. 5) A nation's writers, or a branch of knowledge, and the work they have produced. Sir Nicolás Antonio's library. 6. A collection of analogous books or treatises, similar by reason of the material, epoch, nation, or authors that they comprise. Library of Law and Legislation. Library of Classical Writers.

Another frightening thing that I didn't think to find, or miss: the lack of people, the human element: the service—but let's not get distracted here, because that thing about acquisition, conservation for study, exhibition of books and documents—who does that? Why do they do it? Sure, they do it just to organize books for reading, but whose reading? Customers, users, or readers? I can't resist mentioning what a senior official of Cuban Culture once told me: "That's one of those librarian things: Every time you say 'users' I can't help thinking of a pizza restaurant, and when you say 'customers' I think about the ones at my uncle's grocery store."

And organized how? By size? By the color of the book jackets? Behind each one of those expressions, apparently absurd to young people today, are hundreds of hours of bitter (even violent) arguments some of us had.

Well, since we've already begun to reflect on the dangerous question of reference, let's keep on searching. It could be that the service offered and the person who offers it are described with the same noun. And there goes another button and the flash and the brilliance, responding with 20 definitions and as many links for adjectives – but are they information or informational? It seems that it still has to be approved.

Q.E.D., as one of my students would say, the grandmother who's searching for information about the world her granddaughter is going to enter won't understand anything by means of the dictionary, and in her mind she will only see the sleepy image of the little library from her home town.

But one option still remains to us. The grandmother searches directly for that thing that her granddaughter wants to be or do, or she asks the librarian at the qualifying library—dusty and sleepy moments ago. And I do the search for her again, and I find "Librarian. Noun. A person in charge of the care, organization, and service of a library."

That doesn't much help the imaginary grandmother or us to situate ourselves in relation to our issue of concern.

You see that it's not a simple, isolated problem. A dictionary or encyclopedia is not going to define and exalt the things of libraries, their hidden places, their characteristics, but I still think that it could be a little more descriptive. Because it's a phenomenon that goes to the essence of the work of the librarian. Many years ago I had what we now call a friendly argument with someone who knew much more than I, whom I admired, and whose memory I deeply respect. That person was speaking precisely about this idea. Someone said that the work, the function, the management of the library entity was like a diamond. Given the high level of the meeting, I murmured as if to myself, "Like a pearl…". I didn't mean to be heard, let alone to argue with such illustrious people; it's just that I thought (and still do) that the pearl is hidden, since it has to be taken from the oyster. Once it is obtained or discovered, we find an unparalleled natural phenomenon, but it's hidden, it's hard work, it has a matte sheen, it doesn't stand out, it doesn't surrender itself easily. But it is a prized jewel.

That's why it's difficult to put a value on it when we pass one of our municipal libraries, which definitively does not shine like a diamond, but has the hardness and apparent smoothness of a pearl—which can sometimes look gray. We collect; we don't store. We organize; we don't stockpile. We go to the bottom of the back shelf in the last row, there on the right or the left, wherever it may be, and we retrieve the volume necessary for tomorrow's exam, or find the right verse for the wedding ceremony, or verify the citation for the doctoral thesis.

We serve, we process (we no longer catalog or classify, for all that has been changing in books), one source of information in the function of another, another unknown and not.

Scandinavian countries, where night falls at five o'clock in summer and four o'clock in winter, have converted their libraries into refuges; for the children who finish school before their parents finish work; for the high percentage of senior citizens who are bored and, because of the climate, can't go out to the parks where they would otherwise spend most of their days. So the libraries have developed a form of interior architecture that attracts people and makes them want to stay there, with colorful carpeting and walls covered with the best art—walls where the shelves and books become part of the décor, or the atmosphere. And where the child as well as the adult gains a taste for being, remaining, reading, and learning.

That is to say, the place, the walls, the royal storehouses are suitable and even beautified in order to accomplish the ultimate objective of the library: to serve the community of users or readers.

At one time specialized libraries in the United States, especially those on university campuses, adopted such interiors and architecture to attract readers: the point was to create an even better environment than that of the home. In that way users would feel so comfortable that they would not check out books, and thus the dangerous circulation of unique and rare materials was avoided.

Librarians who attend the next IFLA conference in Helsinki will appreciate some examples of the marvels of architecture. I have already referred not only to libraries but to architecture as an expression of artistic form. And there you will see the big reading rooms that librarians invented to deal with the universal and inevitable custom of university students using library reading rooms as group study rooms and/or play areas.

With the above, I want to say that providing a storehouse of books is as valid and necessary as processing them by hand, by spreadsheet, using

MARC records or LINUX. It doesn't matter whether we process with the new propensity for Dewey or the old (but not forgotten) preference for Ranganathan, if the subject headings are made into keywords and then into metadata. Nor does it matter if books are called documents and journals are no longer published on paper.

What matters is our mission, and our mission (I cite only my own experience) is to provide information to a human being who needs it. I said "need"; sometimes we have to help this human decipher his own need for information, which can range from "Where in Spain is Huelva?" or "How do I tell my child that I don't know where to find the explanation of mathematical functions?" or the tourist who enters a library in the historic district and asks which are the effects of Heber Procter or how to find them. And the doubtful scientist who asks, "Has news of my latest discovery come out somewhere on the Internet?" Or the young man who says, "And how can I know why this historian calls the President the President General?" Or why is Leonardo di Caprio making a new version of Romeo and Juliet or, same question, what are the permanent values Shakespeare put into that work, which never ceases to adapt and readapt itself, without losing the love, the balcony, the lark, or the nightingale?

And that human being who needs, asks, looks, through any medium (manual, automated, or transparent), for a reason to continue his other vital searches. That's the thing. That is one of the best things that we librarians do. That's why Vicentina will continue being right, in spite of all the passages to the virtual unknown.

The things of librarians are, essentially, human.

# Bibliography

Alexa. "How Popular Is Ecured.cu? Alexa Traffic Ranks. " Accessed on June 25, 2014. http://www.alexa.com/siteinfo/ecured.cu.

Alkalimat, Abdul. "Malcolm X Habla En Los 90's / Malcolm X Speaks in the 90's." Malcolm X: A Research Site. Accessed on June 25, 2014. http://www.brothermalcolm.net/2002/mx_1990/.

————. "Sankofa Cuba." *The Black Activist: Journal of the Black Left Unity Network*, no. 2 (Fall 2013): 28-91. Accessed on June 25, 2014. http://jblun.org/issue/2/.

Alkalimat, Abdul, and Kate Williams. "Social Capital and Cyberpower in the African American Community: A Case Study of a Community Technology Center in the Dual City." In *Community Informatics: Shaping Computer Mediated Social Relations*, edited by Leigh Keeble and Brian Loader, 178-204. London: Routledge, 2001. Accessed on June 25, 2014. http://people.lis.illinois.edu/~katewill/cyberpower/.

Anderson, Jon Lee. *Che Guevara: A Revolutionary Life*. New York: Grove Press, 1997.

Argudin García, Angel, and Nícolas Inchaurtieta Casuso. "Vacunación Antivariolosa [Smallpox Vaccination]: Trabajo De La Sección De Medicina Preventiva Del Servicio De Higiene Infantil Municipal De La Habana." *Revista de Sanidad y Beneficencia Municipal* 3, no. 1 (July-September 1943): 43-51.

Bachiller y Morales, Antonio. *Catálogo De Libros Y Folletos Publicados En Cuba Desde La Introducción De La Imprenta Hasta 1840.* Ciudad de la Habana: P. Massana, 1861.

Bonta, Bruce D. "Online Searching in the Reference Room." *Library Trends* 31, no. 3 (1983): 495-510. Accessed on June 25, 2014. http://hdl.handle.net/2142/7269.

Bowden, Russell, and Paul Nauta. "Guust Van Wesemael: A Tribute." *IFLA Journal* 17, no. 3 (1991): 224-26.

Brandon, George. *Santeria from Africa to the New World: The Dead Sell Memories.* Bloomington, IN: Indiana University Press, 1993.

Branson, Ken. "Forty Years Later, Doctoral Candidate Returns to Rutgers to Defend His Ph.D. Dissertation and Earn Degree." *Rutgers Today.* Accessed on June 25, 2014. http://news.rutgers.edu/issue.2012-12-20.2609038638/article.2013-01-11.6369588550#.U5YGDSh3cQp.

Brock, Lisa, and Digna Castañeda Fuertes. *Between Race and Empire: African-Americans and Cubans before the Cuban Revolution.* Philadelphia, PA: Temple University Press, 1998.

Butler, Desmond, Jack Gillum, and Alberto Arce. "US Secretly Created 'Cuban Twitter' to Stir Unrest." *Associated Press (wire service)*, April 4 2014. Accessed on June 25, 2014. http://bigstory.ap.org/article/us-secretly-created-cuban-twitter-stir-unrest.

Butler, Desmond, Jack Gillum, Alberto Arce, and Andrea Rodriguez. "US Sent Latin Youth Undercover in Anti-Cuba Ploy." *Associated Press (wire service)*, August 4 2014. Accessed on June 25, 2014. http://bigstory. ap.org/article/us-sent-latin-youth-undercover-anti-cuba-ploy.

Byrne, Alex. *The Politics of Promoting Freedom of Information and Expression in International Librarianship.* Lanham, MD: Scarecrow Press, 2007.

Cairo Ballester, Ana. *José Martí Y La Novela De La Cultura Cubana.* Santiago de Compostela, Spain: Universidade de Santiago de Compostela, 2003.

Cassell, Kay Ann, and Uma Hiremath. Reference and Informtion Services in the 21st Century: An Introduction. Second ed. New York: Neal-Schuman Publishers, 2009.

Castro, Fidel. "The Havana Declaration, September 2, 1960." University of Texas Latin America Network Information Center Fidel Castro Speech Database. Accessed on June 25, 2014. http://lanic.utexas.edu/ project/castro/db/1960/19600902-2.html.

Castro de Morales, Lilia. *Biografía De La Biblioteco Nacional.* Ciudad de la Habana: Editora Biblioteca Nacional, 1957.

Choldin, Marianna Tax. "Beginning a Conversation on Access to Information and Freedom of Expression." *IFLA Journal* 22, no. 4 (August 1996): 280-84.

Comisión Nacional de Alfabetización de la Ministerio de Educación. *¡Alfabeticemos!* Ciudad de la Habana: Imprenta Nacional de Cuba, 1961.

———. *¡Venceremos!* Cuba: Gobierno Revolucionario, 1961.

Commission on Cuban Affairs. Problems of the New Cuba. Foreign Policy Association, 1935. Accessed on June 25, 2014. http://archive. org/details/problemsofthenew027158mbp.

Coolidge, Calvin. "Address before the Pan American Conference at Havana, Cuba, January 16, 1928." The American Presidency Project. Accessed on June 25, 2014. http://www.presidency.ucsb.edu/ ws/?pid=443.

Cuba, Republic of. "Fundamental Law of the Revolutionary Government." Havana: Publicaciones Lewis / Private Commercial Service S. A., 1959.

Cushing, Lincoln. ¡Revolución! Cuban Poster Art. San Francisco, CA: Chronicle Books, 2003.

de la Torre Molina, Mildred. "Vivo Orgullosa De Ser Maestra: Entrevista a Carmen Almodóvar Muñoz." Espacio Laical [Laity Space] 6, no. 24 (October-December 2010): 73-77. Accessed on June 25, 2014. http:// www.espaciolaical.org/contens/24/7377.pdf.

de Tournemire, Guillaume. "[Genealogy of] Andrès Terry Y Dorticos" Geneanet. Accessed on June 25, 2014. http://gw.geneanet.org/pierfit ?lang=en;p=andres;n=terry+y+dorticos.

Decreto Presidencial Número 177, Publicado En La Gaceta Oficial De 9 De Febrero De 1917." Collección Legislativa: Leyes, Decretos y Resoluciones 55 (1917): 190. Accessed on June 25, 2014. http://catalog.hathitrust. org/Record/010427180.

Decreto Presidencial Número 281, Publicado En La Gaceta Oficial De 9 De Marzo De 1916." Collección Legislativa: Leyes, Decretos y Resoluciones 51 (1916): 339-40. Accessed on June 25, 2014. http://catalog.hathitrust. org/Record/010427180.

Dowling, Michael. "Cuba Update for ALA 2008 Annual Conference." Washington, DC: American Library Association, 2008. Accessed on June 25, 2014. http://www.ala.org/offices/iro/iroactivities/ALA_Cuba_Updte-Annual_2008.

EcuRed. "EcuRed: A Cuban Encyclopedia." Accessed on June 25, 2014. http://www.ecured.cu.

Ely, Roland T. *Cuando Reinaba su Majestad el Azúcar*. Buenos Aires: Editorial Sudamericana, 1963.

Empresa de Telecomunicaciones de Cuba S.A. (ETECSA). "Cable Submarino Alba 1 Está Operativo Y Se Comienzan Pruebas Para Tráfico De Internet." *CubaDebate: Contra el Terrorismo Mediático*, January 24, 2013. Accessed on June 25, 2014. http://www.cubadebate.cu/noticias/2013/01/24/cable-submarino-alba-1-esta-operativo-y-se-comienzan-pruebas-para-trafico-de-internet/#.U9AZDWN3dqx.

Espín Guillois, Vilma, Asela de los Santos Tamayo, and Yolanda Ferrer. *Women in Cuba: The Making of a Revolution within the Revolution*. New York: Pathfinder, 2012.

Farber, Samuel. *Cuba since the Revolution of 1959: A Critical Assessment*. Chicago: Haymarket Books, 2011.

Ferrer, Ada. *Insurgent Cuba: Race, Nation, and Revolution, 1868-1898*. Chapel Hill: University of North Carolina Press, 1999.

Foner, Philip S. *Antonio Maceo: The "Bronze Titan" of Cuba's Struggle for Independence*. New York: Monthly Review Press, 1977.

———. *A History of Cuba and Its Relations with the United States. Volume 2, 1845-1895: From the Era of Annexationism to the Outbreak of the Second War for Independence*. New York: International Publishers, 1963.

Gleijeses, Piero. *Visions of Freedom: Havana, Washington, Pretoria, and the Struggle for Southern Africa, 1976-1991*. Chapel HIll, NC: University of North Carolina Press, 2013.

Grafton Horta, Pilar, and Marta Terry González. *Referencia I*. Ciudad de La Habana, Cuba: Universidad de la Habana Facultad de Artes y Letras Departamiento de Información Científico Técnico y Bibliotecología, 1984.

————. *Referencia II*. Ciudad de La Habana, Cuba: Universidad de la Habana Facultad de Artes y Letras Departamiento de Información Científico Técnico y Bibliotecología, 1984.

Greenwald, Glenn. *No Place to Hide: Edward Snowden, the NSA, and the U.S. Surveillance State*. New York, NY: Metropolitan Books/Henry Holt, 2014.

Grogan, Denis. *Practical Reference Work*. London: Clive Bingley Ltd, 1979.

Guevara, Che. "Che Guevara on the Mistakes of the Revolution; from a Speech Made in Algiers on February 26 1965" In historyofcuba.com (website), edited by Jerry A. Sierra. Accessed on June 25, 2014. http://www.historyofcuba.com/history/che2.htm.

————. "Socialism and Man in Cuba." In *The Che Guevara Reader*, edited by David Deutschmann. North Melbourne, Australia: Ocean Press, 1965. Accessed on June 25, 2014. http://www.marxists.org/archive/guevara/1965/03/man-socialism.htm.

Guillén, Nicolás. *Man-Making Words: Selected Poems of Nícolas Guillén*. Translated by Robert Márquez and David Arthur McMurray. Havana: Editorial de Arte y Literatura, 1973.

Guridy, Frank Andre. *Forging Diaspora: Afro-Cubans and African Americans in a World of Empire and Jim Crow*. Chapel Hill: University of North Carolina Press, 2010.

Harrison, Faye V. "Fernando Ortiz." *International Encyclopedia of the Social Sciences*. Accessed on June 25, 2014. http://www.encyclopedia.com/doc/1G2-3045301836.html.

Hart Dávalos, Armando. *Aldabonazo: Inside the Cuban Revolutionary Underground, 1952-58: A Participant's Account*. Translated by Mary-Alice Waters. New York: Pathfinder, 2004.

Hilton, James. *Goodbye, Mr. Chips*. London: Hodder & Stoughton, 1934.

International Federation of Library Associations and Institutions. "Honorary Fellow." International Federation of Library Associations and Institutions Honours Awards Web Page. Accessed on June 25, 2014. http://www.ifla.org/honours-awards/honorary-fellow.

Kagan, Al. "An Alternative View on IFLA, Human Rights, and the Social Responsibility of International Librarianship." *IFLA Journal* 34, no. 3 (2008): 230-37. Accessed on June 25, 2014. http://www.ifla.org/publications/ifla-journal.

―――. "IFLA and Social Responsibility: A Core Value of Librarianship." In *Libraries, National Security, Freedom of Information Laws and Social Responsibilities: IFLA/FAIFE World Report*, edited by Susanne Seidelin and Stuart Hamilton, 33-43. The Hague: International Federation of Library Associations and Institutions, 2005.

Katz, William A. *Introduction to Reference Work: Volume 1, Basic Information Sources*. New York: McGraw Hill, Inc., 1969.

————. *Introduction to Reference Work: Volume 2, Reference Services.* New York: McGraw Hill, Inc., 1969.

Kennedy, John F. "Speech of Senator John F. Kennedy, Cincinnati, Ohio, Democratic Dinner, October 6, 1960." The American Presidency Project. Accessed on June 25, 2014. http://www.presidency.ucsb.edu/ws/index.php?pid=25660.

Leiner, Marvin. *Sexual Politics in Cuba: Machismo, Homosexuality, and AIDS.* Boulder, CO: Westview Press, 1994.

Lenin, Vladimir Ilyich. "Our Foreign and Domestic Position and Party Tasks: Speech Delivered to the Moscow Gubernia Conference of the R.C.P.(B.) on November 21, 1920." Translated by Julius Katzer. In *Collected Works.* 4th English ed. Moscow: Progress Publishers, 1965. Vol. 31: 408-26. Accessed on June 25, 2014. https://www.marxists.org/archive/lenin/works/1920/nov/21.htm.

Luna Mendoza, Jorge. "Las Ferias Cubanas." La Editorial Electrónica Cubaliteraria, Web Portal of the Cuban Book Institute. Accessed on June 25, 2014. http://www.cubaliteraria.cu/evento/filh/2005/memorias3.htm.

MacIntyre, Ben. *The Napoleon of Crime.* New York: Farrar, Straus and Giroux, 1997.

MacLean, Betsy. *Haydée Santamaría.* Melbourne; New York: Ocean Press, 2003.

Madory, Doug. "Cuban Fiber: Completo?" *Renesys* (blog), January 23, 2013. Accessed on June 25, 2014. http://www.renesys.com/2013/01/cuban-fiber-completo/.

Marquez, Gabriel García. "Operation Carlota." 1976. Accessed on June 25, 2014. http://www.rhodesia.nl/marquez.htm.

"Marta Terry of Cuba Here 'to See US for Myself,'" *The Chicago [Daily] Defender* (National Edition), July 17, 1954.

Martí, José. "Letter to Manuel Mercado, May 18, 1895." In *HistoryofCuba. com* History of Cuba Web page: Sierra, Jerry A., n.d. Accessed on June 25, 2014. http://www.historyofcuba.com/history/marti/mercado.htm.

————. *Obras Completas.* 27 vols. Havana: Editorial de Ciencias Sociales, 1975.

Mayol, Josefina, and Jerrold Orne. "Cuban Libraries." *Library Quarterly* 22, no. 2 (April 1952): 92-124.

Mealy, Rosemari. *Fidel & Malcolm X: Memories of a Meeting.* Melbourne: Ocean Press, 1993.

Montejo, Esteban. *The Autobiography of a Runaway Slave.* Edited by Miguel Barnet. Translated by Jocasta Innes. New York: Meridian Books/The World Publishing Company, 1969.

Moore, Robin. *Nationalizing Blackness: Afrocubanismo and Artistic Revolution in Havana, 1920-1940.* Pittsburgh, PA: University of Pittsburgh Press, 1997.

Morris, Emily. "Unexpected Cuba." *New Left Review,* no. 88 (July-August 2014): 5-45. Accessed on June 25, 2014. http://newleftreview.org/II/88/emily-morris-unexpected-cuba.

Mulgrew, Dominic. "Cuba: A Beacon of Hope for Disability Rights." *Rock Around the Blockade News Blog*, n.d. Accessed on June 25, 2014. http://www.ratb.org.uk/news/campaign-news/211-cuba-a-beacon-of-hope-for-disability-rights.

Murphy, Joseph M. *Santería: An African Religion in America*. Boston: Beacon Press, 1988.

Ortiz, Fernando. *Cuban Counterpoint, Tobacco and Sugar*. Durham, NC: Duke University Press, 1995.

————. "Los Cabildos Afrocubanos." *Revista Bimestre Cubana* 16 (1921): 5-39.

Palmié, Stephan. *Wizards and Scientists: Explorations in Afro-Cuban Modernity and Tradition*. Durham, NC: Duke University Press, 2002.

Pateman, John. "The Development of Public Libraries in Cuba since 1959." *Library History* 17 (November 2001): 189-95.

Pérez, Louis A., Jr. *Cuba under the Platt Amendment, 1902–1934*. Pittsburgh, PA: University of Pittsburgh Press, 1986.

Poey Baro, Dionisio. "'Race' and Anti-Racism in José Martí's 'Mi Raza'." *Contributions in Black Studies* 12, no. 1 (1994): 55-61. Accessed on June 25, 2014. http://scholarworks.umass.edu/cibs/vol12/iss1/6/.

Press, Larry, and Joel Snyder. "A Look at Cuban Networks." *Matrix News* 2, no. 6 (1992): 1-2. Accessed on June 25, 2014. http://som.csudh.edu/fac/lpress/devnat/nations/cuba/cuba2.htm.

Prince, J. C. *Cuba Illustrated*. 6th ed. New York: Napoléon Thompson & Company, 1893/94. Accessed on June 25, 2014. https://archive.org/details/cubaillustrated00prin.

Quiros Moran, Dalía. *Guide to Afro-Cuban Herbalism*. Bloomington, IN: AuthorHouse, 2009.

Ranganathan, S. R. "IFLA: What It Should Be and Do." *Libri: International Library Review* 5, no. 2 (1954): 182-89. Accessed on June 25, 2014. http://www.ifla.org/history.

Romanos de Tiratel, Susana. "El Legado Bibliográfico-Bibliotecológico De Josefa Emilia Sabor (1916-2012)." *Información, Cultura y Sociedad*, no. 27 (2012): 11-33. Accessed on June 25, 2014. http://eprints.rclis.org/19625/.

Sabor, Josefa Emilia, and Ricardo Nassif. *Methods of Teaching Librarianship*. Paris: United Nations Educational, Scientific, and Cultural Organization, 1969.

Sales, William W. *From Civil Rights to Black Liberation: Malcolm X and the Organization of Afro-American Unity*. Boston: South End Press, 1994.

Setién Quesada, Emilio. "Libraries and Library Science in Cuba." *IFLA Journal* 20, no. 2 (June, 1994): 109-19. Accessed on June 25, 2014. http://archive.ifla.org/V/iflaj/index.htm.

Sparanese, Ann. "Statement to the ALA International Relations Committee's Subcommittee on Latin America and the Caribbean, January 8, 2001." *Library Juice* 4, no. 9 Supplement (March 14, 2001). Accessed on June 25, 2014. http://www.libr.org/juice/issues/vol4/LJ_4.9.sup.html.

"Statement of Librarians from the United States and Puerto Rico on US-Cuba Relations, Havana, 1994." *Library Juice* 3, no. 38 Supplement "Good Stuff on Cuba" (October 4, 2000). Accessed on June 25, 2014. http://libr.org/Juice/issues/vol13/LJ_3.38.sup.html.

"Summary by Language Size." Ethnologue: Languages of the World. Accessed on June 25, 2014. http://www.ethnologue.com/statistics/size.

Terry González, Marta. "Address by Dr. Marta Terry to the Opening Session of the 60th General Conference of IFLA, August 21-27, 1994. Conference Programme and Proceedings." International Federation of Library Associations and Institutions. Accessed on June 25, 2014. http://archive.ifla.org/IV/ifla60/60-terry.htm.

————. "Cuba." In *World Encyclopedia of Library and Information Services*, edited by Robert Wedgeworth, 234-38. Chicago: American Library Association, 1993.

————. "The Pioneers: Olinta Ariosa Morales (1921-1999)." *World Libraries* 13, no. 1/2 (Spring and Fall 2003). Accessed on June 25, 2014. http://worlib.org/vol13no1-2/index.shtml.

————. *Referencia: Ejercicios*. Ciudad de La Habana, Cuba: Universidad de la Habana Facultad de Artes y Letras, 1982.

————, ed. *Servicios Comunitarios: Selección De Textos*. Ciudad de la Habana: Editorial Félix Varela, 2005, reprinted 2009.

————. "Special Libraries and Other Information Institutions in Cuba." *World Libraries* 13, no. 1/2 (Spring and Fall 2003). Accessed on June 25, 2014. http://worlib.org/vol13no1-2/index.shtml.

Terry González, Marta, and Isabel Portales Tamayo. *Referencia: Selección De Lecturas*. Ciudad de La Habana, Cuba: Editorial Félix Varela, 2003.

Terry, Kevin. "Terrys in Latin America of Cork Origin." *Irish Migration Studies in Latin America* 7, no. 3 (March 2010). Accessed on June 25, 2014. http://www.irlandeses.org/1003terry.htm.

————. *The Terrys of Cork: Merchant Gentry 1180-1644*. Chicester/ Gloucestershire, UK: Phillimore & Company, Ltd/The History Press, 2013.

Thomas, Hugh. *Cuba: The Pursuit of Freedom*. New York: Da Capo Press, 1998.

Tyson, Timothy B. *Radio Free Dixie: Robert F. Williams and the Roots of Black Power*. Chapel Hill, NC: University of North Carolina Press, 1999.

Unión de Periodistas de Cuba Executive Committee. *A Sketch of the Clandestine and Guerilla Press Covering the Period 1952-1958*. Havana: Instituto Cubano del Libro, 1971.

University of Toledo Africana Studies Program. "Toledo Spiders Go to Cuba." Murchison Center. Accessed on June 25, 2014. http://murchisoncenter.org/cuba/.

Uriarte, Miren. *Cuba: Social Policy at a Crossroads: Maintaining Priorities, Transforming Practice*. Boston: Oxfam America, 2002. Accessed on June 25, 2014. http://scholarworks.umb.edu/gaston_pubs/115.

Viciedo Valdés, Miguel. *Biblioteca Pública Y Revolución: Su Desarrollo De 1959 a 1989*. Ciudad de la Habana: Ediciones Extramuros, 2009.

————. "Biblioteca Pública: Algunos Paradigmas En El Mundo Y Sus Puntos De Contacto Con El Paradigma Cubano." *Bibliotecas*, no. 1-2 (Enero-Diciembre 2001-2003).

"A Wealthy Planter's Will: Don Tomas Terry's Disposition of His Property Contested." *New York Times*, November 21, 1886.

Wedgeworth, Robert. "The Virtual IFLA: Moving Knowledge through Time and Space." Paper presented at the 60th Annual Meeting of the International Federation of Library Associations and Institutions, Havana, August 21-27, 1994.

Wieder, Joachim. "IFLA's First Fifty Years: A Reprise. Extracts from 'An Outline of IFLA's History', by Joachim Wieder, Selected and Edited by Harry Campbell." *IFLA Journal* 28, no. 3 (2002): 107-17. Accessed on June 25, 2014. http://archive.ifla.org/V/iflaj/index.htm.

Williams, Kate. "Literacy and Computer Literacy: The Cuban Experience: Report on a Library Tour of Cuba, February-March 2001 / Alfabetización y Computadorización: La Experiencia Cubana: Informe Sobre un Viaje de Bibliotecarios a Cuba, Febrero-Marzo 2001." Kate Williams faculty Web page. Accessed on June 25, 2014. http://people.lis.illinois.edu/~katewill/cuba/.

## About the Authors

**Abdul Alkalimat** is professor emeritus of African American studies and library and information science at the University of Illinois at Urbana-Champaign.

**Kate Williams** is associate professor of library and information science at the University of Illinois at Urbana Champaign.

# INDEX

CPSIA information can be obtained
at www.ICGtesting.com
Printed in the USA
FFOW01n0536250215
11349FF